LUCK

or Something Like It

KENNY ROGERS

LUCK

—✦✦— or —✦✦—

Something Like It

wm

WILLIAM MORROW

An Imprint of HarperCollins*Publishers*

FIRST EDITION

Designed by Betty Lew

Library of Congress Cataloging-in-Publication Data has been applied for.

ISBN 978-0-06-207181-1

12 13 14 15 16   OV/RRD   10 9 8 7 6 5 4 3 2 1

To Wanda, Justin, Jordan, Kenny Jr., and Chris. They are my rock. They are my reason for living.

CONTENTS

CONTENTS

AUTHOR'S NOTE

I would like to offer a special thanks to my friend, Patsi Bale Cox. Without her, this autobiography never would have happened. I had been asked to do a book for at least twenty years, and it was never something I had any interest in doing, for a lot of reasons.

After being persuaded to meet with Patsi for lunch, I found myself discussing and laughing about moments of my life that I hadn't thought about for years. In that moment, two things happened: I agreed to write the book and I made a new friend. Both were exciting.

Somewhere in the middle of our journey together, Patsi was diagnosed with a form of lung cancer, and I think she knew in her heart it wasn't going to end well. Instead of stopping and feeling sorry for herself, she committed herself to the completion of my story.

There were times when she couldn't type or talk on the phone and when she could barely breathe, but she tried. She worked as hard as she could to live up to her responsibility to me and the publishers, but this disease shows no favorites. On November 6, 2011, the disease won the battle. She had fought it with all she had . . . and lost.

She wasn't fighting so much for me but for what she thought I had to offer to the history of country music. Her first love was music history. As we go on without Patsi, I hope we can do her memory justice and live up to what she had hoped to accomplish in her mission.

I, and all of country music, will dearly miss our friend Patsi Bale Cox.

Special thanks to Allen Rucker for stepping in at an awkward moment and for pulling this whole thing together. Without him, it never would have been finished.

I'd also like to thank Jason Henke for his important contributions to this book. Jason's tireless efforts, attention to detail, and knowledge of my career were vital to getting this book to where it needed to be.

In addition, I would like to thank Matt Harper at HarperCollins for his unwavering dedication to this project. Matt took remarkable care at every turn to ensure a successful arrival at the finish line, and I'm grateful for all of his hard work.

Special thanks also goes to Kelly Junkermann for his help writing this book, for remembering all the good times we've had together, and for taking so many of the terrific photos in this book.

Finally, this book never would have happened without the two people who got the whole process started. Many thanks to Lisa Sharkey at HarperCollins and Mel Berger at WME for helping to convince me that the time was finally right for me to tell my story.

PROLOGUE

"What in the world were you thinking, Kenneth Ray?"

My mom was on the phone. It was in the early months of 1977 and she had tracked me down on the road. Things had been moving so fast with the release of my new single that I hadn't talked to her in a while.

"The very idea! What are people going to think when they hear you singing about your mother leaving her family to run off to some bar?"

I couldn't get a word in edgewise. My mom was on a roll.

"And how dare you write about me having four hungry kids?"

The song was, of course, "Lucille." And as a matter of pure coincidence, my mother's name was Lucille. She had not been amused when she heard those lines coming over the radio airwaves: "You picked a fine time to leave me, Lucille, with four hungry children and a crop in the field."

"Mom, Mom," I said. "First of all, you have eight kids. Secondly, it's not about you. And thirdly, I didn't write it." I paused for a moment, and my mom jumped back in.

"Imagine what your father would say!" My dad, if he'd still been living, would've been having a good time with this one. He really loved to watch my mom squirm.

For a man who had lived a tough and often disappointing life, he could find something funny in nearly everything. My mother had a sense of humor, too, but I could tell she wasn't having fun with this song I'd recorded.

Earlier, I'd told her the story about the song "Ruby, Don't Take Your Love to Town," and how the country star Mel Tillis had written it about a real person. So as far as she was concerned, this new song might be close to character assassination for a woman named Lucille.

And she wasn't the only doubter.

Some of the label executives had questioned the song when they first heard it, thinking it was all wrong for a Kenny Rogers release. But then, the top brass at United Artists had considered me a long shot as a country artist to begin with. It wasn't surprising that a major label might question offering a country contract to a former jazz and rock musician who was closing in on forty years old. For that guy to make it in country, he'd have to beat some big odds.

In fact, Al Teller, the head man at UA, had told my Nashville producer, Larry Butler, to forget this outrageous idea of signing Kenny Rogers and instead sign some guy without a twenty-year history. Butler, being something of an outrageous character himself, said, "Read my contract, Al. I can sign anyone I want to." There was dead silence on the phone. "Hello?" Butler asked.

"You better be right," Teller snapped, and slammed down the phone.

That was the end of the signing debate, and after UA heard our first studio work, they jumped on the bandwagon. But over a year later, we still hadn't found the breakout song. Two singles—"Love Lifted Me" and "Laura (What's He Got That I Ain't Got?)"—had cracked the Top 20, but the one big release that would establish

me firmly in country music was elusive. I agreed with Larry Butler that "Lucille" could be big. I did question the original ending,
thinking it was a downer. But after some rewriting of the last verse,
I thought we had a song that worked for me and would fly on radio
as well.

When my manager, Ken Kragen, first heard the song, he burst
out laughing. "This will either be written off as a novelty song," he
said, "or it's going to be the biggest song in the country." It was a
good thing he gave it at least a fifty-fifty shot, because, once again,
the UA execs disagreed. They thought it was "too country" for what
they considered my middle-of-the-road image. Of course, when I'd
walked in the door, I wasn't country enough. I couldn't win. This
time it was Kragen who stepped in.

"Release it," he said. And they did.

After one performance of "Lucille" on the *Tonight Show Starring Johnny Carson,* Butler got a call from Atlanta: "We just got a
reorder for ten thousand copies of that single."

"*What?*"

"You heard right—ten thousand."

Butler called me and said, "It's exploding."

Seemingly overnight, we went from two shows on weeknights
and three on Sunday in Las Vegas lounges to the main showrooms.
Things moved fast. It seemed like just a couple of weeks earlier, our
road manager, Keith Bugos, was having to get to our shows early to
make sure someone hadn't mistakenly put up an old Kenny Rogers and the First Edition poster or gotten me confused with Kenny
Loggins, who was just beginning a solo career separate from Loggins and Messina. Keith also had to deal with the fact that we only
had the sound equipment for an audience of two to three thousand.
Now the venues had overflow crowds of ten thousand.

"Lucille" changed everything. It went to No. 1 and stayed there for two weeks. It won a Grammy, the Academy of Country Music Song and Single of the Year, and the Country Music Association Single of the Year. In 1977, I was named the ACM Male Vocalist and in 1978 took home that honor again along with the ACM Entertainer of the Year. But maybe the most telling awards came from the jukebox operators, because jukebox sales reflect people going into cafés, drugstores, and bars, dropping their quarters into the slot, and paying to hear a song. It was listeners like that who grabbed ahold of "Lucille" and made it a monster hit.

Once "Lucille" became a worldwide hit, it didn't bother my mom that she happened to have the same name. It didn't have to be about a real person just because "Ruby" was. My mom was nothing if not pragmatic.

More important, she wanted me to be happy and to succeed at whatever I tried. She was never one of those people who drilled it into her kids' heads that they could do anything they set their minds to, but she did believe life was full of possibilities. You just had to be open to opportunity when it showed up.

My mom saw lessons in almost every experience. She had advice for nearly any situation, and it was one of the old adages she so loved that convinced me making music was the life for me: "Find a job you love . . . and you'll never work a day in your life."

One time a journalist asked her if she was proud of me, and she said, "You know, I'm truly proud of all my sons. My other boys had jobs Kenneth probably couldn't do. . . . All that boy ever did was sing."

CHAPTER ONE

A Pair to Draw To

"Kenneth . . . Kenneth . . . Kenneth Ray!"

That sound still rings in my ears when I think of my mom. Like most kids, I could usually count on being in trouble when my mom used both my names together like that. So I ask you: Why would a mother yell this name at her son all his life, after signing a document that says his name was Kenneth Donald? I ask because I actually saw the birth certificate with my mom's and dad's signatures, which I recognized as theirs, with the name Kenneth Donald on it, and I had never, ever heard anyone in my family call me by that name. It was always Kenneth Ray.

I was born on August 21, 1938, at St. Joseph's Infirmary in Houston, Texas, the fourth child of Edward Floyd and Lucille Lois Hester Rogers. I am told that I have Irish and Native American heritage, and I always assumed that my Native American blood came from my grandmother Della Rogers, with her high cheekbones and her once dark black hair that she pulled back in a severe bun in her later years. Whether it was Grandmother Della or someone else, I can't say for sure, but I just took it for granted that I was part Irish, part Indian, and that was that.

I grew up in the San Felipe Courts housing projects of Houston's Fourth Ward. San Felipe Courts, which was later renamed Allen Parkway Village, was built by the city of Houston in the early 1940s. San Felipe Courts consisted of a series of long, two-story brick buildings that faced inward to a courtyard with benches where people gathered to talk and children played. Over the years, many journalists have listed me as growing up in the Houston Heights area, but it was actually San Felipe Courts. The Heights was more upscale than my family could afford.

We were poor people, but living in the projects, we really didn't know it because we were all in the same boat. Our apartment had two bedrooms upstairs, one downstairs, and a kitchen. We basically had a revolving door with people always coming and going; as the older kids moved out, the younger kids came in. I was closest to my sister Barbara, who was two years older than me. The problem was that she beat me up every day of my life. Finally, the day I reached the breaking point, I had her by her hair and was banging her head on the fridge door. Thank God my dad walked in when he did or I would have killed her. Barbara could be both my best friend and my worst enemy.

My brother, Lelan, was ten years older and was gone all the time. Lelan was really slick, smooth talking, a very sharp dresser with his hair slicked back, and one thing was for sure—he knew the streets. Lelan left home at seventeen. My sister, Geraldine, was thirteen at the time, and my sister, Barbara, was nine. My younger brother Billy was four, and Roy was just a baby. At this point the twins, Randy and Sandy, weren't born, but we knew with Mom and Dad, more were coming.

No matter what age we were, our parents would send us outside to play. They had no worries about us being harmed by strangers. We played all over that area of town with no fear. Seems hard to imagine now, and I regret, for most kids today, both that loss of innocence and that loss of freedom.

Prior to the time the city built San Felipe Courts, the Fourth Ward area had been primarily African American, including Freedmen's Town, so named because freed slaves had populated it in the late 1800s. The land was cheap because much of it was low swampland prone to flooding. Initially, there were rumors that African Americans were going to be included in parts of this public housing, but after the Courts were built, the city put up a fence between the Courts and what was left of the black section. At that young age, I didn't know why people were separated or even think to ask. It was just the way things were. I'm sure there must have been some bad feelings among the African Americans about that fence, but I never felt any hostility. I spent quite a bit of time in the black section, going to the friendly, always welcoming Italian store, Lanzo's Grocery, for my mom or cutting through the yards on my way to school, and my memories were of friendly faces, elderly people sitting on their porches and waving as I passed. I'd like to think I've always been color-blind, and my relationship with the people in the black neighborhood next to San Felipe Courts is probably the reason. I can only speak for my family, but in our case, we were all poor people and felt a certain kinship.

Parents know their families are poor, but kids don't until rich kids at school notice. And they did notice and were quick to make fun. My defense was developing a lifelong habit of blocking out painful memories. Not too long ago, though, I got a letter from a grade school friend that brought back one very hurtful moment. Her name was Mary Gwynne Davidson (now Ridout) and we were in the first grade together. She remembered me as someone who kept to himself and was very quiet and very polite. And very self-conscious, I might add.

The occasion that Mary Gwynne remembered was an event in Mrs. Monk's first grade class called May Fete. The tradition was that each girl got to pick a boy as her May Fete partner. For a six-year-old, this was a big deal, and Mary Gwynne has been kind enough to let me share her letter here:

It was April of 1944 in Mrs. Monk's first-grade class at Wharton Elementary School in Houston, Texas.

We were lined up, girls in alphabetical order. The teacher had given us instruction for the girls to select their May Fete partner. My last name was Davidson so I was close to the beginning of the line, which gave me a pretty good position. I remember clearly that I selected Walton Elson for my partner.

I then watched as one by one the other girls selected their partners. It became very clear to me that a shy blond boy was going to be the last choice. The girls in the line had begun to snicker and talk about Kenny as he didn't have any shoes and wore black-and-white-striped overalls. Kids can be so cruel.

I watched as Kenny fidgeted and tried to not show his embarrassment. He was very polite and kept up a brave front, even with all the snickering. His mannerism was very gentle. I began to try to imagine how he must have felt. It hurt!

Kenny was from a family of nine or ten children and lived in a tenement district in Houston called San Felipe Courts. He helped his mother support his brothers and sisters by selling newspapers on the street corner and doing odd jobs that a young lad could do. In his adult life Kenny's mom moved to Crosby, Texas, where Kenny built an adult center where seniors could go and socialize and enjoy life. I understand he provided everything they might need to enjoy their leisure time together and that he also provided for food for the needy in the community.

In 1962 I ran into Kenny again at a little place called "The Coffee House" on Bellaire Blvd. across from the Shamrock Hilton Hotel. He was playing bass fiddle with the Bobby Doyle Three. Bobby played piano and sang, but that night Bobby had a really bad cold and in the middle of a song he stopped and said, "I have punished my throat and my audience enough. We will now find out if these other guys can sing . . . Kenny, it's your turn." When Kenny sang, I knew he "HAD IT." Yes, he had what it takes to make it because Kenny is none other than Kenny Rogers, my old May Fete partner and friend.

Wishing you well . . . you deserve it. I've always admired you . . . your classmate and friend.

MARY GWYNNE DAVIDSON RIDOUT

It did hurt. It took Mary's letter to jar my memory about this particular incident, but I never forgot the pain.

We were always short on money. Meals were usually simple poor-folks food: pinto beans and rice, corn, and collard greens that we picked with our mom along the banks of Buffalo Bayou.

Thinking back, I never had the feeling that our mom really enjoyed cooking. She worked too many jobs and had too many kids to see preparing meals as much more than a daily chore. She worked as a nurse at Jefferson Davis Hospital, and she worked cleaning offices at the Gulf Building; on Sunday, she worked at the church.

As for cooking, she *was* proud of her banana pudding, and she did love to sit and have a glass of iced tea.

My dad was easy to please when it came to food. He was truly happy as long as there was a mason jar full of long jalapeños on the table. Every night he'd crumble his beans and rice with a fork, take a bite, then grab a jalapeño and bite it off at the stalk. He would literally break into a sweat, his face turning so red it looked like it was on fire. He couldn't utter a word for a while after each one. I watched him do that over the years and never failed to marvel at his ability to eat those things. I tried it once or twice and that was it. Once, in grade school, I finally asked him why he ate them. He just smiled, and as soon as he could talk again, he said, "I just love 'em, son. I just love 'em."

Remembering my father is important to me, but it's also pain-ful. I actually knew little about him. Like most men of his day, he was pretty shut down. That was hard, but what was really difficult was that he did not have a happy life and he drank to bury his feelings about it. My older brother, Lelan, once described him as a bitter man. I think that the Floyd Rogers Lelan knew and the one I knew were different, though; by the time I really got to know my father, he seemed more beaten down than bitter.

My dad was an alcoholic, and alcohol costs money—money we didn't have, money that should have gone to buying food and clothes. Drinking controlled his life, and he was always looking for a way to pay for it. After Lelan had left home, my dad would always hit him up for some cash when he came for a visit, sticking out his hand and saying, "Will this be a ten-dollar or a twenty-dollar visit?" It was his game, and we always knew it was coming.

On one occasion when he panhandled Lelan, Lelan snapped back, "You know what, Dad? That question really offends me. I spent a hundred and fifty dollars on a plane ticket to come here. I rented a car in Houston, drove here to Crockett, and took you and Mom out to dinner. Next time would you rather I just send you the money and not come at all?"

My dad thought this over and finally got a little grin on his face and said, "Oh God, son. Don't make me make that choice." He would've hated to admit it, but I think he was truly conflicted over that question.

When I was older and started making a little money, my dad began to treat me the same way—as the golden goose. It evolved into another game he would play to get liquor money. He would start out talking about money in general.

"If I could just get together a hundred dollars . . . ," he'd say.

Or he might mention something specific, like "If a man just had an electric saw."

I'd play along. "So if this hypothetical man had an electric saw, what would you saw with it? Would you build anything?"

Usually my questions didn't get much of a response, but one time my dad said, "I'd build birdhouses."

"Really!" I said. "What're you going to do with them? Put them in the yard?"

"No, I'm gonna sell birdhouses."

"How many of them could you make in a day?"

My dad shrugged. "I don't know. Two or three."

"So at the end of the week you're going to have maybe twelve or fifteen birdhouses. Where are you going to sell them?"

"Somewhere, maybe on the street."

"What if it's raining? Or are you just going to sell them in good weather?"

"Well," he'd say, "hell, son, I don't know!" and off he'd go with some new on-the-spot cockamamie plan. "If a man had a violin . . ."

He knew I was just messing around, but he really did want the money. We both knew it, and we also knew that I would end up giving him money even though I knew I shouldn't because of the drinking. I knew it enabled him. When he brought a paycheck home, if my mom got ahold of it quickly enough, she kept the money to help pay household bills. This was painful to watch because I knew my dad felt completely emasculated at those moments, and I hated seeing him like that. Between us, it was just a couple of guys kidding around. But when my mom stepped in, he felt like less of a man.

Someone once brought to my attention that every time I spoke of my father, the first thing I'd say was "He was an alcoholic." He was an alcoholic, for sure, but the guy then asked, "Was that the most important thing about your father?" That stopped me in my tracks, because suddenly I realized that he was right. Though his alcoholism was a destructive constant in our lives, it was only a part of my father's personality.

For one thing, he was a damn good fiddle player and, for another, he was a damn good storyteller. Although his drinking certainly hurt him, I don't think it left any of his kids permanently damaged. I'm sure my mom didn't love this side of him, but she loved him. Unlike many couples today, when things got bad, they didn't split up. They stayed together. And honestly, he was the best father he could have been, given his addiction and his inability to find a steady job.

I certainly couldn't say his drinking ruined my life or the lives of any of my brothers and sisters. If anything, it kept me from any real degree of substance abuse. I never wanted to get out of control like I saw my dad and his drinking buddies do back in the projects. My dad never beat us and was never violent on any level. He was in fact a good-natured drunk, except when he would argue with his best friend, Mr. Knoe, another alcoholic who lived across the court-yard from us. They'd get into it and yell at each other for hours, then stagger off home to sleep it off. By morning they'd both have forgotten they even argued the night before. It was never about anger with my dad. His drinking and his all-night arguments were about frustration and disappointment.

My father was never much of a disciplinarian. I only remember a few times when he punished any one of us. One occasion in-volved my younger brother Roy and my dad's precious liquor stash at home. My dad hid his liquor in one of the closets, where one day Roy happened to find a bottle. He knew that the minute our dad got finished with dinner, he would slide into the closet, close the door, and take a big hit from his bottle of whiskey.

That night, Roy was a step ahead of him. He excused himself from the table and scooted into the closet before our dad even got up from the table. Then Roy quickly climbed up into the crawl space above and waited. Sure enough, our dad slipped into the closet and closed the door. Then he located his bottle and took a big long swig. Roy, hidden from sight above him, called out in a ghostly voice: *"Floyd . . . this is your conscience . . ."*

My dad almost had a heart attack. He dropped the bottle, jumped up, and hit his head on the shelf. Roy started laughing, but he didn't laugh long once Daddy saw what was up. Roy got such a whipping and then spent about a month being grounded. This family loved nothing more than a practical joke, even one like this, where the truth of the matter hurt.

Regardless of my dad's troubled life, the only thing I ever re-ally wanted growing up was his approval. Every son needs that, and I was no exception. That was true both when I was younger but also as I got older. Much later on—in the mid-1960s—I was in a jazz group, called the Bobby Doyle Three. Jazz was a music my dad neither liked nor appreciated, but our little group was hot and I wanted him to see us. We were invited to play at the Houston Petroleum Club, a private gathering place of many of the richest people in the state of Texas. I invited my dad to come see the show, assuming he'd never accept. It was not his kind of people or his kind of music. Much to my shock, he said yes. I felt great—I wasn't going to let this father-son moment pass us by.

Keep in mind that my dad had only one suit, one tie, one pair of nice shoes, and one dress shirt, and I'm not sure if I ever saw him in them all at the same time. He arrived at the Petroleum Club looking nice. As I got ready to play, I noticed him working the room, introducing himself as Floyd Rogers, the bass player's dad. He acted like he belonged in that club. I was proud of him that night, and I think he was proud of himself.

But as we played, I came to realize that his only interest was the open bar. He shared a drink with every person he met and as he drank, his face got redder, like the Irishman he was, and his voice got louder. *Oh God*, I thought, *what will he do next?* I was afraid he was going to do something stupid and get us both kicked out of there.

As the show ended, I heard him announce, loudly, to the mayor of Houston and some cronies, "Hi, I'm Floyd Rogers. I'm in the oil and gas business; how about you?" Later, when I finally got him out of the place and confronted him about his lie, he said, "Hell, son, I *am* in the oil and gas business. I work at a gas station eight hours a day, don't I?"

At least for one night, and drunk as can be, he hobnobbed with the rich and felt great about it. I did, too.

What I loved most about Floyd Rogers was his constant laughing at life. He was a jokester, for sure. He always swore that the following was a true story. A policeman pulled him over to write him a ticket for speeding. "What's the problem, Officer?" he asked innocently as he handed over his license.

The trooper looked at the license and said, "Mr. Rogers, do you realize you were doing sixty miles an hour in a thirty-mile-an-hour zone?"

My dad sighed. "Officer, that can't be true. This car won't run for an hour!"

The trooper laughed and tore up the ticket. My dad had joked his way out of a big fine.

Through it all, my mom stood steadfastly beside my dad, and I never saw him belittle or threaten her as some drinking men do to their wives. In the fifty years they were married, I don't think it happened even once. My mom was a physically strong woman and she was bigger than my dad. She wasn't fat by any means, just a big strong woman—five foot eight to my dad's five foot six. I don't think he'd have dared to browbeat my mom even if he'd had the inclination. Well, there was one time. I have no idea what caused their confrontation. The kids were all in the living room doing homework when my dad came around the corner yelling, "Lucille, don't do that!" I never saw her actually hit him, but she was wielding a twelve-inch skillet. Submission and compliance were his only options.

I think I open every conversation about my dad with a remark about his alcoholism because I continue to feel a lot of sadness about him. I wish I'd known him better. I knew his funny side, his good-natured response to almost everything. And I knew his drunken side, when he just seemed to be trying to hang on. But there was a lot more to him that I never quite uncovered. He was a

Mason, and it was important to him. One time after I was older, I asked him about it.

"What's it really all about, Dad?"

"If I told you, I'd have to kill you," he said with a quick laugh.

Drunk or sober, he never even gave me a hint about his meetings at the Masonic lodge. It wasn't even that I wanted to know the specific details of their meetings. But something other than drinking tied those men together in friendship and camaraderie. I'd like to have known that side of my dad.

Another thing I know about him is that he never stopped trying to be a good provider, whether he failed or not. One time he hung on to a job for what seemed like quite a while. It was back when Coca-Cola bottles were delivered in those wooden crates with separate compartments. My dad got a job repairing the ones that got busted throughout the week. Every Saturday morning he would go to the plant and rebuild boxes for twenty-five cents apiece. I helped him with that job, and it was a good father-son time for us.

After my dad died, I found out that he once drove to Galveston trying to get a day's work. He slept outside that night, waiting in the line of men applying for jobs, using his shoes as a pillow. It makes you wonder about his drinking. Was it something within him? Or was it the times? I know that back in the Depression, hard times drove a lot of men to drink, and my dad may have been one of them. But whatever the cause, he never lost his sense of humor, his sense of the absurd.

I had a very close and enduring bond with my mother, and I think my dad understood that. I remember when Terry Williams (a member of the First Edition) and I wrote the song "Momma's Waiting" for the album *Love or Something Like It*. The song is about a guy in prison on death row dreaming of making one last trip back home to see his mom, though the listener doesn't know that fact right away. In the song, the prisoner is driving home knowing his mother will be waiting because . . . "I'm all she's got to love since Daddy's gone."

When he first heard that lyric, my dad jumped up and said, "Well, you damn sure wrote me out fast! Seems like you could have waited until at least the second verse!"

That was classic Floyd Rogers.

If I got my sense of humor from my dad, then my sense of values came from my mom.

My mom had only a third-grade education, but she was one of the wisest people I have ever met. She understood the wisdom she found in biblical proverbs and everyday axioms, and she understood how to say a lot with very few words. Some of her sayings were those that she'd heard over the years; others were ones she made up herself. She always managed to find a succinct way of illustrating a lesson or offering a way to look at life.

They say you can reach any child in one of three ways: the written word, which some kids need to see and read; the spoken word, for kids who need to hear it; and the purely physical. My mom mastered all three. She never hurt any of us, but at one time or another we all thought we were going to die.

Some of the lessons she passed along were just plain old common sense—things like punctuality. If I have a meeting, I will always be on time. My mom believed, and so do I, that being late is disrespectful. It was her opinion that the other person's time was at least as valuable as yours. That's one rule I've tried to impart to my kids as they grow up.

Important as punctuality was, sometimes I took it too far. One of my earliest embarrassments in life came about because of my obsession with being on time. At age twelve, I was invited to my first school party ever and I was the most excited boy in the projects. The girl having the party was Shelby Graves. It was her birthday and she lived over on Taft Street, right above Bryant's five-and-dime, where I walked on my way to elementary school every day. Taft Street wasn't in the projects but was a far more upscale place where professionals lived. Shelby's world involved parents who didn't appear to have to work nonstop to put rice and beans on the table. It was a fairy-tale world to me.

Somehow my mom came up with the money to buy Shelby a little present. We wrapped it up and attached a tag that read, "To Shelby from Kenneth . . ." The party started at two P.M. I took my bath, combed my hair, and dressed in the clothes I usually saved for Sunday church and I was ready. To be safe, I decided I should be there at noon.

Shelby's dad looked confused when he opened the door. I boldly announced, "Hi, I'm Kenneth Rogers and I'm here for the party."

"Well, Kenneth," he said, "aren't you just a little early?"

I felt completely idiotic, but saw no way out. "Maybe," I said. "But I'm here now."

Mr. Graves ushered me in as he mumbled something about things not being quite ready and hoping I didn't mind waiting a while. I didn't mind a bit. I sat there in the living room for two full hours, staring at the wallpaper, until Mrs. Graves got everything in order. I never dared say a word, just sat there with a smile on my face, waiting for the party to start.

Clearly I had to learn the hard way that there was such a thing as being too early, but my mother was always teaching me about the importance of respect. Respect was important to her. From the time I was a kid, my mom taught me to be respectful of others and to try to be thoughtful and fair in my dealings. I live and do business that way, too. I want to play fair with people, and I want them to play fair with me. Karma can be a bitch. Because of my mother, I have been a rule follower all my life. If you aren't supposed to be using the cell phone in a movie theater, then don't use it.

Mom also encouraged me to understand what I was saying and why. Once when she told me I couldn't go to the movies with my friend, I got mad. As I was leaving the room, I mumbled under my breath, "I hate you!" Instead of getting mad at me or shaming me, my mom sat me down and said, "No, son. You don't hate me. You hate the fact that I won't let you do something you want to do. That's a lot different from hating *me*. You need to always understand what you are saying, and why. Use the right words."

As I got older, I realized that she always tried to make things right before we parted. Considering how many people lose parents in accidents or a sudden heart attack after having harsh words, it was a thoughtful thing to do.

My mom believed in teaching her kids about values early. We rode a city bus to church three times a week, rain or shine. I wasn't more than five years old when one night I dug my heels in and said I didn't want to go. My mom said, "Son, I want you to listen to me and remember what I say. You can never be anything more as an adult than what's put into you as a child. So get on the bus and let's go."

She was right. Character is formed early. That's when our personalities and our values take shape and begin to solidify. You can't build a solid house without a strong foundation.

Just as important as her wisdom was her outlook: my mom was the most positive person I have ever known. She had this perpetual optimism about her that got her through even the hardest times. That outlook and an ability to stay hopeful have helped me stay on an even keel throughout all these years. The lows don't throw me into a massive depression, and the highs don't cause me to turn cartwheels. I've tried to look at them with my mother's eyes and find something meaningful—something useful—in each experience.

I believe, in many ways, that has been a key to the way my career has unfolded. I have had many different music careers and many levels of success. And I enjoyed every phase of my journey. I never allowed myself to become content or complacent. I never said to myself: *I can quit trying now. I've had success.* While my mother had a belief that things could always be better, she taught me that part of the trick in achieving that was understanding the difference between happiness and complacency. She would say, "Son, you've gotta be happy where you are. If you're not happy where you are, you'll never be really happy. Never be content to be there, but be happy where you are."

This optimism was with her throughout her whole life, even in the most trying of times. After my dad died, she felt imprisoned in her own house because she had no car and had never even learned how to drive. When anyone left her house to go anywhere—the grocery store, the drugstore—they always invited her to go along. I think she felt we were either feeling sorry for her or making fun of her. "You just go ahead and make fun of me, Kenneth Ray," she said. "I am going to have a car, a brand-new car, too."

"Oh, you are, are you?" I asked with a smile. "You may want to learn to drive first." And she said, "Oh, I will, don't you worry. Just so you know: I'm going to win a car from a contest that Lee Trevino is having. I entered and I am going to win right here in Crockett. Then I'm going to learn how to drive."

And what do you know? My mom won that car in a National Lee Trevino Good Guy Contest, right there in Crockett, Texas. She chose a fire-engine-red Dodge Charger with a white leather top. The seats were all protected by plastic when it was delivered, and she never took that plastic off. She learned to drive, too, just like she said she would. She'd drive from Crockett to Houston to see her grandkids and back again. She was a dreamer, but for Lucille Rogers, dreams did come true.

I have often smiled, knowing that something I did may have made her proud. Not every time, though. Even after her death, I have worried that she might be looking at me right now from somewhere, her eyes narrowed a bit.

"What in the world were you thinking, Kenneth Ray?"

CHAPTER TWO

———————— ✥ ————————

Music and Country

Our family may have lived in Houston, but we had our roots, both musical and historical, in a little unincorporated town called Apple Springs in East Texas. Apple Springs was where our grandfather Byrd Rogers had a farm, and it was on his front porch that I heard live music for the first time.

Grandfather Rogers was steely eyed with a long white handlebar mustache. He wore khaki pants, starched shirts with rolled-up sleeves, and suspenders that he called "galluses" or something close to that. He was darkly tanned from working in his fields. For years, Byrd just barely scraped out a living on a small plot of ground outside of Apple Springs, where he had a house with a long porch in the front and a lone outhouse in the back. That land allowed him to grow a few vegetables—snap beans, watermelon, and corn—and keep a few chickens, while also hunting and fishing. That was enough to keep Byrd and his wife, Della, going, but not enough to support their kids once they grew to adulthood, married, and began having families of their own. There were eight kids in their family as well.

My dad ended up in Houston because he had dreamed of something better than sharecropping in East Texas, but though Houston promised a better life, my dad's eyes always lit up when he'd load us kids into the back of his old pickup and head back to East Texas for a weekend of playing music with his brothers and sisters. Live music in Apple Springs meant the Rogers brothers had come back home from Houston.

My uncles all brought their instruments to these family reunions. My dad brought his fiddle, one of his brothers had an organ—I think it was a B3 or the equivalent—that he pulled out on the porch to play, and my uncle Willie and uncle Judd both played guitar. This was a band. All the kids would sit around and listen to the music and feel the closeness of the family. I would sit with my feet under the front of the house and play drums with my hands on the old wooden porch, as if I were part of the group. I doubt if I had any talent at that age, but one thing's for sure—I had an instant love for music.

A lot of the songs were hymns, and sixty years later they would inspire my 2011 album, *The Love of God*. A number of the songs on the album were ones my dad and uncles had played on their porch in Apple Springs: "Will the Circle Be Unbroken," "Amazing Grace," and "What a Friend We Have in Jesus," as well as "In the Sweet By and By," which I always remember as my mom's favorite song. She sung it over and over ad nauseam, but when you love a song, you love a song. Others are hymns and songs that I'd loved the minute I heard various artists' versions: "I'll Fly Away," with The Whites, and "Circle of Friends," with Point of Grace.

Uncle Willie, my dad's brother, bought me my first musical instrument, a Dobro. When I was twelve, I was sick with the measles and had to stay inside in a darkened room for two weeks. That was the routine treatment back then. Uncle Willie thought it would be a good time for me to learn to play an instrument. The trouble was, Dobro is a difficult instrument to play. It has a solid metal body, and the strings are about a quarter inch off the fingerboard. But I had two weeks in seclusion and so I learned a little riff I could drive my dad crazy with. I must have played it over and over and over again. That's where I started getting the feel of playing an instrument and how much fun it could be.

Although we had fun on Byrd Rogers's porch, Grandpa Rogers was a tough man. He was abrupt and succinct when he spoke. He minced no words.

"Two of the happiest days in my life," he once told me, "are when you come and when you leave." I'd like to think he didn't mean that literally, but with him you could never tell.

Grandpa Rogers believed in teaching tough lessons. He had two animals that he dearly loved, an old horse named Blue, which he refused to work on Sunday, and a dog named Joe. I always felt Byrd, once his kids were gone, loved that old dog like a brother or even a son. They went everywhere together. Byrd never got into his pickup truck without whistling for Joe, who raced from wherever he was in the yard, jumped the fence, and leaped into the truck bed.

One night Byrd, for some reason, strung an extra line of wire above the fence, raising the height by about six inches. The next morning he got in his truck and whistled. Joe ran, jumped like he had for years, hit that wire, and fell back into the yard, momentarily stunned but otherwise unhurt. As he drove off, my grandfather yelled back with a smile, "Joe, don't ever assume today is like it was yesterday."

That was my grandfather's lesson for the day. His sons might not listen to him, but by God his dog would. And his grandson, for the next fifty years.

I remember I had an opportunity one day to impress Grandpa

Rogers, whom we called "Gran'sir." I failed. He was a hunter, a skill that kept his family fed over the years. He decided it was time for me to learn to shoot. In his world, a man never knew when being able to bag a squirrel for dinner might be necessary for survival. So, after some slight weaponry training, into the Piney Woods we went. It didn't take long for him to spot a squirrel in the trees.

"There you go, boy," he whispered. "Let's get us some dinner."

I quickly aimed and wrapped my finger around the trigger. The squirrel looked up, froze in place—and so did I. I couldn't do it. There was no way I could shoot an animal. It wasn't that I had anything against hunting or that I didn't love the taste of meat with my meals. It was just that I couldn't do the shooting myself. My grandfather grabbed his gun, shot the squirrel, and headed back, just that quickly. He was clearly disappointed in me, and I knew it.

I've since wondered, at times like that, if my grandfather ever realized that, music aside, there was a huge chasm between him and his grandchildren—or at least this one. Grandfather Rogers was rural East Texas, and I was Houston. Big difference.

Even to this day, I'm not much of a hunter and I've never felt comfortable around guns. The only gun I ever remember owning was a .22-caliber rifle. When my first wife, Janice, and I were married, I ended up with that gun, though I have no idea where I got it. My brother Billy, who was probably fourteen or fifteen at the time, came to spend the day at our house while I went to work. While he was sitting in our living room holding this gun, it accidentally fired, glancing off the top of the coffee table and lodging itself in our neighbor's house across the street. Billy was too young to see the danger. He was really worried about having scratched the coffee table. Later in my career, I had to do a number of gun scenes in the *Gambler* movies, and even though I knew the rounds were blanks, it still bothered me.

Because my grandparents grew their own food, our meals out there were usually homegrown vegetables and freshly killed game. Sometimes during the day I'd sneak away to my grandpa's watermelon patch and eat a melon while it was still attached to the vine—delicious as long as I didn't get caught. Those visits to Apple Springs were really special to me, filled with memories of great food, great music, good fun with all the cousins, and exploring in the woods. That's an experience you can never forget, especially at night, by yourself.

Even when I wasn't in Apple Springs, music came to me from all directions growing up, and on one occasion it actually changed my life. I was walking home from grade school one day, and like most days, I stopped by Lanzo's Grocery, where Mr. Lanzo would sometimes give our family food that hadn't sold or had to be thrown out. Lanzo was a good man. There was a little black gospel church just down the street from Lanzo's. Sometimes I could hear music coming from that church, music that was far different from what I heard every week when my mom and the family took the bus downtown to First Baptist Church. I loved going to our church. It was huge, with maybe a thousand members, and it had youth and sports programs. I sang in the junior choir, and on special occasions we got to stand in front of the main choir of adults, resplendent in their immaculate robes, and sing our songs. It was a beautiful, spiritual sound.

But the music I heard coming from that little church down from Lanzo's was something else. The power of those voices was so strong, and my curiosity became too much to resist. One day I crept up to the window of the small wooden building and peered inside, wondering if I was doing something wrong and hoping no one caught me spying. The whole congregation was standing, clapping, singing, and some of them were dancing in praise of the Lord. Some of the hymns had the same words as ours, but there was so much warmth and honesty and rhythm in this sound.

Although I didn't realize it at the time, listening that day to that gospel choir was a defining moment for me. I could hear the same songs played in different ways and appreciate both. I could see that everything about the music was in the approach taken. I have always loved all kinds of music and love hearing them played separately or merged together into a kind of fusion. I'm no purist. I just love the music.

As I said, music was always around. Besides the fiddle playing in the country, our house seemed to always have music playing on the radio. I remember Mom ironing in the kitchen, a glass of iced tea on the end of the ironing board, and Hank Williams on the radio. My mom may well have been the worst singer I have ever heard in my life. I feel guilty about saying so, but the fact is, it's true. She was not only bad, she was loud.

My brother Lelan got married at seventeen, and even young as I was, I recognized that his wife, Hazel, was a hot girl. Unlike other members of the family, Lelan and Hazel could dance. They would come into our living room, put on a record, and jitterbug for the whole family. The minute they left, my sisters Geraldine and Barbara would get up and pretend they were Lelan and Hazel. They weren't very good, but it sure was entertaining.

It was a thing to behold—music and dancing, people having a great time. My sister Geraldine had a special musical influence on me, though she didn't often sing and wasn't thought of as a particularly musical person. It was Geraldine who taught me to sing harmony. In church both of us would move away from my mom—sometimes to the other side of the church—because she sang so poorly. I wasn't always sure that was even far enough. One day while singing "The Old Rugged Cross," I noticed Geraldine wasn't singing the melody, but it sounded really good. I asked her what she was singing, and she said they called it "harmony." It changed my musical ear forever. I started listening to and appreciating variations of the melody from then on.

I found that I loved singing this thing called harmony. I loved it so much, in fact, that I didn't envision myself as a solo singer for years on end, just as a harmonizing member of a group.

My mom's family lived in nearby Crockett, Texas. There was Uncle Ocie and Aunt Dimple, Aunt Bill and Uncle Barton, Aunt Mildred and Uncle Pete, Aunt Beulah, Aunt Marie and Uncle Ted. They took great pride in never letting me get too big "for my raisin'," as they loved to say. Uncle Ocie looked every bit the part of an East Texas farmer in his striped overalls, flowered shirt, and brown felt hat. When a film crew working on a TV special about my career came to Crockett and interviewed Uncle Ocie, he later told me: "All these people makin' a fuss over you, sayin' they're glad to see you. Hell, I don't know what makes them think you're so special!"

It was hot in Crockett in the summer, and the homes were cooled by window fans. All the younger cousins would crowd into beds and make small talk late into the night. Our dreams were pretty cut-and-dried back then. The most anyone hoped for was a red Chevy convertible. Most of our days were spent down at the local Dairy Queen, the social center of Crockett, Texas.

My mother's father, Wily Hester—we called him Papa—later

shared a house with us on Clay Street in pretty much downtown Houston. Some of my best memories of early childhood were in that house with Papa, who was as much a character as Byrd Rogers. Papa had epilepsy and was also in what seemed to be the early stages of Alzheimer's. Like Byrd, Papa was a man of few words. I remember him sitting in a rocking chair on the porch of the house we rented, watching us kids run and play. He'd watch as long as he could stand the commotion, then stand up and say "Can that fuss!" at the top of his voice. And believe me, we did.

My most unusual memory about Papa Hester was the time I took a late-night trip with him. Perhaps it was because of Alzheimer's or just senility, but he had taken to walking in his sleep. The trouble was, he slept with me. I must have been three or four years old when he decided to take me on a nighttime excursion.

I remember waking up as he lifted me out of bed, stood me on the floor, and took my hand. Then we went to the screen window, which was open on that hot, humid Houston night. Papa unlatched the screen and out we climbed. My parents found us much later, blocks away, just sitting in the middle of Root Square Park. Grandpa Hester was sound asleep at a picnic table, and I was sitting there just watching him and looking around.

Other than the sleepwalking episode, he was not a problem. He was quiet, kept to himself, and was prone to staring off into space for long periods of time. Sometimes my mom would stand there looking at him, and say, "Well, I guess Papa's crossed over again." That's an expression we all used affectionately when my grandfather checked out.

Papa Hester was a sweet old guy. He used to say, "Son, youth only happens to you one time, so if you should miss it when you're young, you can still have it when you're old." Although Papa just sat there on the porch all day long, doing nothing, I thought his words of wisdom were so thought provoking that, years later, they inspired me to write a song about him.

There's an old man in our town,
I guess he's been around
For years and years,
At least it seems that way.

Wrinkled hands and rocking chair,
Growing old just sitting there.
Every year he had the same old things to say.

Youth only happens to you one time,
And so I've been told,
If you should miss it in your young time,
Have it when you're old.

Papa wasn't an overtly affectionate person, so it was hard to tell him just how much he meant to us. That tribute in the song was the only way I knew how to do it.

He was a true product of Depression-era America. He lived through it, and consequently was, let's say, careful with his money.

When I was in my late twenties, playing music for a living and scouting opportunities in California, we decided to take Papa, who had never been out of the state of Texas, on a trip. We all piled in my 1957 Chevrolet Bel Air and drove for five days, taking our time because Papa Hester was thoroughly enjoying this bucket-list trip across the country. We stopped all along the way, filling the hours with diners and donuts, eating our way to L.A.

Once we got there, Papa Hester pulled me aside, as if to spare me any embarrassment in front of the rest of the family, and handed me $313.38 in small bills and a big pile of change, along with some grandfatherly advice: "Son, you'll never have any money if you keep leaving it everywhere you go."

Unbeknownst to the rest of us, Papa had been picking up all the tips I had left in diners and cafés along the road.

He smiled at me and said, "One day, boy, you'll thank me for this."

CHAPTER THREE

Lovesick Blues

I started grade school at Wharton Elementary School on West Gray Street with the hope of blending in with all the other guys. I didn't want to stand out for any reason, good or bad; I just wanted to be accepted. My goal was anonymity. Being considered an average student was plenty good for me, and that's what I was. I think I probably had a little attention deficit disorder, but of course there was no such diagnosis back then. I was just considered a hyper kid. I had a lot of energy and was a little scattered.

The problem that faced me early on was this: although I wanted to remain anonymous among the guys, I still wanted the girls to notice me. I was, from age six, girl crazy. The love of my life in elementary school was Colleen Mays. I thought she was the coolest girl I had ever seen. She didn't live in the Courts, either, but in a very wealthy area near school. Colleen was really beautiful and pretty impressive in her brightly polished brown-and-white saddle shoes. I noticed them every morning as we sat in class. While all the other kids were doing their work, I was totally mesmerized by her shoes. They looked brand-new every morning! Maybe that's why I was a C student.

If Colleen had agreed to be my girlfriend, it would have been a classic case of dating up. Her father was a federal judge. Their yard was huge and full of pecan trees. Every day on my way home, I would ask her parents if I could pick up pecans for my family and also a few for *her* family.

I also had a pal named Ronnie Sherrod who was a real jock and played shortstop on the school softball team. Since Ronnie was on the team, I always came to the games, and it didn't take me long to notice that Colleen was there, too. She never missed a game. So I started practicing fast-pitch softball with Ronnie. I worked and worked and finally got good enough to be the pitcher on the team. It got even better when we started winning.

One day after I had pitched a big win for the team, I swaggered over to where Colleen was standing. "Hi, Colleen!" I said, ready for her to tell me how great I was and start up the romance of my young life. At the very least I expected a hi or a giggle. Instead I got, "You are such a show-off!"

I was mortified.

It hurt so much because she was right. I had developed a big windmill pitch that helped get batters out but was really designed to impress Colleen. Obviously it didn't.

I'll let you in on a secret: entertainers—no matter how old they are—should never take themselves too seriously. Years later, in the early 1980s when I was at the peak of my success, I came to Houston for a show. You always want to look good for your hometown, so I was excited about playing before eighty thousand people at the Houston Astrodome. The show was great. The crowd cheered with every song and laughed at all my jokes. It couldn't have gone better.

As I was leaving the building with my mother, it suddenly got a *lot* better. There she was . . . Colleen Mays! I recognized her immediately. I hadn't seen her for years, not since we were kids. What a rush! She'd come to see her old friend, the boy with the razzle-dazzle windup who used to pick pecans in her yard.

I stopped the procession leaving the arena and went over to her, thinking, *This is so cool.*

"Hello, Colleen!" I said.

"Hello," she said, with a completely blank look on her face.

"I'm Kenneth Rogers. We went to Wharton Elementary together. I used to pick pecans at your house." I was feeling a little less cool. It appeared that Colleen had come to a Kenny Rogers concert, advertised as a show from a hometown boy, and never made the connection to the Kenneth Rogers she knew as a child. She really had no memory of that little awestruck boy from the projects.

"Remember, I pitched on the softball team?"

"Yeah, I kind of remember that."

You bitch! I thought. *You "kind of remember that"? Come on! Throw me a bone, Colleen. My mom is standing right here! You could at least pretend that you remember me!*

I guess I had been more successful at being anonymous in grade school than I thought.

If a celebrity likes people to read about his successes, he should be willing to share his humiliations as well. In my life, more than a few have fit the pattern set by Colleen.

As early as grade school, I began to see music and singing as a respite from all the awkwardness and embarrassment of growing up poor, shy, and often an outsider. Developing a little confidence from singing and playing around the house, I entered my first talent show in Houston. It was 1949, and I was ten years old. The event was sponsored by Foremost Dairy and held just prior to a big Eddy Arnold appearance at the Texan Theatre, where I later worked. Eddy was a big country star at the time, at one point that year having five hits on the charts at the same time. The grand prize of the competition was a half gallon of vanilla ice cream, quite the prize for a ten-year-old from the projects. And the grand *grand* prize was that the winner would get to meet Eddy in person.

I marched out on that stage and sang and yodeled a song called "Lovesick Blues." Originally a show tune from the 1920s, this song had been released by the great Hank Williams and became his first No. 1 hit. I heard it on the radio and figured that if Hank had hit the jackpot with it, maybe I would, too. I threw myself into the performance, even the yodeling parts, and ended up winning first prize. Either I was better than I thought or the other kids were awful. In any case, that half gallon of Foremost Dairy's finest ice cream was mine. Plus a face-to-face meeting with Eddy Arnold! It would take another thirty years or so for me to become a true country singer, but I sure felt like a country star that day.

I was ushered backstage to meet Eddy, and he let me play his big blond Gibson L5. I got a chance to talk about how much I loved his No. 1 hit ballads like "What Is Life Without Love" and "It's a Sin," and he said something nice about my yodeling. What a night.

That contest was one of the first times I felt the thrill of performing, but it also produced, years later, another one of those don't-take-yourself-too-seriously moments. I was in Knoxville to receive a career achievement award, "The Froggy," from radio station WIVK, and as fate would have it, Eddy Arnold was the presenter. By this time he was a legend, having spent more than 145 weeks in the top spot on the country charts, a record at the time. This was the second high honor Eddy had presented me in my life.

His speech started off on a high note: "I like this guy. He's had so many big hits. He's done so many good things for country music." He kept going on and on about how I so richly deserved this award, until he finally said, "I really do like this guy, but for the life of me, I can't remember his name!"

That line took me right back to grade school.

CHAPTER FOUR

Moving On Up

None of the Rogers family minded hard work, including me. I'm still a hard worker, though it's not the hard physical kind these days. My seven sisters and brothers were all workers, too. Before my older brother, Lelan, got involved in the music business, kind of leading the way for me, he worked at Wormser Hat Store in downtown Houston, selling hats. When I was eleven, he got me a job down there sweeping the floor and squeegeeing windows. At a dollar and a half a day, six afternoons a week, I brought home a weekly paycheck of $9, money my mom used to help keep the family afloat.

Every day, right after school, I'd catch the bus downtown for a nickel, put in my hours, then ride it back home for another nickel. One payday before I caught the bus home, I decided to stop in at the penny arcade down the street. Just this once, I told myself, I deserved it. I walked in planning to spend a dollar, tops—and walked out penniless. I had blown my entire $9 pay. This presented two problems: How was I going to face my mom? And how was I going to get home?

I started panhandling on the street, and in an hour collected about fourteen dollars. In a very short time I had gone from *"just this once"* to *"boy, I have blown it"* to *"look at all this money!"* The last guy who stopped was my bus driver. He looked at me with a stern face, and said, "I won't give you any money, but I'll give you a transfer pass. Use it to get home."

It was a humiliating end to my short career as a panhandler.

I started hitchhiking to school every day once I entered junior high school at George Washington Junior High on Shepherd Drive, something no one would do today. If that makes me sound like a tough, daring kid, I wasn't. In fact, I was still afraid of the dark. As shy and self-conscious as I was, though, I realized by junior high that the only real way to attract girls, my continuing passion, was either to be a star athlete or to play in a band. I had loved music since I first saw my dad play the fiddle on Grandpa Rogers's front porch, but I thought sports would be a faster way to gain recognition, so I went out for football. I was excited about being a player because I was particularly interested in a gorgeous cheerleader named Leah Ray Bloecher and being a jock seemed like the path to her heart.

Late summer in Houston was hot and humid, the pads and helmet were heavy, and sweat was running off my face in sheets. Convinced I was ready for the punishment, I went out on the field and started running laps with the rest of the guys. Ten minutes later I was passed out cold on the ground. The next thing I knew, I woke up on a bench in the dressing room, with a doctor telling me to lie still. To me that was a signal from on high that maybe football wasn't my destiny. I called it quits. As I realized very quickly, there's a big difference between being athletic, which I was, and being an athlete, which I wasn't.

I came up with a better Plan B: I would be a cheerleader. That way I got to be at every game, right next to Leah Ray, and never had to risk passing out on the field. I practiced hard but really paid more attention to Leah Ray than I did to the finer points of cheerleading. During our practice sessions, we worked up a cheer with a big ending, where I threw Leah Ray up in the air, then caught her. On the night we rolled this trick out for the football fans, my brother Lelan showed up to watch me cheer. I threw Leah Ray into the air as planned, turned to give a proud look at Lelan, and promptly dropped her on the ground. After that, she kept her distance from me, in every way.

If you come from a family of eight kids, many of them older than you, then there are always people around to show the way. At sixteen, like all red-blooded American boys, I was itching to drive. My sister Geraldine's husband, Eddie Houston, one of the best guys in the world and the rock of Geraldine's life, agreed to teach me. Eddie had a stiff leg from childhood polio, but that never kept him from living his life. The first time we went out in traffic in his old Model T Ford, I turned too quickly, hopped a curb, and busted the right front tire, a disaster in those hard times. Eddie, with no money for a new tire, said, "Don't worry, we'll fix the thing." Which is exactly what we did, with a tire-patching kit. To this day, when someone on the crew has an accident, I can hear Eddie's voice saying "Don't worry, we'll fix the thing."

A few years down the road, I sent Eddie a couple of hundred bucks with a note attached. "Hey, Eddie, this is for that tire I busted when I was a kid." He got a big kick out of that.

As a complete aside—it's a habit of mine—Eddie worked as an accountant for a box company called Gaylord Containers and said he had a gift for numbers. I was instantly impressed. One day, hanging with him at his office, he challenged me to give him some numbers to add in his head. I started reeling them off.

"$6,241."

"Okay." Eddie closed his eyes as if he were The Amazing Kreskin.

"$4,911."

"Okay."

"$16,221."

"Okay."

And the last one," I said, "is $18,000."

"Got it." Short beat. "$62,535 is the total."

I was so amazed. It was so cool that he could just add a group of numbers in his head like that without even writing them down. Just to make sure, I re-added the numbers on his calculator while he was doing something else.

He wasn't even close.

When I confronted him, he smiled and said, "I told you I had a gift. I never said it was a good gift."

That's what I loved about him—an accountant with a sense of humor, and boy, are those hard to find. My first professional accountant/business manager, Michael Gesas, also had a droll sense of humor. As we became close friends, he and his wife, Helene, would come and visit me when I had my farm in Georgia, Beaver Dam Farms. He always had this dream of riding horses. Now there's a great picture, an accountant cowboy from Beverly Hills on a horse. Far be it from me to deny him his dream. In the stable was a big black thoroughbred named Mikey. It was his choice to ride Mikey.

It all started as planned. We mounted up like cowboys and hit the dusty trail. As we were riding, the path took us down by the creek. Michael had no sooner said, "I feel like John Wayne today," when Mikey decided he had had enough. He headed to a sand bed alongside the creek and politely lay down on his side with Mike's leg underneath him. We were all laughing so hard, we didn't even realize he might have been hurt when he asked, "What's the signal for get up?" So we all answered, "How about 'get up'! See if that works." All we heard was the meek voice of what sounded like a seven-year-old saying, "Get up, horsey, get up," but Mikey just lay there. It was a perfect match. Mikey the accountant and Mikey the horse. We all chose to ride off and leave him, knowing Mikey the horse would get up and follow us. When Mike caught up with us, he kept saying unconvincingly, "Boy, that was really fun. It doesn't get any better than this." That's as close to a sense of humor as a business manager/accountant is allowed to have.

Another in-law, my sister Barbara's first husband, Sonny Gibbs (who is not to be confused with the NFL player of the same name), had a big role in at least two experiences that changed my life. Sonny was, in his time, a legendary high school athlete in Houston, and Barbara was crazy about him. When I was twelve, the two of them got roped into babysitting for me on a night they were to attend a really special concert. Having no other choice, they dragged me along to the concert. The main attraction: Ray Charles. I was both wowed by the stage performance and stunned by the love and admiration the audience showed him. They applauded his music and laughed at his jokes. I left that place that night wanting very much to do the same thing.

I also realized for the first time that night something essential to being a performer. People will sometimes clap to be nice, but no one ever laughs to be nice. They laugh when they think something is funny. It's either there or it's not.

My brother-in-law Sonny was a great athlete, but he was also something else: a drug addict. Everyone, including Barbara, knew this, but no one talked about it. One day, out of the blue, he asked me to sit on the front porch and talk for a few minutes. I had no idea what he wanted to talk about, but it soon became apparent. He wanted me to promise him that I wouldn't make the same mistakes that he had made that had sidetracked his whole life. He wanted something good to come from his life, and warning me off drugs was, in his mind, a good start. He asked for a solemn pledge to avoid drugs and I gave it to him. And, with a few infractions along the way, I have largely kept that pledge.

I now had the example of my dad to keep me away from alcohol and that promise to Sonny to stay away from the very drugs that had consumed so many musicians and entertainers over the years. Once again, someone had taken the time to care about me enough to change my life.

In 1954, a good thing happened. With my mom working extra jobs and with Lelan, Geraldine, Barbara, and me all contributing to the family income, the Rogers clan was no longer poor enough to qualify for public housing. We had moved up a notch on the economic scale. We moved out of San Felipe Courts and over to the north side of Houston, right across the street from Jefferson Davis High School, just as I was starting high school. I was coming up in the world.

My paperwork to transfer from my old neighborhood high school, San Jacinto, to Jeff Davis hadn't come through by the first day of school, so when I showed up at San Jacinto, I knew I was in for a wasted day. Rule follower that I was, I had never before had the audacity to skip school, but now was my big chance. Some friends and I decided to drive to a place called Spring Creek, about twenty miles north of Houston.

What a day! We had borrowed a brand-new red Mercury convertible from my brother Lelan's friend Frank, just back from a tour of duty in the military, swam in the creek, and then headed home at sundown. We all went back to San Jacinto the next day, where we were politely greeted by four city detectives and promptly arrested and taken to jail in handcuffs. That was a shocker, to say the least.

As it turned out, a delivery truck from Ben Wolfman's Furs had been robbed the day before in the same area and someone had reported the license number of our flashy red convertible as the getaway vehicle. That was the bad news. The good news was that we were cleared right away. The best news was that when I got back to San Jacinto High, you would have thought I was a convicted felon and hardened criminal in the eyes of the other students. Though all we really did was lounge by a creek all day, we had been arrested, and we deserved respect.

When I then showed up for my first day at Jefferson Davis, my tough-guy reputation, despite my soft-guy nature, had preceded me. That was good, because the Jeff Davis crowd was all new to me, and it was better to be seen as a tough guy than just another nervous teen. But the moment of truth came when the resident bully, Wallace Connor, chose me as his next victim. For whatever reason, he thought that I needed to be taught a lesson. I was sitting on a stool at Dube's drugstore one afternoon with none of my backup crew when Wallace accosted me. He punched me in the back of the head with his fist, snarling, "Hey, tough guy, I want you outside. I'm gonna whip your ass."

"Well," I said, "now is as good a time as any," shaking like a leaf but seeing no way out of it. "Let's get it on."

That appeared to shock Wallace, and he hesitated a moment before he said anything else. Finally he shrugged and said, "I guess we don't need to do this. I just wanted to see what you were made of."

Standing up to Wallace Connor was a big accomplishment at Jeff Davis, and no one bothered me again, with or without my tough-guy reputation. I don't know if Wallace was really the badass he made himself to be when I first met him, but a few months after he got out of high school, someone shot him through the screen window of his home, thinking he was a drug dealer. He died instantly.

I ended up buying my first guitar with money I earned while working as a busboy at the Rice Hotel in downtown Houston. Throughout high school, I continued to take as many part-time jobs as possible, including working as an usher at the Metropolitan Theater and rebuilding Coca-Cola boxes. Finally, after I'd been at the Rice Hotel for a bit, I'd saved enough to actually buy an instrument.

At the local H&H music store, a salesman named Red Novak had set up a kind of "pickers' corner" in the store where you could go in and play one of their instruments. He'd let you pick out a guitar and try it out as long as you were responsible. Red's rule was "You Break It, You Own It!"—but he at least gave you the chance to play really good instruments without having to buy them. There were other pickers who hung around the store. We all learned chords and technique from each other. There was a great camaraderie at those guitar pulls.

The guitar I loved was a Les Paul L5, the same guitar Eddy Arnold had let me play years earlier. It cost $500. I ended up putting it on layaway and paying for it, bit by bit, with money I earned working my part-time jobs. But I practiced on it, learning the chords, in Red's pickers' corner.

I guess you could say that from a professional standpoint, it all started for me when I went to a talent contest at Jeff Davis and saw a really bad band get up onstage and play. Once I saw how little it took to be in a "talent contest," I figured I could do better. I had learned a lot from all those sessions at the music store, and I believed I could put together a band that *could* be professional.

One of the greatest things for me at Jeff Davis was singing in the glee club, where Mrs. Leifesti encouraged my singing and gave me a lot of solo parts in school performances. By this time, some friends and I had formed a vocal group called the Scholars, an interesting name for four C students. Nevertheless, we were serious. As a cover band, we sang whatever was popular on the radio, like songs of the Penguins ("Earth Angel") or the multihit group the Drifters, or anything else that sounded good with four-part harmony. I played my Les Paul guitar for that group. The four of us went to the First Baptist Church together and joined the Texas National Guard at the same time. We were having fun making music and getting better at it. We were a group. That's where I felt most comfortable.

We took turns singing lead and sang a lot of harmonies, because doo-wop and R&B harmonies were the music styles of the times. Although I played guitar, we were primarily a vocal group. I think I was the only musician in the band. We rehearsed in the basement of the church and ended up playing for sock hops at every school around. We were in high demand, or so we thought. Performing for free added a lot of luster to our career.

It wasn't long before we felt that our sound was good enough to play for bigger audiences. My brother Lelan was a clothes salesman at the time, but he agreed to be our manager. Now we were pros. We had a manager.

Lelan was something else—a good-looking, slim, five-foot-eleven guy who always had a smile on his face. Nothing ever seemed to get him down. He always had a hello or a pat on the back when someone needed it. He was also a bit of a street hustler. If you weren't streetwise back then, you'd get chewed up in that world of indie labels, major labels, promoters, producers, and clubs, both paying and nonpaying. Nobody chewed up Lelan Rogers, and he never tried to chew up anyone else. If anyone could help me maneuver through the mine fields of this business, it was Lelan.

Somehow, Lelan got us booked for a show at the officers' club at a military base in San Antonio. So off we went, in a 1956 Ford Fairlane, for the 340-mile round trip. After playing two twenty-minute sets, we each got paid $13. Hell, we were professionals now!

What was important to us was that those air force officers had no idea that this was the band's first real-for-sure paying gig. They treated us like professionals, and I believe that when you're treated like a professional, you become a professional. After that night at the San Antonio officers' club, we were off and running, at least as a cover group.

The hottest venue the Scholars ever played was a strip joint in Dallas allegedly owned by Jack Ruby, the mob-connected guy who shot Lee Harvey Oswald. This was a club where patrons would put up with twenty minutes of band music to see the main attraction: dancers like legendary Texas stripper Candy Barr. We would put in our twenty minutes, then trip over each other racing to the balcony to see Candy in action. And not one of us was of legal age.

Life was good.

CHAPTER FIVE

Goin' Solo

The Scholars formed in 1956 and developed throughout 1957, but in the middle of all this, an abrupt, unforeseen event turned my life upside down. The first girl I had ever had sex with got pregnant. Her name was Janice Way and I met her at one of the high school talent contests, where every band in the area took a shot at local stardom. Janice was beautiful and truly one of the sweetest girls I had ever met. She was a dancer, and a good one, a student of Patrick Swayze's mom, Patsy, a fixture in the Houston dance community long before her son became a movie star. Janice and I had a few dates, and while we weren't looking down the road to a future, we did care for each other. We didn't know it at the time, but we had a future looming that read "big time." This was the same time my brother Lelan decided that I should try to make it as a solo artist, as I'll explain in a moment. But first, Janice and I had an appointment with a justice of the peace.

I got the call from Janice's mother on a Wednesday. "You better get over here right now, Kenny," Mrs. Way said. "I need to talk to you."

"How about Saturday?" I replied, thinking foremost about my music.

"I don't think so," she barked. "You need to get here right now. We have plans to make. You and Janice are getting married on Saturday.

My daughter is pregnant and you are responsible. Come tonight and be prepared to get married on Saturday, young man, do you understand?"

My response, as weird as it may sound now, was simply, "Well, okay."

My family was stunned at the news that I was getting married in four days, to say the least. My dad sat at the table with his head in his hands. They thought they should go to Janice's house with me.

"My God, son," he said, "just when you are old enough to help out around here, you let this happen."

"You're the one," I told him, "that taught me, 'If you're man enough to get yourself in trouble, then you need to be man enough to get yourself out.'"

So I went alone. Having no understanding of the seriousness of this moment, in some perverse way I was proud of myself.

Prior to Janice, when I was still the rule follower, I had always stopped before consummating the act. I understood how girls got pregnant and that guys had an obligation when they did. When my Janice got pregnant, I was fully prepared to take the step into married life. It never occurred to me to walk away from the responsibility. I was my mother's son, after all. Not only was this Lucille Rogers's personal moral code, it was mine, too. It was not for nothing that Kenneth Ray Rogers had taken the downtown bus to the First Baptist Church with his mom all those years.

The fact that I stood up to take responsibility at that moment did not mean my parents were happy about my getting married. They saw it from the perspective of losing another wage earner in the family. Our family hadn't been out of the San Felipe projects that long. Both Lelan and Geraldine had quit high school to start working and help the family out, and my mom had hopes that with a high school degree, I could earn even more. She wanted me to be happy and pursue my dreams—something a teenage marriage threatened—but she was also determined to bring her family out of poverty, and I was part of the plan.

I saw the marriage in a different light. When I got married, I thought that having a wife just meant a guy could have sex anytime he happened to think about it, which in my case was *all* the time. I can still see the look on my dad's face when I told him my all-sex/all-the-time theory of wedded bliss. He looked at me and shook his head.

"Just know this, son," he said. "Sooner or later you'll have to get out of bed."

Janice and I were married on May 15, 1958, and our daughter, Carole, was born the following September. At the time, I honestly didn't feel "trapped" or cheated out of anything. I thought the idea of being married was pretty cool. The Scholars were going strong, plus I was sitting in with groups around town and even playing in some recording sessions. We moved in with Janice's parents for a year until I had a job that paid enough to rent an apartment. We bought furniture for the living room, dining room, and bedrooms. We were playing house.

Around the time Janice and I were married, I graduated from high school. I became the first person in my family to walk across the stage and pick up a high school diploma. My mom and dad and seven siblings were so proud that day. It seemed like a turning point for my family and its hope for a better future.

Now out of high school, I took any musical job I could find and also worked a series of day jobs, trying to earn enough for rent and diapers. It was important to me that we had our own place and furniture we could call our own. I even saved up enough to buy a brand-new "pea green" 1959 Chevrolet. I did everything I could to pay the bills and still keep my hand in the music business. I had a dream; I was married; I had a beautiful wife and a beautiful daughter. I was happy.

I landed a day job selling office supplies, carbon paper, and typewriter ribbons. I was determined to make a success of both the sales job and my so-called music career, so I planned my schedule carefully. I played music at night, then came straight home and got some sleep. At eleven A.M., I was off to the day job. I started by making appointments with people working at offices in the Gulf Building in downtown Houston. I would begin on the top floor and work my way down to ground level. Even though I was only showing up for three hours a day, I was the company's top salesman. I figured that I was doing pretty damn good. Unfortunately, my boss, Ed Benson, saw it otherwise and fired me.

First he called me in and demanded that I work a regular nine-to-five schedule. "But I'm already selling more than anybody else," I said.

"That doesn't matter," Ed said. "Just think how much you could sell if you put in a full day. Look at the commissions you could be earning!"

"I don't care about the commissions," I countered. "I'm doing just fine."

"Well," he replied, "you're bringing down the company's morale. You're the top salesman and only working three hours a day!" I found that to be a position I couldn't argue with. Ed had a point. I had to go.

Ed Benson was actually a good guy. He and his wife, Elaine, liked me and no doubt just thought I was undisciplined. The trouble was, it wasn't discipline I lacked. It was time. I needed every hour I could squeeze out of a day to become a musician.

The truth is, Janice's parents never got used to the idea of their son-in-law being a musician, whether I was making money with a series of day jobs or not. Once they saw that I wasn't going to change my career ambitions away from music, they wanted little to do with the marriage. They wrote me off as a long-term bread-winner, and our marriage turned sour and lasted only until the next October of 1959.

The whole thing ground to a halt one day when our daughter, Carole, was about six months old. Janice and I were having what some might call an argument, but it was actually more of a difference of opinion. I don't even remember what it was about. I am capable of getting pretty heated during an exchange of views, and Janice was the kind of person who hated confrontation.

The one thing I didn't want to happen was to say something that would hurt Janice or fill me with guilt and regret down the line. I loved Janice and had no intention of hurting her. Plus, remember, I never saw my dad, even in his most drunken state, fight with my mom. I hadn't grown up around parents who yelled at each other or said nasty things. So I decided to take a walk and cool off.

"I'm gonna walk around the block," I said. "Let's not say things that will be hard to take back." I left, walked around a while, and returned to the apartment to find Janice's mother there helping her pack.

"You've ruined my daughter's life," she snapped. "I'm taking her out of here, and don't you ever call her again." I was so shocked I honestly didn't know what to think or do. Afterward I kept trying to get Janice on the telephone, but I never could make it past her parents. Finally one day I called in the middle of the day and Janice answered. I had my speech prepared.

"This is crazy, Janice," I said. "I love you. Let's go somewhere with Carole and get a sandwich or something and try to work this out. I know we can."

"Just a second," she replied. "I have to ask my mother." When she came back to the phone, she said, "I'm sorry, Kenneth, but Mother won't let me go."

Janice's parents obviously thought I was worthless. That's when I decided to just walk away. That's how I have always been with unresolved, and seemingly irresolvable, situations. I give some-one every chance, but if the situation turns bad, I completely shut down. I close myself off to that person and it's never the same for me. It's like a light switch. I click it off and walk away.

In April 1960, less than two years after we married, our divorce was finalized, with Janice having custody of Carole and me paying $80 a month in child support. The divorce was hard enough, but losing Carole was extremely painful.

Soon after, Janice married another high school boyfriend, David Billingsley, and she asked that Carole be adopted by them. She also wanted to change Carole's name to Billingsley. I reluctantly agreed. I wasn't happy with the decision, but I truly believed Carole would be better off with a dad in the house with her, whose name she used, rather than trying to explain where her real father was. I made a conscious effort not to create problems for their family. Consequently, my daughter and I never had a chance to really bond. I'm not sure I handled the situation in the best possible way, but I was very young and simply made what I thought was the best decision at the time.

So that was the end of that intense, emotionally confusing teenage marriage. I have said this often: music, at least for me, is like a mistress, and she's a difficult mistress for a wife to compete with. It took me five tries to find the right woman and get this marriage thing all worked out in my life. Looking back, I think the failure of each of my first three marriages was 85 percent my fault. If success—and I'm not talking about dollars but about professional acceptance—had been less important, I could probably have stayed with any of the three. But at the time, especially with Janice, the need to succeed was more important than holding a marriage together.

I've long thought about my marriages and about being so career-driven. Just the other night, I sat up in bed and thought, *You know, Kenny, there's a fine line between being driven and being selfish.* And I may have crossed that line.

Even before my days with Janice were over, the Scholars had their shot at fame and fortune. Lelan arranged for us to record a tune called "Poor Little Doggie" on Jimmy Duncan's local Houston label, Cue Records. Soon after, we recorded a follow-up, "Spin the Wheel." Neither went very far, but they got us some national distribution. Then Lelan set up a recording deal with Imperial Records in L.A., the people who brought you Fats Domino and Ricky Nelson, among other '50s stars. We cut a couple of forgettable tunes before we got to what would become the group's swan song, a tune called "Kan-Gu-Wa." This was written by the then-famous gossip columnist Louella Parsons. The idea was that if we cut her song, Ms. Parsons might help promote us through her column.

"Kan-Gu-Wa" was as close to the big time as the Scholars got.

The record company flew us out to Los Angeles to record. That was my very first trip outside of the state of Texas. It was quite an experience for a bunch of greenhorn kids still in high school. The label booked us rooms at a hotel and hired some of the top studio musicians in town for the sessions. In addition, we were each paid the princely sum of $150.

"Kan-Gu-Wa" went nowhere, but the experience of being in Los Angeles, a world away from Houston, stayed with me. I knew that despite how rich the music scene in South Texas might be, everything I wanted for the future was happening in Los Angeles, California. That trip just fed my ambition to shoot for the moon.

Like most teenage bands, even those who got the thrill of cutting records, the Scholars soon went by the wayside. One guy decided to go to college. The L.A. experience had convinced another that he should try to become a solo singer. I wasn't sure what I was going to do when "Kan-Gu-Wa" flopped and the band broke up. Remember, I was never the lead singer of the group—I sang first tenor and played the guitar. But still, all I knew was that I wanted to keep singing and playing my guitar.

Though nothing came of it, my brother Lelan succeeded in steering the Scholars from Cue, a local label, to Imperial, a national one. And though the Scholars disbanded, Lelan was sticking with me. Like a lot of promoters, Lelan himself wasn't musical. But he *loved* music, especially R&B. He knew everybody on that side of the business, and he later became heavily involved in the careers of some terrific talents, including Big Al Downing and Esther Phillips. He may not have been credited with everything he did, but he was there pulling strings. I am still in awe of him.

While I was working at being young and married, Lelan was spending time with a local singer-songwriter named Ray Doggett, who was writing songs for guys named Jimmy Duncan and Larry

Kane there in Houston. Ray was on Decca and trying to decide what material to record when he asked Lelan for advice on his songs. The minute Lelan heard Ray's "That Crazy Feeling," he thought it was right for me, so, under the more formal-sounding name of Kenneth Rogers, we released the song on the Carlton label.

Larry Kane had a local television show in Houston using the *American Bandstand* format. I was scheduled to perform "That Crazy Feeling" on that show as Kenneth Rogers. Larry graciously told me, "You can't use Kenneth Rogers; it's too formal. You need to be Kenny Rogers." I said I really didn't want to do that because it would break my mom's heart. But once the show started, Larry Kane introduced me as Kenny Rogers, against the best instincts of both my mom and me. Every little girl in the audience clapped and screamed "We love you, Kenny!!!" With that, the decision had been made—I was now Kenny Rogers.

Late one afternoon my sister Barbara told me to listen to KNUZ radio because they were playing my record. I turned on my little Motorola and listened for three hours before I heard it. It wasn't in heavy rotation yet, but it was there. It was strange; I remember thinking that it didn't even sound like me. I was from the projects and now I was on the radio.

Lelan went to work promoting the single, and when regional radio started playing the song in heavy rotation, local sales took off. Lelan said that Carlton sold a million copies of "That Crazy Feeling." I never saw anything from those million copies, if in fact that's what sold, and in all fairness I doubt it sold that. But it did become a big enough hit that I was invited to perform on the premier rock-and-roll TV show of its time: *Dick Clark's American Bandstand*. When word of this got out, I got my first-ever write-up as a solo artist in the *Houston Chronicle*.

The headline was "Kenny Rogers, Local Boy, Is on the Way," and the story read, in part:

> A 19-year-old Houston singer whose tunes have been set-ting the record circuits on fire will take to the tube Thurs-day on *Dick Clark's American Bandstand.* Fans who watch the rock 'n' roll stint on KTRK-TV (4 P.M. daily) likely will hear Rogers sing his hit, "That Crazy Feeling." Rogers, who once sang with the popular Houston-based the Scholars, has ventured out on his own. Reports are that his hit tune is currently the No. 2 best seller in this area. It has done landmark business in other areas of the country, too. Kenny is a graduate of Jeff Davis High School here and is currently attending the University of Houston.

It was the most exciting thing I could have ever dreamed of—flying to Philadelphia to appear on *the* teenage star-making TV show of the era. When I got to the studio, the producers had me sit in a soda shop set, eating a hot fudge sundae, singing "That Crazy Feeling." I have no idea whose idea it was for me to be at a table eat-ing ice cream, but I didn't care. I was on *American Bandstand* and the whole country was watching.

This performance set me up for yet another of those "Who did you say you are?" moments like I'd had with Colleen, the judge's daughter. Years later, I was talking to Dick Clark, who by then I had become good friends with, and I brought up that appearance. Dick looked a little confused. He obviously didn't remember me.

"Come on, Dick," I said. "You have to remember that show. Ed Townsend was there, 'For Your Love.'"

"Oh, I remember Ed Townsend," Dick said, brightening up.

"It was the same show!" I said excitedly. "I was wearing a gray suit and a white shirt and I sang 'That Crazy Feeling' in a soda shop."

Dick frowned and shook his head. "I'm sorry, Kenny. I just have no memory of you being there." I was crushed. (I found out later that he was teasing me the whole time.)

Lelan was now promoting records for both Carlton and Pearl Records, but he was still thinking of new ways to push me as a solo singer. So we formed Ken-Lee Records and cut another couple of songs written by Lelan's pal Ray Doggett. The A-side was "So Lonely Tonight," backed by a song called "Beach Party." We also recorded an old Cajun standard, "Jole Blon," using a saxophone instead of an accordion. We were so clever—not successful, but clever.

It was important to me to get the Cajun pronunciation correct in this song, so we brought in a real live Cajun from Louisiana. He coached me phonetically on every syllable until I had it right. A few years ago when I was in Quebec, I thought it would be fun to do something that sounded "French" that the French Canadians could relate to, so I picked a guy from the front of the row and started singing "Jole Blon." The guy kept shaking his head, saying "That's not French" every time I blurted out another line. Obviously my "flawless" Cajun French wasn't French enough for the Québécois.

When those destined-to-be-but-never-were classics "So Lonely Tonight," "Beach Party," and "Jole Blon" went absolutely nowhere, I did yet another song for Carlton, "For You Alone," backed with Ray Doggett's "I've Got a Lot to Learn." Again, no traction—I had no hits for Carlton Records. Now divorced from Janice, I met Anita Bryant, who was on the same label at the time, and had a couple of dates with her. She had already been the second runner-up to Miss America in 1959 and was riding the wave of a genuine hit, "Paper Roses." I was pretty impressed with her.

You'd think that not having a hit by then, after more than a few tries, would have gotten me down, but it didn't. I had that positive Lucille Rogers attitude, believing that hard work and perseverance would in the end win out. . . . something would come along. After all, I had dated Anita Bryant. I had had a crackerjack write-up in the *Houston Chronicle* that all my friends and family could read. I had changed my stage name to Kenny, and to top it all off, I had been on *American Bandstand*!

Things weren't all that bad. I have never forgotten the adage I learned in childhood that the wind can shift most any time. Like Grandpa Rogers had said all those years ago: "Never assume today is like it was yesterday."

CHAPTER SIX

Where It All Began . . . Jazz

As has happened often in my life, just as things seem to hit a low point, a little bit of luck kicks in. After my first brush at a recording career and TV stardom, I started meeting a series of people around Houston and getting a run of gigs that would eventually lead to an entry into the world of jazz. I've often heard my various career moves—from jazz to folk to rock to country—described as "reinventions," and I may have said that myself once or twice. I think a better way to put it is that I have always left myself open to change; I went where the music took me.

While attending the University of Houston for a brief period, I started hanging out at a lot of studios, playing guitar and singing on sessions, including ones where we harmonized on advertising jingles for local businesses such as hardware and furniture stores. Every one of them seemed to give the same message, "Don't spend more than you have to," when of course the real message was "Just spend it on us." In any case, I was getting experience.

When an acclaimed regional jazz pianist named Bobby Doyle heard me play in a club one night in 1959, he asked me to join his group as a bass player. There was one big problem.

"I appreciate the offer, Bobby, but I'm not a bass player. I play guitar, and I'm not even that great at guitar!"

Bobby's reply: "There's more demand for bad bass players than bad guitar players."

I figured Bobby wasn't hiring me for my musicianship, and though I knew little about playing jazz, I jumped at the chance to work with someone so well respected. He heard something in my work that made him believe I could learn to play stand-up bass well enough to pass muster even with the professional jazz musicians who followed his work. Plus, he wanted more from me than simply the bass playing. He liked my ability to harmonize, and that three-part harmony was important to the sound he wanted for his group, the Bobby Doyle Three. This period marked a major shift in how I approached music in general.

It's true that I started playing in bands for two reasons: a love of music and a desire to attract girls. It was my ticket to ride in high school. But when I started playing with Bobby Doyle, and his very savvy crowd of jazz fans began to give us feedback, my ambition changed. Now, instead of impressing the ladies, I wanted to impress my peers. It became important to me that other jazz musicians see me as a professional and not merely some kid along for the ride and the harmony singing.

I learned how to be a musician from Bobby Doyle. Many years later, David Letterman asked me to name the best musician I had ever worked with, and without hesitation I said, "Bobby Doyle." Bobby had been blind from birth, and his entire world was music. In fact, we used to laugh and tell him after hours of rehearsal, "Bobby, some of us have to take care of things at home once in a while." The "some of us" were drummer Don Russell and me. We'd keep at it: "Bobby! Some of us have to mow the lawn!"

He'd laugh, too, then continued to push us relentlessly to practice. The fact that we were ever taken seriously as a jazz trio was because of Bobby's drive for perfection. I could never remember where B-flat on the bass was in the early days. We'd be playing along and he'd turn to me and say, "B-flat, goddammit!"

I'd go "Okay, okay," and play the B-flat. It took rehearsal after rehearsal, but I finally got it.

We played our first show at the Saxony Club in Houston shortly after we formed, and the response was great. After word got around, we got bookings throughout the entire region. I needed the money to pay child support for my daughter, Carole, and for another reason: I'd gotten married again.

I married my second wife, a beauty named Jean Massey, less than a year after breaking up with Janice. The marriage to Jean lasted a little longer—about two years, this go-round—and probably ended for a lot of reasons, but the main one again was my obsession with music. At that stage, I was working six hours a night and rehearsing four hours a day and in between, looking for any work to survive. That is not a recipe for a healthy marriage.

That I loved being married should be obvious by now, given how many times I've tried it. I like almost everything about marriage. What it all boils down to, I guess, is I'm a nesting kind of person. The only one of my seven siblings who has anything vaguely negative to say about marriage is my sister Sandy, who has turned out to be the great caregiver in the family. She never married and laughs when she says, "There's no need for *everyone* in this family to be miserable!"

The Bobby Doyle Three got booked at a Houston after-hours place named the Showbiz, owned by the Fenburg brothers, Paul and Freddie. The club held only about fifty or so people, but it was a hot spot because it was right across from the Shamrock Hotel and drew a great clientele because of the location. A lot of name acts played the Shamrock, and when their shows were over, they came across to the Showbiz to unwind. The Bobby Doyle Three could have found no better venue for getting our name out in front of other entertainers, jazz lovers, and musicians from all over the country. People like George Carlin, Buddy Greco, Lorne Greene, and Liza Minnelli came to listen to us.

One of my favorites was Tony Bennett, who came by every time he was in town. There were times when Bobby would get sloshed, then go onstage. Tony would say, "Bobby, can I come up and sing a song?" and Bobby would say, "In a minute, Tony." I'm surprised Tony stayed our friend, but he did.

Lorne Greene, a huge star on the long-running network TV series *Bonanza,* used to stop in the Showbiz every time he was in Houston. Over a period of time, I got to know him on what I thought was a personal level. Maybe I wouldn't have classified him as a close friend, but certainly an acquaintance. Every time he left the Showbiz, on his way out of Houston, Lorne told me to give him a call "the next time you come out to L.A." He gave me his phone number several times, just to make sure I could reach him. Boy, it was *great* to have such a fan. As it turned out, I did get out to L.A. with the group and I did use that phone number to call my fan and friend Lorne.

"Hello, Lorne? This is Kenny Rogers from Houston. You said to call you when I got to Los Angeles."

"Who did you say this is?"

"Kenny Rogers, from Houston. The Bobby Doyle Three—we played at the Showbiz."

"How did you get this number?"

"You gave it to me. Remember? It was when you came to one of our shows over at the Showbiz. You told me to call."

"I would never have given out my private home number," he said frostily.

Oops, I thought. "Sorry," I said, and hung up.

Not long after that I saw him on an airplane as I was walking through first class to get to coach. I decided to give it another try after the plane had taken off. A lot had happened between the time he'd come to hear us play at the Showbiz and the time I'd called him in L.A. This was at the very beginning of the 1960s, and *Bonanza* was on its way to becoming a number one TV series. Maybe if he actually saw me, he would remember all the times we sat together at the Showbiz and talked about music.

I made my way up to first class, and smiled at him. "Hi," I said. "It's Kenny Rogers."

"So?" Lorne looked up at me over a pair of little half-glasses. Then he went back to reading his newspaper. I nodded, smiled, and quickly went back to coach, embarrassed that I had given it a second try.

But not everyone forgot me from the Bobby Doyle days. Liza Minnelli and I first met there and then later on, as my career blossomed, we'd bump into each other at one event after another. Along the way we became social friends, and when I was in L.A. in the mid-1980s, she invited me to a party at her home in Beverly Hills.

I showed up at this flashy Hollywood affair and immediately felt like a fish out of water. These were Broadway people, people who knew everything about Liza's famous mother, the great Judy Garland, and her equally famous father, Vincente Minnelli, the Academy Award–winning director of classic film musicals like *Meet Me in St. Louis* and *An American in Paris.* I knew a little about Liza's mother and father but otherwise was a country singer in a Broadway world. They were all very nice, of course, especially Liza.

At one point I noticed a frail little man sitting alone in the corner. He was all alone but didn't seem to mind it. As I started to go introduce myself, a group of partiers came in, immediately surrounding him and treating him like the pope. This was Hollywood royalty, no doubt about it.

Liza came by, grabbed my arm, and said, "Have you met Vincente?" She walked me over to meet her legendary dad, explaining on the way that he was in the advanced stages of Alzheimer's. Like everyone, I said hello and extended my hand. He shook it, chuckled, and instantly disconnected from me, as he had with everyone else. As I turned to leave, I mentioned how much I had enjoyed his movie *An American in Paris*, and he immediately perked up. He started reliving the whole production of the movie. I had opened up a floodgate to the past, and he wanted to talk about it for the next thirty minutes. He couldn't remember what had happened five minutes before, but he knew every detail of a movie made in 1951. I'm sure he never knew who I was—just a guy in a gray beard asking him questions—but later, when he died, the family asked me to be a pallbearer at his funeral. I was incredibly honored to do so.

And it all started with Bobby Doyle.

For someone just getting started in the music business, I was in paradise. Between gigs with Bobby Doyle and any pickup work I could find, I was making up to $800 a week, a sizable amount of money for the early 1960s. I ran right out and bought a brand-new Lincoln. People have pointed out in some articles that I had actually bought a Cadillac, but that's not quite the story.

I did drive a Cadillac around Houston for a while in those days, but it wasn't mine. It was borrowed from the infamous woman named Candace "Candy" Mossler. In 1964, Candy, a platinum blonde and ex-model, had been arrested for murdering her millionaire husband in his Florida condo. It was a nationwide scandal and fodder for every tabloid in existence. She and her partner/lover in this situation, her husband's nephew, Melvin Lane Powers, were defended by a famous lawyer named Percy Foreman and acquitted of the killing. Foreman later defended Martin Luther King's killer, James Earl Ray.

Things do get tangled up down around the coast of Texas.

Candy needed cash and her son loaned me her Cadillac with the hope I would buy it. By the time she found the pink slip two years later, I was in my new Lincoln.

"You should put your money in the bank and buy a Chevrolet," my mom advised, forgetting that I already had had a Chevy that was repossessed in high school. I loved those flashy cars, but also figured that if I drove one to a club to negotiate a salary with an owner or a promoter, it would make me look good by appearing successful. At that stage of my career, I was convinced that what you had was sometimes not as important as what people thought you had.

Of all the people who stopped in to see the Bobby Doyle Three at the Showbiz, the luckiest break for me came in the person of Kirby Stone, a trombone player who fronted a group called the Kirby Stone Four. Kirby was a mediocre trombone player who made up for it by being a great entertainer and by finding very good musicians to work with.

Kirby traveled with musicians on guitar, accordion, and drums, but since his music spanned big band and pop, he needed a larger band and picked up extra players wherever he was booked. He had hit the national charts with a song called "Baubles, Bangles and Beads," which meant he got a lot of bookings—good bookings. He was a name.

In 1961, about three years after I started playing with Bobby, Kirby happened to hear us at the Showbiz one night and was so impressed that he came back every night that week. He especially loved Bobby's voice, which sounded a little like a Ray Charles vocal. Kirby thought our drummer, Don Russell, had a Sinatra-type sound, whereas my own voice was high enough and versatile enough to do many kinds of material. There are some groups, like the Bobby Doyle Three, which are made up of singers who can play. Kirby took us under his wing because he needed more versatility in his band. He liked to take show tunes and make them into pop or big-band songs.

Teaming up with Kirby was an opportunity for the Bobby Doyle Three to be heard by audiences all over the United States and Canada. With every appearance with Kirby, and endless hours of rehearsal with Bobby, my bass playing got better. Kirby was the lead, and the band backed him up. For twenty minutes of every show, we, the Bobby Doyle Three, would be featured on our own. Then Kirby, the main attraction, would come out and we'd be part of the backup band. We played a lot and learned a lot about harmony, arrangement, and stage performance. I carried all of these things with me as I later moved from genre to genre.

Kirby took us to New York to record the inaugural Bobby Doyle Three album, and we stayed at his house in Paterson, New Jersey, throughout the process. It was a jazz album with standards including "Come Rain or Come Shine," "Fly Me to the Moon," and "I Got Rhythm." As it turned out, we played on very little of the record. Most of the music was played by a big band Kirby brought in. We were certainly not studio musicians, and at the time Kirby recorded the Bobby Doyle Three, that's how things were done. It's been reported that I felt the album didn't work because bringing in outside musicians was a mistake. I don't know if I ever said anything like that, but it is doubtful.

The album, *In a Most Unusual Way,* was released on Columbia Records in March 1962. It produced nothing that made any waves, so we then signed a deal with the Houston label Townhouse and sent a song called "Don't Feel Rained On" to radio. Once again, the release didn't go anywhere. Kirby had good bookings, and we came with the package, so we kept working whether we had a hit record or not. I was a gainfully employed, twenty-three-year-old jazz bassist and loving it.

After the album came out, we were performing in Winnipeg, Canada, with Kirby. It was minus fifty degrees and I told Don and Bobby I would go to the club on Saturday morning and pick up our check. I walked out of the hotel, went about thirty yards, then turned around and came back. Now remember, I'm from Texas. I had on a sweater and a pair of jeans. When I returned, the doorman said that if had I gone all the way to the club and back, I probably would have had frostbite on my ears and nose. I had no concept about that kind of cold, but I did after that.

Aside from working with Kirby, we had managed to book a few jobs without him. One of them was at a little piano bar/jazz club on Sunset Boulevard called the Melody Room, better known today as the Viper Room, the same club where River Phoenix died. After a few nights there, we realized there was a regular customer at the bar every night. The customer was Clint Eastwood.

CHAPTER SEVEN

It's Not All Wet Towels
and Naked Women

I divorced Jean in 1963, and not too long after, I met my next wife-to-be, Margo Anderson, at Houston's Bunny Club, the local equivalent of a Playboy Club, where she stood out as far and above the most interesting woman—quite an accomplishment for that place. She was different from anyone I had ever met. Not only was she beautiful, she was smart. I mean Mensa smart.

She had been married to an undercover narcotics officer from Corpus Christi before we met, so she was very street smart as well. By this point, Jean Massey and I were struggling to see what it was we had seen in each other in the first place. To say the least, I was susceptible, so I let Margo take full advantage of me. I really loved Margo's parents. Her father was like an old salt—Scandinavian, I think—a big guy with a heart of gold. Her mom, Doris, gave you the feeling that she knew the whole story about life in general. They were always exceptionally nice and treated me with great respect.

Margo and I had an explosive relationship right from the start. When it was good, it could not have been better, but when it was bad—stand back. Margo didn't really like to argue, she liked to fight, and she knew how push my buttons. She loved to regurgitate problems, things that happened from years before. Once I heard "do you remember," I knew what was coming next and I knew it wasn't going to be pretty. There is no question I must have overreacted at that point. She had strong opinions about things I didn't even recall, and she could remember the smallest details. If I had to guess, most of the arguments we had at that point in my life were about money, which was pretty typical of people of that age. It doesn't make them less attractive or less explosive, but it does make it typical. I don't ever like to blame someone else, but in this case, they were all her fault. The good news is, I didn't have to remember my shortcomings because she did and didn't hesitate to remind me. Other than that, our marriage was damn near perfect! I guarantee that if I walked up to her today, she would find something we could argue about.

Now I know I've been kind of hard on Margo, and in some instances she probably didn't deserve it. And for that I apologize. However, some of our "misunderstandings" were, at the very least, comical. Sometime near the end of our marriage, which I might add this story had nothing to do with, I was working in Lake Tahoe, Nevada, in the dead of winter. Snow was everywhere and all the roads were frozen solid. I had absolutely no experience driving under these conditions.

So as we reached the top of the hill on a very narrow and icy road, I noticed I had no control over stopping the car. We were at the mercy of gravity and sliding sideways. Fortunately we were barely moving, but I could not stop. I don't know about Margo, but I knew the outcome was not going to be good.

Aside from the slide, the road dropped off some twenty to thirty feet on my side of the road, and we were headed for the edge. I knew we had to do something. I said to her, "Get out, you can make it," and I knew she could. At times she could be very athletic, and this needed to be one of those times.

Margo opened her door, jumped out, and started running alongside the car as I slowly headed for the inevitable. I was so impressed with her concern for my safety, and it really touched me. Could I have been wrong all this time?

I watched this little 110-pound woman hold on to the car door, dig her heels into the ice, and struggle to keep the car upright at the same time yelling to me: "Throw me my mink!" I guess she felt she needed that coat so she could live and go tell someone what had happened to me.

I didn't throw it . . . she would have to freeze to death and I would have to die anonymously.

I have to admit we had some great times. We dated about six months and then we got married. It was in early 1964. Our son, Kenny Jr., was born on May 24, 1964. Do the math.

Getting to know and work with Kirby Stone during this period turned out to be so important on so many levels. For example, Kirby was the first person to encourage me to take a serious interest in photography, something I have developed a deep passion for over the years. The Bobby Doyle Three—Bobby, Don, and I—were staying at Kirby's house with him and his wife, Julie, in New Jersey sometime in the early 1960s while doing some performances in the area. It was fall and the landscape was beautiful. I don't know that I had ever seen a fall day in that part of the country before. For a boy from Texas, it was really something.

Kirby's backyard was full of colorful fall foliage and I really wanted to photograph it. I was using an old camera that I'd had for I don't know how long, a Brownie Hawkeye, nothing fancy, but it worked.

"Why don't you use my Argus C3?" Kirby asked. "It'll give you a sharper image."

So we spent a little time going over it, and he showed me how simple it was to use. I tried it, and I must admit, those were some of the best color photographs I've ever taken. To this day I can remember the thrill of seeing those pictures, even though at the time I had to wait seventy-two hours for the film to be developed. It just felt good knowing I had taken them.

This was the starting point of my lifelong love of photography. Kirby believed that most musicians did themselves a disservice by getting so far into the music that they had no outside interests. Because of him, I have tried to get involved with other things, like photography and sports, that could motivate me. Boredom is a huge factor in the lives of most musicians. The onstage show gives you such a high that the rest of the day can't compete with it. So, feeling down, you start experimenting with things that you hope can match the feeling you have onstage, but you just can't. Performing is a high like no other.

Kirby was also the first person who was adamant about me seeing the business side of music. I think it was at the Thunderbird Hotel in Las Vegas that he first broached the subject.

"You've got to look at music as a profession," he told me, "not as a path to fame or instant wealth. See it from a business standpoint and treat it like business.

"Remember this," he went on. "You pass the same people on the way up that you pass on the way down—and people don't forget."

It was an important lesson. After all these years, I am still amazed how much some people will do for a person they like and how little they will do for a person they don't. Kirby's attitude was, you'll be able to work longer in this business simply because you treated people fairly. And you'll hang on to more of the money you make if you approach it with the right attitude.

My mother's advice about finding a job that I loved helped me choose music as my career, and Kirby Stone explained in one short sentence that I was entering into a business, not a lifelong party. In his immortal words: "It's not all wet towels and naked women."

There's no question that a lot of guys start out playing in bands to party and attract women. I understand it all too well, because that's exactly what I did all through school and when I played with the Scholars. I was always a sucker for a pretty face, and playing at parties every night seemed like a smart way both to make a living and to pursue my passion. The passion was intense from a very early age and only got stronger over time, especially when my focus shifted to earning the respect of fellow musicians. At some point, though, if you want to survive and grow as a musician, you need to get serious about the business side of the music industry.

Kirby was as much an entertainer as a musician. The Kirby Stone Four included a lot of humor in their stage shows, and Kirby explained to me early on the showbiz etiquette that you never tell a joke or make a gesture that excludes your audience. No inside jokes. But go for the laughs, he said, even if they are at your own expense. If people are laughing, you can pretty much assume they're having a good time, and having a good time is really all they ask when they pay their money. It took me back to the Ray Charles concert I had gone to with my sister when I was twelve and the way the audience had loved both his music and his jokes.

Despite the solid performances alongside Kirby, things at this point were not looking great for the Bobby Doyle Three. Little by little, the group was falling apart. Bobby was depressed and dealing with a lot of personal issues. He was drinking a *lot*. There were times that I was afraid he might fall off the stage. His alcohol consumption was at a level that made me increasingly uneasy. At his worst, though, he was still better than anyone I had ever heard. The three of us, feeling the constant tension, thought that if we opened our own club in Houston, it would create a more comfortable atmosphere where we wouldn't be constantly traveling yet could continue to build a following. That kind of a work situation would still allow us to work out on our own, away from the Kirby Stone group. If we needed to hook up with Kirby to generate extra income, that was always an option.

The Act Three Club, as we called it, was our own after-hours place. Unfortunately it didn't last long. The waiters got rich, and we made nothing. When you're onstage, you can't watch everyone who works for you and they knew it. You can't stop the hired help from stealing if that's what their mission is. We fed them as long as we could; then we quit.

Finally the Bobby Doyle Three closed up shop and moved on. Don Russell and I, without Bobby, joined another pop/jazz vocal group, The Lively Ones. The lineup was Don; Don's sister Leigh; her husband, Paul Massaro; and me.

To set the stage, Leigh and Paul were Jehovah's Witnesses and didn't believe in things like singing "Happy Birthday" for religious reasons. Now I understand that, but I'm telling you, at three o'clock in the morning, most good ol' Southern boys don't. If Bubba wants you to sing "Happy Birthday" to Sally, by God, you better sing "Happy Birthday" to Sally.

One night, at the stroke of midnight just as we were packing up, Bubba wanted to hear "Happy Birthday" and wasn't going to take no for an answer, religion or no religion. To their credit, Paul and Leigh stood up for their principles, which I truly admire, and just about the time Bubba was coming over the piano bar for Paul, he chose to make a quick exit. I admired that, too. Now that left just Don and me—a drummer and an upright bass player—to sing "Happy Birthday" to Sally. It actually sounded pretty good in two-part harmony, with just bass and drums, and Bubba decided not to kick our asses, which he would have had no problem doing.

In 1966, Kirby's group was managed by two entrepreneurs, George Greif and Sid Garris, who had recently purchased controlling interest in the very successful folk group the New Christy Minstrels. Greif and Garris had just begun looking around for new talent to replace the original members who had either quit or become too expensive for them to continue paying. The Christys had already launched the careers of some of their earlier members to a national stage, including Barry McGuire, who had a big hit with a protest song, "Eve of Destruction," and Gene Clark of the legendary rock group The Byrds.

Hearing about their recruiting, Kirby advised his managers: "You ought to call Kenny Rogers. He's a very versatile singer and plays stand-up bass."

So as a courtesy to Kirby, they did just that. When they caught up with me, however, I was in a busy hotel lobby. They asked if I would sing something for them over the phone so they could get a sense of my range and the quality of my voice. So here I am, in the lobby of the Houstonaire Hotel, people everywhere, on a pay phone, about to start singing. It doesn't get any better than that, in my book. I took a deep breath to start.

"Hold on," someone said. "Let me put Mike Settle, our musical director, on the phone."

Mike was a well-respected folk singer and guitar player as well as a great songwriter. So Mike comes to the phone.

"Okay, Kenny," he said. "Whenever you're ready."

There was no "Hello, I know this must be awkward for you," just "Let me hear you sing."

I'm not sure you're ever ready for that, but like a fool, I start singing.

"Green, Green, it's green they say . . ."

Now people were starting to turn around and look at me singing a folk song in the lobby of a hotel on a pay phone. I was trying to sing softly so as not to create too much of a disturbance, but Mike wouldn't have it.

"Can you sing a little louder, Kenny? I'm having trouble hearing you."

I said to myself, *You bet I can. After all, this might be the difference between having a job and not having a job next year.*

Lobby or not, I started singing at full volume:

" . . . *on the far side of the hill! . . .*"

That's about all I got out, thank God, when Mike interrupted me.

"Okay, you've got the job. I'll see you in L.A."

But things weren't totally finalized yet. Greif and Garris wanted me to leave Houston, move to Los Angeles, and join the Christys, all for the grand sum of $500 a week. I told them I couldn't do it for that. Once they said that was their best offer, I didn't even stick around for any further negotiations. For obvious reasons, I wanted out of that lobby. Quickly.

Kirby Stone was my mentor. He's the guy that took me under

his wing, and when he said, "Pay attention to me. You need to do this," I usually did whatever he recommended. But, come on, as a twenty-year-old I was making $600 or $700 a week in Houston. I had been making $500 at the club where I was working, plus I had a couple of other jobs a week. This was 1966 and I was now twenty-seven. I needed more than $500. I needed $750 a week or I couldn't go.

Finally, Greif and Garris agreed to match that offer. Actually, when I went to the club in Houston where I had been working and told them about the Christy Minstrels' offer, and that it was a great opportunity for me, they really shocked me. They offered me $750 to stay. As much as I appreciated the offer, it was too late. I was now up to the challenge of performing folk music, which was, after all, much closer in form to the country music I heard as a kid. And I wasn't afraid to explore a new form. I had already done that with jazz.

The Christys were basically a folk group, but not of the Joan Baez or Bob Dylan political bent. They were more along the feel-good folk lines—more like the Kingston Trio. That was how they'd always seen themselves, and that's how they wanted to remain. Going in, I was excited that I'd gone from the complexity of singing jazz to finding the beauty in songs that didn't have to be complicated. What the folk music of the time said was important worldwide. I also liked that it was uplifting, about the strength and tradition of this country, and not just more love songs. The group at that time consisted of Thelma Camacho, the girl with a pixie haircut who TV legend Ed Sullivan later fell in love with, along with a Japanese girl, Kyoko Ito. Kyoko spoke no English but sang English song lyrics with absolutely no Japanese accent. Then there was Michael McGinnis, who was the Barry McGuire of our era.

He actually carried a shillelagh, an Irish walking stick, wherever he went. This guy was proud Irish. Finally, there were Mike Settle, Terry Williams, and me. Soon after I arrived, the group started changing. Kim Carnes came in to replace Thelma Camacho. Kim's husband-to-be, Dave Ellingson, also took Michael McGinnis's place as banjo player.

To be perfectly candid, when I had the chance of going national with the New Christy Minstrels, I was hungry to join because they were an accepted group and so I'd be accepted, too, by both the commercial music business and by their fans. In a way, it was a calculated gamble to get my name out there, always in the context of a group, of course.

We played mostly places where you would find folk singers—some little theaters, but generally state fairs and big venues. We traveled hundreds of miles on a Greyhound bus with just regular Greyhound bus seats. If you want to make friends, just try that sometime. You have no choice. Even with all the hardships we had to endure, we generally loved it.

I think Kim Carnes got a little depressed sometimes. She had no female friends to talk to. While Kyoko was an incredibly sweet girl and we all felt very protective of her, she couldn't really carry on a conversation in English and we couldn't speak Japanese. So there we were. We were like a Double A baseball team—no perks included.

I do think it was a special time for all of us. The shows were exciting, and we were all learning our trade. The first show that included me, in 1966, however, was a bit of a disaster. Here I was doing a show with the world-famous New Christy Minstrels—Kirby would be proud of me. I knew those folk songs backward and forward. What I didn't know was the choreography, because no one told me there would be choreography. You don't have moves in a jazz band. You just stand around and play. So here we are, doing a command performance for Michigan's then governor George Romney, and at the end of one number, we were all supposed to jump in unison. No one had told me this and so I just stood there like a dummy, watching as everyone else jumped.

The shift in musical styles was not as hard as you might think. Jazz was a complex form that I had to learn from the bottom up. The folk music I was learning to sing and play, like Woody Guthrie's "This Land Is Your Land," wasn't a whole lot different from standard hymns like "Will the Circle Be Unbroken" and "I'll Fly Away" that we sang on my grandfather's front porch.

In late 1966, we appeared at the Canadian National Exhibition in Toronto, Canada, with the Smothers Brothers. Called "The Ex," this is Canada's largest fair, and we were excited about being in Canada and performing with the Smothers Brothers. We were all big fans. It was a special Veterans Day performance and required some unique staging. We were asked to walk along with the crowd on the street, then one by one gradually merge with the veterans' parade before our show. I don't know where the signals got crossed, but I assume someone had cleared this with the veterans. So here we come, long hair and all, proud and excited to help Canada celebrate its special day. The moment we appeared to be moving into the crowd, the vets among them took us for hippie protesters and started beating us on the head with their signs. What was this about? They hadn't even heard us sing yet! Somehow we instinctively knew this was not the time to start singing "Green, Green . . ."

We had some fun times on the road, but within a few months I realized that, other than making the move to Los Angeles, my career was never going to go anywhere with the New Christy Minstrels. We had two big issues. One, we realized they were never going to record Mike Settle's original songs, and two, even if they were recorded, the powers that be would use studio singers and not us. "I guess they don't want to pay us royalties," Terry surmised. Since Kim Carnes and I both went on to make hit records, maybe they should have been more accommodating. Our names in the 1980s would have helped them sell a lot more albums.

With the writing on the wall, Mike, Terry, and our first female singer, Thelma Camacho, began putting a new group together in early 1967. They started practicing and rehearsing some of Mike's songs whenever they could. They sounded great—kind of an early fusion, I guess, of folk and rock—but a three-piece vocal group couldn't do the full harmonies we had all gotten used to hearing, and they knew that because of my background in jazz, I heard those harmonies better than anyone they could find.

It was clear that they didn't want me in the group originally. Nothing personal, mind you, but I was a good deal older than the others and probably looked a little staid for the hipper group they had envisioned. But guess what? I decided there was no way in hell I was going to let them escape "Christy Prison" without me. I would make them want me. This became another defining moment in my life. In much the same way I felt when auditioning for the Christys, I wanted to be accepted in the group. And I wanted to be accepted *by* the group—peer approval mattered more to me than public acceptance.

So I went about changing my look. I started parting my long hair in the middle, put a gold earring in my ear, and found a pair of rose-tinted glasses to wear. This would ultimately become my '60s trademark—I mean, I was *stylin'*.

The good news is, it worked. They lowered the bar and let me in. This was a great day for me that I knew I was going to remember for a lot of reasons. "Onward and upward," we said.

Now we had a group with no lead performer and a plan.

Our contracts with the Christys were up on July 10, 1967. We had decided we would shoot for that date to make our move. So tell me, what are the chances of an as yet unformed, unnamed group getting a record deal? It took some incredibly good fortune, that's for sure.

Terry Williams was our guitar player, and his mother, Bonnie Williams, happened to be secretary to Jimmy Bowen, the A&R director at Warner Bros. Records. Lucky break number one. Bonnie had once been the female singer with the Tommy Dorsey Orchestra when Frank Sinatra was the male singer. She had maintained her friendship with Frank over the years. When Frank merged his own label, Reprise Records, with Warner Bros. in the early '60s, he saw to it that Bonnie was hired to be Jimmy's secretary, and Terry had actually worked for a stretch in the mailroom as well.

The only problem, Terry said, was that Bonnie herself was a little concerned for her job at Warner Bros. Their sales had been lagging and everyone was feeling really insecure. But, as the story goes, once Jimmy produced "Everybody Loves Somebody," a huge record for Dean Martin, everyone there felt more secure, including Bonnie. Break number two.

Both Frank's Reprise Records and Warner Bros. Records were housed in the same building in L.A. So, as any mother worth her salt would do, Bonnie marched into Jimmy's office and told him that her son, Terry, was starting a band. Jimmy, in his ultimate wisdom, said, "Well, bring 'em over and let me hear 'em."

CHAPTER EIGHT

Just Dropped In

Okay, here we are, heading off to Warner Bros. Records like four elementary school kids going to our first "invited" school party. We were all at least an hour early and we were excited. We were about to meet and possibly record with the guy who had produced records for the likes of Frank Sinatra, Sammy Davis Jr., and Dean Martin. And maybe he was going to produce us!

None of the rest of us had actually met Jimmy Bowen, but when Terry had been working in the Warner Bros. mailroom a couple of years before, he had encountered him a time or two. The rest of us had all seen pictures of Bowen on the back of Dean's, Sammy's, and Frank's albums, so at least we knew who to look for. This would be one of those moments none of us would ever forget. We went into his office, sang for him, and he signed us. I guess Terry knew him better than we thought.

Our plan was to leave the very day our New Christy Minstrels contract was up, on July 10, 1967, and head to Warner Bros. to begin our new album at nine A.M. on July 11. What else did we need?

Oh, yeah. We needed a name. We must have thrown around a thousand different ideas, but none of them felt right. Then Mike Settle was looking through an old book from the library hoping to find something unique, and in the front were the words *First Edition.*

That was the first name that had everything we were looking for. It had an image. It was then we all decided it would be in keeping with the name if we would wear all black and white on stage, like newsprint. Now we had a name, a dress style, a record contract, and some great Mike Settle songs to record.

It was only after we got to the studio and started rehearsing the band for our first song to record, Mike Settle's "I Found a Reason," that we noticed a guy our age or younger directing the operation. It didn't take long to realize this unknown kid, and not the legendary Jimmy Bowen, was to be our producer. His name was Mike Post, and I'm not sure anyone, even the musicians, knew who he was at the time. As disappointed as we were, we realized very quickly that this guy was very good and very contemporary.

Jimmy Bowen had now given us two gifts: our first record contract and Mike Post.

Once we started to perform, the group immediately realized that two guitar players, a bass player, and a girl singer did not an exciting group make. There *was* something else we needed. We needed a drummer. So we started asking around for suggestions. The name Mickey Jones kept coming up everywhere we turned. He had great credentials. He had been the drummer for Trini Lopez for many years and had most recently spent a few years playing with Bob Dylan, accompanying Dylan on his first world tour the previous year. We set up an audition for this guy we had heard so much about and played songs with him for several hours that day. Mickey was amazing. He was a flamboyant, energetic, stick-twirling, hard-playing rock drummer who kept incredible time. We knew we wanted Mickey with us after the first song he played. He was just what we needed.

Over the next several years, we all came to appreciate Mickey not only for his musical talent but also for his willingness to jump in and lend a hand, no matter what we needed. He was the ultimate team player, and when you're in a start-up group, that's crucial.

Mickey was there from the beginning to the end of the First Edition, and we never got a review that didn't praise him. He has since become a very accomplished actor and has been in many commercials; movies, such as *Sling Blade* and *Tin Cup*; and TV shows, such as *Home Improvement* and *Entourage*.

Once we added Mickey, we felt more comfortable playing clubs around L.A. One of our frequent stops was a Westside club called Ledbetter's, a good place to be seen in L.A. by people who could make things happen in the music business. We played it often and almost always drew really good crowds. This was about the time comedians like Steve Martin and Pat Paulsen and groups like the Carpenters were coming up and were working at Ledbetter's as well.

In the audience at Ledbetter's one night was a guy named Ken Kragen, a Harvard-educated businessman who had become the manager for several well-known acts, including the Smothers Brothers, John Hartford, and Pat Paulsen. By this time our old friends from the Veterans Day parade in Canada, the Smothers Brothers, had begun the *Smothers Brothers Comedy Hour* on CBS television and were stirring up quite a following. Ken really liked what we were doing and insisted the Brothers come see us. That chance encounter would become the catalyst that exploded the First Edition onto the national stage.

Almost immediately they invited us to appear on their show.

Ken Kragen not only signed on to manage the First Edition, he also became my personal manager for the next thirty-three years. He was the driving force in developing my career and giving me the stature I would later acquire.

Ken was a very dynamic person, and the fact that he was managing the Smothers Brothers certainly gave him credentials. We liked that someone was interested enough in us to say, "Hey, let me work with you. Let me help you if I can."

Ken was a manager with vision—not just locally, but globally. He was a big-picture guy. He never thought small. He began by getting us every television show he could. People knew they could trust Ken, so he had access to everybody. This was the era when there were variety shows on TV almost every night, a great platform for a new band. During the first year alone, 1968, we were on *The Smothers Brothers Comedy Hour, The Perry Como Show, The Pat Boone Show,* and *Rowan & Martin's Laugh-In.*

Shortly after Ken became our manager, he worked out a deal with Reprise Records, our record label, to give us a promotional budget of twenty thousand dollars to promote our name. We did the only sensible thing we could with our newfound wealth—we threw a party.

And what a party it was! We invited more than three hundred writers, deejays, record-store owners, booking agents, distributors, and all the Warner Bros. staff. We tried to include anybody who had any tie to the music business who might be instrumental in helping us on down the line. Tommy Smothers secured us the free use of a CBS soundstage and hosted the party. We had all the hors d'oeuvres and cocktails anyone could want. At one point we stopped the food and did a thirty-minute concert for our guests, complete with a backdrop of huge blown-up individual photographs of the band. It was great. People in the industry were talking about that party for months afterward—and, more important, about us.

Tom and Dick Smothers became close friends of the First Edition, so we ended up on their *Comedy Hour* quite frequently. I can't stress enough how much Tom and Dick helped us during that time. You have to remember, we had little name recognition and no big hits when they began having us as guests on their show. We also became Pat Paulsen's official "Presidential Band" when he ran for the office in the '68 election. He actually blamed us for not being elected. We all loved his warped sense of humor.

As a group, we thought we had a great sound and a big company behind us and we were ready to set the world on fire. The first song we rehearsed was "I Found a Reason," a terrific tune by Mike Settle. Mike also sang lead vocals. We watched the charts daily, to no avail. Our first try went nowhere. However, we weren't all that worried. Mike had been writing songs since he was in diapers, and we knew how good he was. To this day, some of my favorite Mike Settle songs that the First Edition recorded were not the hits they should have been. But that doesn't mean they weren't wonderful songs. They were and are.

When we started looking for songs for our first album, one kept coming back to me over and over. And it started in high school.

When I was a senior back at Jeff Davis in Houston, I met a guy named Mickey Newbury. Mickey started school at Jeff Davis in our junior year. He would come around every now and then to listen to the Scholars practice. He begged us time and time again to let him be a part of our group, but there was one small problem at the time: he couldn't sing or play an instrument.

But Mickey liked to write music, and one day when he brought us a song he had made up, I honestly don't think we took him seriously. You'd have to know Mickey to appreciate this, but he wasn't insulted in the least. This guy never met a problem he couldn't solve if he put his mind to it. His solution was, he would go home and lock himself in his bedroom for a month or two and practice. No one saw him for the entire summer.

I don't know how he did it, but the next time he sang and played guitar for us, we were dumbfounded. He could play and he could really sing!

He was now way too good for our group, and he knew it. For those of you who don't know him, Mickey went on to become one of the premier singer-songwriters in any genre of music in his generation. In 1966 alone, he pulled off the incredible feat of having written three No. 1 songs and one No. 5 song across four different categories—Pop/Rock, R&B, Country, and Easy Listening. If you have never heard Mickey sing, you owe it to yourself to find one of his albums and just sit down and listen to this guy.

Mickey sang and played one of those songs for me years later, long after high school. It was called "Just Dropped In (To See What Condition My Condition Was In)." I was with the Christy Minstrels at the time, but it was way too bizarre and psychedelic for their image, and it had apparently already been promised to Sammy Davis Jr.

But the song kept coming back to me. There was something about it that I thought made it perfect for the First Edition's first album. Remember, I had long hair, an earring, and rose-tinted glasses, and our drummer, Mickey Jones, looked like a wild man. We kind of fit the image of a song about altered consciousness. Once I got in touch with Newbury, he said he was sure it would be fine for us to record it. Sammy never did anything with it, and Jerry Lee Lewis had already recorded the song, but never released it.

An interesting side note: Glen Campbell played guitar on the recording of "Just Dropped In" as a studio musician not long before he began singing on his own records. Several of the best-known musicians of that era became regulars on First Edition records. Aside from Glen Campbell, there was Hal Blaine, probably the best-known drummer in the country at the time; Glen D. Hardin, who later played piano for Elvis and also produced a couple of our records; and my favorite electric bass player for studio work, Joe Osborn, who took great pride in not changing the strings on his bass for over a year and would not let me wipe them off with a cloth in fear of, as he put it, "wiping off some of his cool licks."

Another interesting side note: Mike Post, the unknown producer we met that first day in the recording studio, did not stay unknown for long. He would go on to enormous fame and success, writing and producing theme songs for many of the country's biggest television series, including *Hill Street Blues, Law and Order, L.A. Law, The Rockford Files,* and *Magnum P.I.,* to name a few.

After all was said and done, "Just Dropped In" was released as the First Edition's second single and the first with me on lead vocals. I'll never forget when it started to make its way up the charts. We were playing in St. Louis at a place called Ruggles' Cabaret, a joint so small it didn't have a public phone. This was obviously before cell phones, so every day for three weeks, at exactly six o'clock, we got on the office phone at Ruggles and called Terry's mom at Warner Bros. to find out how sales were going.

"You sold ten thousand records today," she would say, and every day the figure went up. Fourteen thousand, then sixteen thousand, until finally one day it reached thirty-eight thousand. This was an unbelievable figure to us. It climbed to No. 5 on the *Billboard* charts, and we were ecstatic.

And the song has continued to hang around for the more than forty years since its release as a kind of anthem to the drug era of the 1960s. When the Coen Brothers wrote and directed the cult classic *The Big Lebowski* in 1998, they reportedly had "Just Dropped In" in the back of their minds the whole time. A new generation of young people know of the song only from that movie.

With a hit record, our TV exposure only increased. The legendary creator/producer of *Rowan & Martin's Laugh-In,* George Schlatter, found a way to use us and our psychedelic hit song. *Laugh-In* was strictly a comedy show with no music acts prior to our appearance. George put the First Edition in a taxidermy shop, in our black-and-white outfits, and shot some bizarre angles of us singing "Just Dropped In." It was a weird song with an even weirder approach, and reputedly the first music video. The weirdness was right up *Laugh-In*'s alley. They loved it.

But the success of "Just Dropped In" all came back to the original sound. We were originally signed by Jimmy to Amos Productions, which was his production company, and then he signed us to Reprise Records. It turned out that Mike Post ended up producing our first three albums and was responsible for the unique sound of our first hit. In a song that heavily referenced the LSD experience, Mike made the whole feel of the recording psychedelic. It was unlike anything the record business, or radio for that matter, had ever heard.

Mike was always striving to do something innovative and different. Typical of his willingness to take chances, one day, while rewinding the tape, Mike heard and loved the sound of Glen Campbell's guitar "backwards." He compressed these backward licks, added a tremolo effect, and that was it—the "something different" that he had wanted. The sound for "Just Dropped In" and the First Edition was born.

It was an exciting time to be in the music business, right at the beginning of a wave of new '70s groups. Los Angeles was then a hotbed of new bands like The Byrds and new singer-songwriters like Gram Parsons, Jackson Browne, and Warren Zevon. The First Edition was right in the middle of the L.A.-based musical style that became known as country-rock. I'll tell you about the origins of one of the biggest of all '70s country-rock groups.

I was in Dallas visiting a friend of mine, Billy Bob Harris, in the late '60s when he took me to a clothing store to look at some leather shirts. While standing at the rack, a young long-haired guy named Jerry Surratt approached me and asked if I was Kenny Rogers. He said he was with a band named Felicity and wanted to know if I could come see them perform that night. I told him that I didn't go to clubs to see new groups. He said he thought I would really like them, and it would mean a lot to them if I came. Don't ask me why, but for some reason I went.

I have to admit this little group of young guys from Linden, Texas (about 150 miles east of Dallas), was worth the trip. It was Jerry on piano, Mike Bowden on guitar, Richard Bowden playing bass, and a guy named Don Henley playing drums. They really were, as Jerry had promised, exceptional.

I was so impressed I went back to Jimmy Bowen and suggested he might want to sign and produce them. Once again in typical Bowen fashion, he said, "I won't produce them, but I will sign them, on your word, and give you $10,000 and you can produce them." Now that was pressure. So I brought the gang out to L.A. and the first thing we did was change their name to Shiloh, which we all felt was stronger than Felicity. And as part of the deal, I owned the publishing rights to their songs and produced their first album.

Two weeks later, while I was back in Texas, we all went out on dirt bikes and in a freak accident, Jerry, the guy I had met in the clothing store, was hit by a car and killed. A group can't lose a partner, a friend and musician like Jerry, and stay the same. I don't know how long the group lasted, but we all stayed in touch. I ran into Don Henley one day in L.A., and he said he had a chance to be part of a new group that was being formed, but he needed his publishing back in order to be a part of the group.

I was glad to return it to him. The group he was forming was the Eagles. I hope one of the songs I gave away wasn't "Desperado," but I was happy for him then and I am happy for him now. (Later on, Don would sing a Grammy-nominated duet with me, "Calling Me," on my *Water and Bridges* album.)

"Just Dropped In" was on our first album, along with Mike Settle's "I Found a Reason." Mike had written eight of the twelve songs for this album. In my estimation, the album should have done better than it did. It didn't do that well, even though Tom Smothers had written the liner notes for it. Guess who won the Best Album of the Year for 1968? Our buddy Glen Campbell, for *By the Time I Get to Phoenix.*

Despite the modest album sales, being on the road with the First Edition was a blast. First, we all got along, which doesn't happen that often with musical groups on tour. I remember one of our first trips going to Boston from Los Angeles. We packed up our station wagon and van with just the five band members and Keith Bugos, our soundman/roadie, and headed cross-country. What seemed like an eternity at the time had a charm written all over it in retrospect. On the road we stayed two or three to a room. We were living the life. Our first night at the club, at least for the first show, we outnumbered the audience. But a true phenomenon was about to take place. A group that drew no people was actually on national TV that night. So we talked to the manager and he agreed that what few people were there would be more impressed to sit in the room with us and watch us on TV than see our show. So the *Smothers Brothers Comedy Hour* came on and the First Edition, managers, waitresses, and a few patrons pulled up chairs and watched us perform on a fifteen-inch TV. It was pretty impressive, even at that size. Interestingly enough, maybe because of the TV show or maybe because the patrons told their friends, we had great crowds from then on.

Long before the First Edition had success, we were driving all over the country in minivans, sometimes pulling a trailer, sometimes not. Mickey Jones and I traveled together most of the time. I didn't like to drive, but once I got a hundred miles under my belt, I was golden. I could drive for twenty-four hours nonstop, and Mickey had the muscle to do the heavy lifting of equipment. We were a good team.

I can now confirm that in the two weeks of my college education, engineering was not offered. I'm pretty sure Mickey missed it as well.

A classic example of our engineering knowledge (or lack thereof) took place one night in Arizona. The group had landed in Phoenix at eight P.M., in a twin-engine prop plane that we had literally bribed the porters in New York to get our equipment on as luggage. Mickey and I had not even discussed what we would do with it once we got there.

After we landed, we rented a van with a nice big luggage rack on top. We had lowered the seats and were completely loaded in the back of the van; I mean completely. We were so proud of our packing skills—we had gotten a lot of stuff in that van—proud that is, until we realized that sitting on the curb like a big monolith was my Dual Showman.

A Dual Showman, just so you know, is a huge leather-covered, high-powered amplifier for a bass. It is about four feet high, eighteen inches deep, and twenty-four inches wide, with a gross weight of maybe two hundred pounds. A true electronic behemoth. After a long deliberation, Mickey and I decided that, as heavy as it was, if we could just muscle it onto the top, where it fit perfectly, it would ride there safely. We tipped a porter to help us get it up and on. We were convinced that sucker wasn't going anywhere. Okay, we knew this much: we could not leave without it. We had three hundred miles to travel to the next city for a show the next day and no alternative but to get it on the van.

So now for the good part. We hadn't gone twenty miles before we had both forgotten about our passenger on top. We're laughing and telling jokes when we hear what sounds like an airplane crash behind us. We both snapped around to see what had happened and how much danger we were in.

At seventy miles an hour, the two-hundred-pound amplifier had become airborne. I can honestly say I have never seen leather spark like that before, but it looked remarkably like an asteroid shower behind us. It was very impressive.

Thank goodness there was no one behind us for miles. We must have driven back half a mile to get this mangled thing, and you can just imagine what kind of shape it was in.

Apparently two hundred pounds is safe on top up to a certain speed, but we had exceeded that speed. By a lot.

The next day when we were setting up onstage, Terry asked, "What happened?" We didn't have the heart to confess how truly stupid Mickey and I were, so we did the next most honorable thing. We blamed the airlines.

More groups fall apart because of drugs and alcohol than any other reason. Even though we looked wild and woolly and had a drug-themed song as a hit, the First Edition was a relatively tame outfit.

Once in a while we would smoke a little pot, but that was about it. I remember one time, someone encouraged me to unwind and smoke before a performance. I decided to try it. I was fantastic onstage. I was witty, charming, and breezed through all the songs with ease.

This is great, I thought. I was in tune with the universe, and I sounded wonderful—at least to me.

The next day Terry and the guys reviewed my performance from the night before. My supposedly clever banter with the audience went like this. "Uh . . . Uh . . . how are you guys? Like this, this next song, uh, uh, is called 'All That I Am.'" That was it.

And my vocals were completely out of tune.

That was the one and only time I have ever gone onstage not completely clearheaded. I'm sure there were times that people thought I was high, but I promise you, I wasn't. As I mentioned earlier, I've stayed away from drugs and alcohol for the most part. Partly because of a promise I made to myself as a young man, and partly because it is impossible to be professional if you're stoned out of your mind. No one wants to have a conversation with a person whose scintillating contribution is "Hey, dude!"

But abstainer that I generally am, you never know what is going to happen when Mickey Newbury is involved. First, he couldn't even sing or play when he wanted to join my no-name high school band; then in a matter of months, he turned it all around to become a brilliant vocalist and a solid guitarist. After that inauspicious beginning, he gave us "Just Dropped In," which in turn gave us street cred during 1968, a time of massive social change, when music was expected to be edgy and in many cases, drug related. The First Edition was not made up of a bunch of druggies, especially when it came to me and Mickey Jones. On the other hand, I did my first and only hard drugs with Mickey Newbury. He was my friend and I trusted him.

Mickey was staying with me at my house in California when he brought out what he said was LSD, but in reality was psilocybin, a naturally occurring compound often found in "magic" mushrooms. It wouldn't have made any difference to me what he'd called the stuff, because I wouldn't have known the difference.

"We gotta try this," Mickey said.

"Well, okay." He didn't get any argument from me. Maybe he was paying me back for rejecting him in high school. He was going to send me on a trip I would never forget.

Then we did the psilocybin, went into another psychic realm, and sat there listening to Cat Stevens's song "Sad Lisa" for *hours*. Just that one song, over and over again. For eight hours it was magical. I could hear every instrument on that song, and I fell in love with it. We took a pause, then listened for *another* eight hours. During that period of time, I found myself beginning to really dislike "Sad Lisa." We then sat and listened to it for a few *more* hours. The whole experience scared me to death. That's why I never did the drug again.

The worst thing of it all was when I realized that I still had to drive Mickey to the airport. I swear to God that I never drove faster than twenty-five miles an hour the entire way, and yet there was Mickey sitting beside me shouting, "Slow down, man! Slow down!"

So much for my crazy drug days.

---※---

CHAPTER NINE

Ruby, Don't Take Your Love to Town

After starting out so great with "Just Dropped In," in 1967, 1968 turned out to be brutal for us. We were working steadily, but we couldn't buy another hit. Plus, it was a strange time in America. We were working with Richard Pryor at Mr. Kelly's Club in Chicago when Martin Luther King Jr. was shot. I remember that out of respect for Dr. King and the seriousness of the event, we canceled the rest of our engagement there. There was a lot of unrest in the country in 1968, what with the Vietnam War and peace demonstrations all over the U.S. and Robert Kennedy's shooting, plus the King assassination and the North Korean capture of one of our ships, the USS *Pueblo*. In many ways, it was a nightmare of a year.

It was a strange time for the group, too. As I mentioned earlier, Thelma Camacho was this hot little lady with the pixie haircut. Everyone who met her fell in love with her. That probably explains what happened to us during an appearance on *The Ed Sullivan Show*. Ken Kragen had been trying to make the First Edition into a household name and we were all excited to be doing *Sullivan*, then the number one variety show on TV. We had a rehearsal in the afternoon and it went fine. "Ladies and gentlemen, please welcome the First Edition," Ed said, and we came out and did our song. The second go-round, for the actual nighttime show, he says, "Ladies and gentlemen, please welcome . . ." and he couldn't remember the name, so he says, "Thelma and her boys!" So much for name recognition.

Thelma was such an integral member of the band, but she became conflicted about touring. Finally, in 1968, we had to let her go. I'm not sure she wasn't happy about our decision. She was tired of traveling and had fallen in love, so I don't think it came as much of a shock or disappointment to her.

Now we had to replace her. She was very charismatic, and we knew it wouldn't be easy. We held a vocal casting call. We must have auditioned at least thirty or forty female singers, and not one of them seemed right for the group. One of the people we auditioned was, believe it or not, Karen Carpenter. She was obviously great, but her voice just didn't work with our sound. After all the panic, the right person was right in front of our eyes. Thelma had had a roommate for the last two years of her tenure with us named Mary Arnold. We all knew her and liked her very much. Sensing our frustration, Mary spoke up one day and said: "Can I try? Believe me—I know these songs backward and forward."

We were all a little taken aback by Mary's request, not remembering that she had heard all our songs every day for two years and had previously been with a group called the Young Americans. She knew her way around a stage.

Mary came in for literally one rehearsal and started doing shows with us right away. She picked up right where Thelma left off. What a lifesaver she was. Mary would eventually marry a man I introduced her to, the legendary singer-songwriter Roger Miller. They were still together when he passed away.

Despite smoothly replacing Thelma with Mary, our calling card, "Just Dropped In," had actually become a bit of a monster for us. It had given us a hip, young, mind-expanding image, which wasn't really us personally or musically. It had also given us, we thought, a springboard to showcase who we really were and to promote our choice of music. We could not have been more wrong. The music community wanted more of the bizarre, and we had nothing similar to offer.

We tried recording several ballads after "Just Dropped In," but nothing seemed to work. The feeling was that we had squandered a great opportunity by not following our big hit with the right kind of record to keep the momentum going. Now we weren't certain which direction we should go. Then, low and behold, Mike Settle gave us another chance at radio, and a more comfortable image for the group, with "But You Know I Love You," a great song he had written that went on to become a BMI Award–winning song, which was later recorded by Dolly Parton, Bill Anderson, and Alison Krauss, among others.

With the surprise success of "But You Know I Love You," we had found new life on radio, and we were taking no chances this time. We asked Mike to write us another song as a follow-up. He did—"Once Again She's All Alone." It was perfect. It was vintage Mike Settle. We released it as our next single. It was doing very well on the charts, which, ironically, soon created yet another problem for us. We seemed to have an affinity for making things difficult when by all appearances they should have been easy.

Mike Post had produced our first three albums, but his phenomenal success, and our lack of it at the time, forced him to move on with his career. So now Jimmy Bowen stepped in to produce us.

A friend of mine with Mercury Records, Frank Luffell, had come to my house to play me a Roger Miller recording of a song written by Mel Tillis entitled "Ruby, Don't Take Your Love to Town." This was one of the most powerful songs I had ever heard. Although Mel claims it was actually written about the Korean War, people assumed, I guess because one lyric referred to a "crazy Asian war," that it was about Vietnam. In all fairness, the song never specifically mentions either Korea or Vietnam. It is the story of a paralyzed, bedridden war veteran who, while he understands the needs of his young wife, agonizes over her infidelity. If he could, he would get out of bed and shoot her for cheating. He begs her not to take her love to town. The song is in his tormented voice:

> It wasn't me that started that old crazy Asian war,
> But I was proud to go and do my patriotic chore.
> And, yes, it's true that I'm not the man I used to be.
> Oh, Ruby, I still need some company.

This soulful narrative became an anthem for the unseen victims of war, those who were injured but not killed. They were unnoticed and unheralded.

I think Jimmy understood the country-rock genre where this song belonged better than Mike Post, which was so fortunate for us. We were so much more comfortable in that category than being psychedelic head-benders. It was a natural evolution, much in the same that drug-related music gave way to the Eagles and Jackson Browne in the 1970s. At the end of one recording session, we had twenty minutes left. In those days, you had three hours to do three songs, then you went into "overtime" and that was expensive. Plus, there were others waiting to use the studio.

As we were about to leave, I asked Jimmy if I could use the time we had left to do a song I had heard that I thought would be great. After I told Jimmy the concept of the song, I think he saw what had attracted me to it, but his words were "Because of the depressing lyrics, you will never get that song played on the radio." I agreed, but then assured him, "Yeah, but if we do, it could be huge."

So he said, "You have twenty minutes. . . . Have at it."

We had performed this song in the live show so many times we knew we could do it. So Mickey, Terry, and I played on the track to save time. Mickey did some amazing things on the drums. Terry played a trademark scratch guitar, and I focused on the vocals. Twenty minutes later—and in one take—"Ruby" was done.

"Ruby" fit the mold of a classic story song or ballad, a song that was a narrative tale set to music. Such ballads have been a mainstay of traditional folk music since medieval minstrels went from village to village singing the adventures of Robin Hood. Many of the most memorable songs in both pop and country are ballads like this, from the Beatles' "Eleanor Rigby" to Johnny Cash's classic "A Boy Named Sue." Having sung a lot of story songs in my folk days with the Christys, I had an affinity for the form. A story song, to have any impact, demands that you listen to the lyrics and imagine the scenario in your head. I had the kind of voice and vocal style that could make those lyrics both understood and felt. Later, when I became a soloist, story songs became an essential part of my success, from "Lucille" to "The Gambler" and back. I guess I was born to sing these kinds of plaintive, often tragic tales.

As I've often said onstage, many of them are about dysfunctional families. And like "Ruby," the narrator is often someone who has been badly hurt by life. Think of "Reuben James," "Lucille," or "Coward of the County." What that says about me or the appeal of the songs, I don't know.

Now, for the problem "Ruby" created. While "Once Again She's All Alone" was starting to get some traction on radio, a few pop stations had discovered "Ruby" and were starting to play it in regular but light rotation. It was probably a test to see if their audience would accept the hard-core lyric of a paralyzed man watching his wife go to town to cheat on him. As you can imagine, the record company started to get excited. We went from no airplay to two records on the air at the same time.

Whenever a situation like this arises, there comes a point where one record has to be sacrificed for the sake of promoting a potentially bigger record. No station is going to play two songs at the same time by the same artist. Unless, of course, you have someone around who thinks outside the box. That was Jimmy Bowen. Jimmy came up with the idea of putting my name in front of the group on "Ruby" so as to separate the records from each other. "Once Again" was by the First Edition. The label for "Ruby" would now read Kenny Rogers and the First Edition.

Well, now, nobody understands group dynamics better than I do, having been in so many groups and watched so many dissolve for reasons just like this. It's the kiss of death for a functioning group of musicians to suddenly be renamed with one name in front. Jimmy put a different spin on it—having two songs on radio at the same time—and that seemed to help. Believe me, it is not something I fought for or particularly wanted. I liked being in this group on equal status with all its members. We were friends first, musicians second. By framing it as a wise business decision, and not simply favoring one performer over the others, Jimmy took some of the sting out of the adjustment.

Bowen's rationale for the name change was the audience needed one person they knew and could like or dislike when they heard the name. They needed a face and a voice they could recognize. It had been my lead voice on "Just Dropped In" and now, "Ruby." He compared the switch to then-noted examples like Paul Revere and the Raiders and Frankie Valli and the Four Seasons.

The audience didn't have to like that person in particular, but the name in front helped them remember the group and ultimately their music. I can only assume this logic didn't apply to groups like the Rolling Stones and the Beatles. Again, in our case, the concept worked only if it allowed radio stations to play two of our records at the same time.

Unfortunately, that's not what happened. "Ruby," with its topical war reference and tragic narrative about a forgotten soldier, went to No. 2 on the charts with the new group name. We, and America, never heard about "Once Again She's All Alone" again.

We decided to try to find another story song of a similar ilk to follow "Ruby." The ballad that we picked, "Reuben James," came to us in a very bizarre way. After the success of "Ruby," songwriters were pitching their music to us on a daily basis. We were spending a lot of time listening to demos, trying to find a good, strong follow-up tune. One day I was playing in a Jimmy Bowen celebrity golf tournament in Calabasas, California, and this guy started running alongside me. Between shots he would say, "Kenny, I've got a great song for you!" Trying to be polite, but a little miffed that some joker would interrupt my golf game to pitch a song, I tried to brush him off.

"Well," I said, "I appreciate it, but as you can see, I'm playing golf right now. Maybe you could wait until I'm done." I did my best not to sound sarcastic.

"No," he insisted, "let me tell you about it now . . ." Normally, that kind of rude behavior wouldn't have gotten the guy a handshake, let alone a fair hearing of his song, but damned if he didn't follow me to the next hole . . . singing! And even though I didn't want to be, I was drawn into the song. It was clearly unique and compelling. "Reuben James" was a song about a black man raising a white child. When it came out, it continued our musical trend of doing songs that made some kind of social statement. I wasn't on a crusade, mind you. It wasn't the politics of these songs that meant as much to me as the raw, human emotion.

> *The gossip of Madison County died with child,*
> *And although your skin was black,*
> *You were the one that didn't turn your back*
> *On the hungry white child with no name,*
> *Reuben James*

As it turned out, the guy who pestered me on the golf course wasn't even the writer! He was just pitching the song for writers Alex Harvey and Barry Etris. They should have given him a raise. It's hard to find that kind of commitment anymore.

Thankfully, "Reuben James" was a success. It didn't soar quite like "Ruby," but it was a solid hit. Our fourth album, entitled (naturally) *Ruby, Don't Take Your Love to Town,* and including "Reuben James," was released in October 1969. With four popular songs out there—"Ruby," "Reuben," "But You Know I Love You," and our old stalwart, "Just Dropped In"—1969 was a very good year. These songs consistently put us in the Top 40, not only in the rock market, but in pop as well. This was quite a change from the stagnant year of 1968. A good part of this success was due to the efforts and the genius of Ken Kragen.

Ken knew the work involved in building a music act and continued to wheel and deal us onto the most popular television programs in the country. In '69, we appeared on *The Red Skelton Hour*, *The Jonathan Winters Show*, and *The Andy Williams Show*, among others. We even hit talk shows like *The Tonight Show* and *The Merv Griffin Show*.

A few years later, the First Edition appeared on Mac Davis's variety show on NBC. While in the studio, we told Mac, the first-rate songwriter responsible for Elvis hits like "A Little Less Conversation" and "In the Ghetto," that we were looking for new material for our next album. Soon after, Mac invited me to come by his house so he could play me some new songs he had written.

When I arrived, Mac proceeded to play me five or six songs, all of which were great. Then the seventh was one of those songs that you know is going to be something special the minute it starts. He said he had played it for a bunch of other artists before me, but they were afraid of it, because the lyrics were too sexual. Well, that immediately piqued my interest.

If I wasn't going to do drug-related songs, maybe I could get away with some serious sexual content. Once he started the lyrics . . .

> *You lie in gentle sleep beside me.*
> *I hear your warm and rhythmic breathing.*
> *I take your hand and hold it tightly.*
> *Listen, can you not hear our young hearts beating?*

. . . I knew this song was made for me. And I was even more convinced when he got to the pulsating chorus.

Can't you feel it, baby?
Can't you feel it? . . . here it comes.
Feel it! Feel it! Fire! Fire!
Something's burning, something's burning,
Something's burning, and I think it's love.

I loved the fact that "Something's Burning" was blatantly controversial. "Ruby" and "Reuben" were both controversial songs for pop radio at the time and were embraced, I think, because of their frankness. I knew "Something's Burning" would stand out in the mix of new songs constantly being released. It fit the times. After all, a movie all about sexual freedom, *Bob & Carol & Ted & Alice*, was one of the big hits of 1969. I was chomping at the bit to get in the studio. Jimmy Bowen said, "If you feel that strongly about this song, you should produce it yourself." I clearly felt that strongly.

Still, there's a big difference between making a suggestion or two during a recording session and being responsible for the end result. I was excited and frightened. Whatever Jimmy thought about the song, he clearly believed in me, so I had to give it a go.

My plan was simple—to make this the sexiest record ever made. Instead of playing down the sexuality, I would play it up. This was a bit before the massive success of romantic crooners like Barry White or Luther Vandross. Otherwise, I would have never tried to shoot so high.

I wanted this song to open with an actual heartbeat. So we found a recording of an actual heart—*Thump THUMP, Thump THUMP*—but it felt weak. So I tried playing it backward, like Mike Post had done with Glen Campbell's guitar, and damned if it didn't work.

We were off and running on my first production project. After the success of the songs where I was singing the lead vocal, I had developed more confidence in my own musical instincts. Plus, the rest of the group could sense my passion and went along with it.

Finished, with all the vocals pounding this "orgasmic" message and the track as exciting as I could make it, we headed out to radio. I could not wait to hear the praise from the people who would be playing this hot song for a sexually pent-up nation.

Much to my surprise, Mac was right. Everyone was afraid of it. Real heartbeat or not, American radio stations would not play this song.

Initially I was totally deflated. I had put my heart and soul into this record and it wasn't working. Then I asked myself, *What would Jimmy Bowen do?* Of course! He would do an end around and think of an outside-the-box strategy, just as he had done on "Ruby." So, after consulting with Mike and the others, I asked Ken Kragen if he could book us on *Tom Jones* in London to do this song. *Tom Jones* originated from the ITV Network in Great Britain, but also played on ABC in the States.

My thinking was that England was much less afraid of sexuality than this country at the time, and an English audience would at least give the song a fair hearing. The producers agreed to pay me to come but not the entire group. We all agreed it was worth a try. So off I go to jolly old England alone, to do "Something's Burning" on British TV.

My little scheme worked. Once the song was heard in the States on *Tom Jones*, there was no stopping it. Radio, so afraid of it before, now pounced on it. I think station managers were secretly looking for a way to play it all along and needed a little ammunition like a successful TV appearance. So, thinking like Jimmy, I gave them a way.

Sometime after I appeared on *Tom Jones,* the First Edition was touring in Europe. While we were there, we were invited to the wedding reception of Bee Gee Maurice Gibb and pop star Lulu, along with eight hundred others. We didn't really know them well, so we were seated in the top tier of a theater. As the reception was breaking up, I spotted Tom Jones sitting down at one of the floor tables. The group was so excited and asked, "Can we go down and meet him?"

"Sure," I said. "We got pretty close when I was doing the show."

As we made our way through the crowd to his table, I turned back to Terry and the rest of the group for a split second, at which point "my good friend" Tom stood up and walked away. I'm sure he wasn't being rude; he just hadn't seen me. So, as persistent as I am and as important as it was to the band, we followed. At the bottom of the staircase, we looked up and saw Tom. As I raised my hand to him to try again to introduce the band, he turned and walked away. Now I am beginning to take it personally. Being this close, I was not going to give up. He went into a room at the top of the stairs where Lulu and Maurice had gathered with all the Bee Gees and the Beatles. Tom was trapped. There was nowhere he could go.

As only Mickey Jones could do, he reached out to shake hands with Tom at the same time Ringo Starr was pointing to something. Ringo's finger ended up in the middle of his handshake and stayed there through the entire hello and handshake process. I'm not sure Ringo even noticed. Nevertheless, I'd lived up to my promise and introduced the guys to Tom Jones, not to mention Ringo's finger.

The songwriter Alex Harvey, one of the men behind "Reuben James," soon became one of my best friends. He was one of those writers, like Mickey Newbury, who wrote from a place I could really appreciate but could never seem to get to with my own writing. I wrote or cowrote some hits, like "Sweet Music Man" and "A Stranger in My Place" (with Kin Vassy), but my accomplishments in this regard are modest compared to those of soulful writers like Alex. A great example is the song he wrote for the First Edition called "Tell It All Brother." Here is a song that asks people to take a look deep inside themselves and examine their own conscience— at least to internally "tell it all."

His opening line spoke volumes:

How much you holding out on me
When you say you're giving all?
And in the dungeons of your mind
Who you got chained to the wall?

Tell it all brother . . . before we fall.
Tell it all brothers and sisters.
Tell it all.

The first time we ever performed this song was at Kent State University in 1970, shortly after what has since become known as the Kent State Massacre, where four students protesting the American invasion of Cambodia were gunned down in a hail of sixty-seven bullets by the Ohio National Guard. Nine others were severely wounded.

In the middle of "Tell It All Brother," the entire audience stood up and sang along with the chorus. People were crying and waving their arms in remembrance of their fallen cohorts. It may be one of the most moving moments of my life. I was so proud to be a part of something so spontaneous and heartfelt. That doesn't happen often.

It was clear that we were impacting people, but within the group we were encountering our own problems. That year, Mike Settle decided to leave the group to try and save his marriage, but it was too late. The damage of years of travel and estrangement had been done, and unfortunately he and his wife divorced anyway. It's always a tough situation for a musician—to be torn between the desire to play and make music and the knowledge that the only way to make a living doing this is to be on the road all the time. It's not easy on anyone—certainly not a husband or a wife.

Mike wrote so many great songs for us, among them, "I Found a Reason," "Rainbow on a Cloudy Day," "But You Know I Love You," "Shadow in the Corner of Your Mind," "I Just Wanna Give My Love to You," "Once Again She's All Alone," "If Wishes Were Horses" (one of my favorite lyrics), and a host of others. We knew the band would sorely miss him. Mike would continue writing songs and at last count had more than 130 BMI songs to his credit. He is now a journalist and music critic.

I don't think the group was ever the same after Mike left. He and Terry were the organizers and the heart and soul of the group. Now Terry and I became the principal decision makers. Mike was replaced by Kin Vassy, a great singer and guitar player from Carrollton, Georgia. Kin brought with him an incredible amount of unbridled energy. Sometimes a guy like Kin can reincentivize a group. He was a great singer and rhythm guitar player and a good friend. What an asset he became.

In the fall of 1971, we embarked on a completely different journey. After a successful hour-long music special, we were given our own TV show on Canadian television (CTV) called *Rollin' on the*

River, later shortened to *Rollin'*. It lasted two years, was filmed on a Mississippi riverboat set, and was syndicated on 192 stations in the United States and Canada. Again Ken Kragen worked his magic and took a special and parlayed it into a series.

It was a weekly variety show, and Canada had no other variety shows at that time. Anyone having a record to promote had to do our show—there were no options. We had the biggest names in pop music every week—Ike and Tina Turner, Bo Diddley, Billy Preston, and Canadian rocker Ronnie Hawkins, to name a few—and no executive ever second-guessed us. It was a star-studded lineup every week. We did the entire run of the show from Toronto.

Some of my favorite shows were with Gladys Knight and the Pips, where I got to duet with Gladys, or when Helen Reddy came on and sang with Mary Arnold. *Rollin'* was the last show that singer Jim Croce did before he died in a plane crash in 1973. As we went along doing the TV show, we added new members to the cast, like my friend from the Kirby Stone days, Gene Lorenzo, a classically trained piano player and naturally funny stuntman.

We really enjoyed watching other groups perform in rehearsal. Some were peaceful and quiet, did their music, and left. Others were considerably more volatile and unpredictable. To say we were shocked when Ike Turner reached in the front of his pants and pulled a gun on his own drummer for not playing well during rehearsal is an understatement. I got the feeling it wasn't the first time. But Ike knew how to get someone's attention. His drummer was rock solid after that!

B.B. King, on the other hand, just emitted soul and inner expression. He is a man who loves his music and totally exemplifies simplicity. Along with me and the band, all the stagehands in the studio wanted to watch B.B. play. While playing along with his original background track of "The Thrill Is Gone," the director noticed that his fingers didn't match his original guitar solo. This meant that he couldn't edit between the rehearsal and the show performances if he needed to. As politely as he could, he asked, "Is there a chance you could play the same solo so it matches?" B.B.'s answer was like his music—short, sweet, and soulful. "No, sir, I can't be there but once." He got no argument from anyone.

One of my high school buddies, Larry Cansler, a cowriter with Michael Martin Murphey on *The Ballad of Calico*, an album we did later, was brought on as musical director for the show. Larry had a great feel for comedy as well. He wore pink glasses, so we used them in every comedy skit that we did. Between Larry, Terry, Mickey, Mike, Gene, Mary, and me, we took the current hits on the radio and did parodies of them. They were really fun for us, and the people loved them.

Rollin' served a lot of different purposes at a time. It allowed us to do comedy as well as music and gave us a constant TV presence. It was a unique opportunity, given that it came right at the end of the era of TV variety shows of any kind. All in all, doing this show was a great opportunity for us to meet and spend time with some of our musical heroes and to create some lasting memories.

Over the eight years of our existence, all of us First Edition members had some incredible experiences we would have never had on our own. One special one for me happened in the mid-1970s. The First Edition was working the lounge at the Hilton Hotel in Las Vegas, and Elvis was working the main showroom. Out of nowhere, he showed up at my dressing room door one night after our show. I have to admit that was a bit of a shocker. For some reason I remember seeing him standing there and I subconsciously looked back over my shoulder. I have to confess for a moment I thought I was in the wrong dressing room for Elvis to be there.

I don't remember what I said. I'm pretty sure it was some sort of incoherent babbling, but I remember specifically what he said. He said "Hey, man—I really like your music." I was so shocked I don't think I even invited him in. I said, "Yeah . . . I like yours, too." Once we were over that awkward moment, he came in. We had a chance to sit and talk.

I was truly surprised by his candor. He told me he would slip into the back of the lounge and watch our show after his and said how much he really enjoyed the group. It was a thrill but a hard moment to get past for me. Here was Elvis Presley telling me how much he enjoyed the show, and I hadn't been to see his yet.

He invited me to come see him the next night. Needless to say I was thrilled, and needless to say I did. Every time I went to see him he would always introduce me as "his friend" and invite me to come backstage after the show. I think he realized that I wasn't a hanger-on and I assume he appreciated that.

Because I was an employee of the hotel, I could get straight back to the dressing room before the crowd could descend on him, so I would always have four or five minutes by myself with him. Interestingly, looking back, I never saw him in street clothes; it was always stage clothes or his famous robe. He was always soaking wet with sweat.

This was at the time he was dating Linda Thompson. She and I later became good friends when she started doing *Hee Haw*. I'm sure what I got was only a snapshot of his life, but that much success seemed so lonely. I think he just enjoyed having someone to talk to.

As the crowds started building up one night I excused myself and told him I was going to play blackjack. He actually said to me how much he would love to just walk out and play blackjack some night, but Colonel Parker had convinced him he couldn't, that it would be too dangerous. At the time, I thought how sad that must be, and that the colonel was just trying to control him. In retrospect, I think the colonel was probably right. The public has no mercy or respect in that situation.

Several months after Elvis died, I was on an airplane with his last girlfriend, Ginger Alden, who I had met with him in passing. She told me she thought I would like to know Elvis had told her many times that a song I had written called "Sweet Music Man" was his favorite song. I can see where he could relate to it as he got older.

Those are very treasured memories to me, and I thank Ginger for sharing them with me.

The experiences of the First Edition weren't just about who we met, though; they were also about where we went. If you ask any one of us, one of the highlights you'd hear about would be our trip through New Zealand, which we did for a public television show there called *Rollin' Through New Zealand*. We took a minibus from Dunedin to Auckland and did concerts in about thirteen cities along the length of the country. We were treated like superstars. They *loved* us in New Zealand. We could always depend on our songs doing well on the charts there, even if they hadn't done so well in the United States. We made friends with some of the Maoris, the indigenous people in New Zealand, ate some incredible local food, and Mickey Jones and I stayed way too long in the sulfur baths in Rotorua. We couldn't walk for an hour afterward, because our muscles were so weak from the sulfur water.

Memories like these are immeasurable perks in the gypsy life of a touring musician.

Around this same time, Larry Cansler and Michael Martin Murphey started writing songs for the album I mentioned earlier that they called *The Ballad of Calico*. They were fresh from writing a huge hit entitled "Wildfire," so they stayed with the concept and excellent musical chronology of a ghost town named Calico, located in the Mojave Desert. After most of the pieces were sketched out, they brought Terry and me a few songs, which convinced us that this should be our next album. For a couple of months we recorded the tracks and vocals almost around the clock at Glaser Studios in Nashville. The solos and background vocals were incredible, and we pushed ourselves to the max. We then took the project back to L.A. and used a full studio orchestra for the opening—"Sunrise Overture" and "Calico Saturday Night." Kin Vassy sang a song on the album called "School Teacher," which we all thought would be a big hit for us.

Calico was a groundbreaking album, and the songs stood up against anything on the airwaves at the time. Although the album didn't do that well initially, it has since been revived with a large cult following. I only wish Kin had lived to see it. He passed away in 1994 from cancer.

Kin was a good friend, and as much as anybody else, he put his unique stamp on the First Edition, both vocally and as a writer. Being from Georgia, he sang with all the passion of a Georgia country boy. Every time I think about Kin, I think about a song he wrote called "Pocket Change." It was a story that I had related to him about how when I was a child, I always felt better when I knew my dad was in the house. I could always tell when he came in late at night because when he took off his old khaki work pants and dropped them on the floor, I could hear the change in his pocket. Only then did I feel safe. The original title was to have been "My Father's Change." A lot of people, myself included, took their turn at trying to translate this image into a song.

Los Angeles in the early 1970s had a burgeoning music community where many singers and songwriters collaborated or at least shared ideas. Once, I remember, at a small affair at Rod Stewart's house in Beverly Hills, I told this story to the group and how I struggled with trying to capture the essence of the emotion. A few minutes later, I heard Elton John on Rod's piano trying to figure out the song version. Like the rest of us, he couldn't quite get it, which is why I am so grateful to Kin for sticking with it until he came up with the right tune and lyrics to match my childhood experience.

Little by little, the entertainment roller coaster called the First Edition started taking its toll on the members of the group. As much as we truly cared about one another, we all saw the writing on the wall. Even with our success, it was a hard life. After almost a decade of great laughs, good friendships, incredible experiences, twelve albums, and nine charted records, including "Just Dropped In," "Ruby," "But You Know I Love You," "Something's Burning," "Tell It All Brother," and "Heed the Call," the First Edition had run its course.

At one time we all thought we'd stumbled on a magic success formula and would ride it forever. We've since learned that our attitude was unrealistic. This business is mountain climbing. You don't just go to the top and stay there. Sooner or later, you've got to come back down.

CHAPTER TEN

Back on My Own

The First Edition played our last scheduled shows in Las Vegas in the fall of 1975. The breakup was more of an evolution than a falling apart. Terry Williams wanted to try to go solo. Mickey Jones had aspirations for an acting career. Mike Settle, one of the mainstays of the group, was long gone. The group simply lost its collective purpose and momentum.

The two years surrounding the breakup of the First Edition was a dark period for me, both personally and professionally. Everything I had built for at least a decade or more seemed to be falling apart, and there were no easy answers about what to do next. Was my short but exhilarating ride in the pop music business over? Would I have to settle for singing "Ruby" and "Reuben James" on an oldies TV show thirty years from now?

Not having a career direction was just one of my problems. My ten-year marriage with wife number three, Margo, always rocky and tempestuous, was now officially over and a nasty divorce loomed.

My marriage with Margo Anderson had lasted since 1964, a lifetime in my matrimonial history up to then. It was great for about the first ten years, but I was constantly on the road during that whole long period, first with the Bobby Doyle Three and Kirby Stone and then later for years with the First Edition. Little by little trust became an issue for both of us. After we had made the move to L.A., Margo got bored or something and began to experiment with psychedelic drugs with some of the guys she had met in a drama class at L.A. City College. That got just a little too "hip" for me. I came home unexpectedly one day after being on the road, and a young guy had his clothes in my closet.

Somehow I just knew that arrangement wasn't going to work. I tried to do the right thing for the marriage. I told her, "If you can forget him, I can forgive you."

She said she would. She said she could. But she couldn't. A few days later I saw them together and I knew right away.

"Another one bites the dust."

I don't really hold a grudge. It was truly a sign of the times. It was, after all, the late '60s and early '70s, and a lot of marriages fell victim to the upheavals in sex, drugs, and outlandish lifestyles. Plus, as I said, I was so blinded by ambition in those years, so pre-occupied with making it in the music business every minute of the day, I wouldn't have seen a problem in the marriage if you'd hit me in the head with a two-by-four. I identified with my career and not much else.

Margo and I were divorced in 1976. Everything I had went into making a final settlement with her, because I didn't want to be in a situation where I would be making payments forever to someone who no longer was part of my life. Consequently, I gave her what-ever she asked for and gambled that I would be better off in the long run. Of course I still had child support payments for Kenny Jr., then eleven, who I had wrongly assumed would continue being a part of my life.

Through much of that period, a bloody battle raged in the

Hollywood divorce courts of Los Angeles. Once I graciously offered to give Margo everything, she decided even that wasn't enough; she wanted more than everything. So the battle lines were drawn. She is the mother of my son Kenny, so I will choose my words carefully.

I had really strong feelings about Margo at that time, and none of them were good; I thought she was an absolutely uncompromising *bitch*. I have reason to believe she didn't care for me very much either. When all was said and done, though, we both got what we deserved. It was a hard-fought fight, but it ended fair. We ended up with an amicable split.

In 1976, Margo moved away with Kenny and I wouldn't see him again for several years. I went back to the courts to see what could be done, because I missed Kenny more than I can even talk about. But I received a phone call from his grandmother, Margo's mother, and she asked me to be careful because it was hurting Kenny. She told me he did not want to see me anymore, and that the court battles were tearing him apart. I agreed to stop my court proceedings, a decision I have always regretted. I should have fought for my son. I thought at the time I was doing what was best for him, but later I would discover how much my actions had hurt him.

I have seen Margo once since then, and she seems to be much more sensible now. Funny how these things are never my fault. I always thought we brought out the worst in each other, except for Kenny. He has always been, and still is, an amazingly brilliant and talented young man. She deserves all the credit for that. I am very proud of him, and I thank her.

Kenny at one time told me he wanted to be in the music business and asked if I had any suggestions about how to get started. I recommended that he do what I did—put a group together, work locally, and start getting a feel for what this life was about. Then he could make a more informed decision as to whether music was what he really wanted to do with his life or not.

My advice to him, as to anyone considering music as a career, is "Don't do it for the money." Most people who set out just to make money don't last long enough to actually see the money. They get discouraged and quit. Longevity is based on your ability to accept rejection and keep trying. Most people can't do that. Those who do survive do so because they feel music is their calling. These people are hard to discourage.

Kenny then informed me that he felt music was his calling, but he still didn't want to go on the road. He was stubborn, just like his mom, but in the end he was right. He stayed with it until it worked for him. As a father, you have to love that.

I personally had no idea how to generate income without traveling and performing, so I wasn't much help. Kenny did land three record deals and released an album on EMI titled *Yes, No, Maybe*. He realized he didn't want to continue as a touring musician and, through his manager, had the opportunity to write the scores for some sports-based videos. I heard the music he was writing and I loved it. So we brought him on board to help with the music on *Gambler V*; the director, Jack Bender, agreed that the music Kenny was writing was great.

He had found his place in the music business. He was now a "scoring machine," which got him in the doors to the studios. He went on to work at Paramount Television, and his career took off composing TV themes and underscores. In fact, that's his voice heard around the world singing the iconic "Extra, Extra" on the television show *Extra*. So when you hear "Extra, Extra" before and after that show, just remember: "That's my boy!" He never left L.A.

and has done very well. I am extremely proud of the man he's become and the life he's carved out for himself.

As if the First Edition disbanding and my divorce weren't enough, during that time, my dad passed away.

Everything is relative. Bands breaking up and bad divorces are pretty meaningless when stacked up against this event of July 7, 1975.

I think my dad was scared to die. In my thirty-six years he had never told me he was frightened about anything, but then again, I guess dads aren't supposed to be afraid of anything, are they? My dad was facing major surgery, a surgery he didn't really want. He knew he needed it, but nevertheless he didn't want it. Maybe he had a gut feeling, but something, whatever it was, was out of the ordinary for him, and everyone in the family could feel it. You could see it in his eyes.

I remember that I didn't understand it at the time, but my mom had once called for an ambulance for my dad when I was very young. He had had heart problems for years, and that emergency was heart related.

Awaiting the ambulance, I remember he said to my mom, "Lucille, I don't care how sick I am, when that ambulance comes here to get me, I don't want no damn sirens! If I die, I die, but no sirens, please!"

And he meant it. That had been really important to him for some reason. Something about sirens meant "serious" to him, and he wanted no part of broadcasting his health problems to the other people in the projects.

Along with his heart ailment, my dad had diabetes so bad

that his left foot had turned black. That's not a good sign. This is what the 1975 surgery was about. The time had come to operate or amputate—those were his two choices. He wasn't excited about either one, but it was out of his hands now. My mother had put her foot down, and around our house, that was the law, even for my dad.

On his first day in the hospital, he tried to keep his sense of humor up. When someone would knock on his door, he would always say, "Friend or enema?"

The nurses all loved him. On this particular occasion, our dad had asked my brother Lelan to get in touch with all the kids in the family and ask them to be sure and come see him before his surgery. This was so unlike him. He never cared for a lot of hoopla around him. If anything, he discouraged it. But this time he wanted everyone to be there.

The surgery was a standard procedure that even the doctors weren't worried about. They told us they did three of these surgeries a day. It was a vein transplant from the inner thigh to the ankle. This would increase the blood flow to the foot and solve his problems. He was supposed to be up and around in a matter of days.

My dad's stay in the hospital was the first time in years all the kids were together in the same room. There were eight of us, plus my mom, so that was no small feat. We were all married by then and had moved far away from our mom and dad. It was much more difficult now to gather than when we were young. But we did it.

I remember all of us around his bed before he went in for the surgery, laughing and telling jokes. This was nothing to worry about. The doctors had made the family feel very comfortable about it. But my dad wasn't laughing like he normally would be. I think he must have felt this wasn't going to turn out well.

The surgery lasted about three hours, and when the doctor came out, I instantly felt, as you sometimes do, that the news wasn't going to be good. It wasn't. When we saw the look on the doctor's face, I guess we just assumed the vein surgery hadn't gone well and they elected to do the next best thing. We thought they had decided to amputate his foot. That in itself would have been a death sentence for my dad.

It was much worse than that. My dad was seventy-two years old and smoked a pack of cigarettes a day and drank heavily most of his life. He was in worse condition than any of the doctors had led us to believe. Once they had anesthetized him to operate, they hadn't been able to get any of his vital organs to start up again. He had advanced cirrhosis of the liver, his heart was damaged, and his lungs were severely compromised by those decades of smoking.

When the doctor said, "I'm sorry, he's gone," I swear the entire family thought he had gotten up off the operating table and left for somewhere. We wanted to ask, "Gone where?" Then it hit us almost all at once. Our dad had died.

This man who had been married to our mother for as long as any of us knew and who, with all his problems and disappointments, had done what so few fathers in the projects had done—been there for his children—was now gone.

He had just been here talking to us a few hours ago, and for the first time we all realized he was the first family member to die and none of us knew how to feel or really what to do. The silence was deafening. Finally my older sister Geraldine said, "What do we do now?"

I think it was Lelan who suggested that we not go view the body at this time. He thought we should take a moment and make sure our mom was okay. She clearly was not—her level of pain was more than any of us could imagine. Geraldine volunteered to drive Mother home while we went to the waiting room to begin making a whole new order of family decisions. It seemed like we were moving so fast, but this was obviously what needed to be done.

Without saying as much, Lelan knew he was the man of the house now and had to do what none of us knew how to do—make the funeral arrangements. Once that was begun, the family settled in and told Floyd stories. Roy talked about catching our dad with his vodka bottle in the closet and pretending to be "Floyd's conscience." Lelan and I talked about our $10 or $20 visits. Barbara talked about our dad catching her smoking one time and how she claimed the cigarettes were mine. I was ten at the time, but my loving sister had no problem throwing me under the bus at that age. The storytelling went on for four hours. It was sad but somehow joyous at the same time. Dad would have liked it, had he been there.

At the Crockett funeral home where Dad had said he wanted to be buried, we got together for the last time with aunts, uncles, and more cousins than we even knew we had and again told Floyd stories. Some we were sure weren't even true, but they had the "Floyd flavor" and they made for good memories and good laughs. As we all gathered around the casket for a final viewing, I realized I didn't even really know my dad, not like I should have. There were so many questions I should have asked but didn't. I had never taken the time to ask him what he did as a child, what things he liked, whether he was a happy kid, and whether he was truly proud of us.

I did know this: he was a good man who had to face things that I wouldn't have to face because of him. Like all the other people that day, I was there simply to say good-bye and let him know I loved him very much. We all did.

———— ➤•◄ ————

In the fifty years I have been in this business, I can honestly recall only once when I felt uncertain about my future. When I left the Bobby Doyle Three in Houston, I went straight to Los Angeles and started getting a paycheck from the New Christy Minstrels. When Terry, Thelma, Mike, and I left the Christys for the First Edition, we left on a Friday and started our new life the Monday after. I was broke at the time, but I had the possibility for a future and a musical family to support me.

But when the First Edition called it quits, I felt—for the first time—totally lost and alone. Those first two years after the breakup, I hardly worked at all. I had always been a group singer. I loved singing harmony and I loved the friendship. Now I was suddenly thrown into a situation of being, in effect, a solo singer. There wasn't another group in the offing to join. Having been the lead singer for most of the First Edition hits, I hoped to keep singing without them. But the truth is, I didn't know how to be a solo singer. When you are in a band and things aren't going well, you can say, "Hey, we're not doing very well, are we?" But when you are by yourself, you can only say, "I'm not doing very well, am I?"

I remember the first night I went onstage by myself. For almost twenty years, I had played bass and stood behind a microphone and sang. All of a sudden, there was no bass to hide behind and I had to walk and sing. I found out I didn't even know *how* to walk. Every step was awkward and I just knew I was going to trip and sprawl out across the stage. Worse, I found myself walking to the tempo of the song, which certainly looked strange.

As I looked around, I realized there weren't any obvious options. I had very few job skills and I couldn't imagine in my heart doing anything that wasn't music related. It's times like this that you find out who you really are, what you're made of, and how important your dreams are.

I was actually lying in a bed in a funky little rent-by-the-day hotel on Van Nuys Boulevard in L.A., remembering all the good times I had had and how lucky I had been in my life, when something dawned on me. With the exception of "Just Dropped In," the First Edition had really been a country-rock band. With hits like "Ruby, Don't Take Your Love to Town," "Reuben James," and even to some extent, "Something's Burning," we had created a bit of a following in country music.

It was at that moment that I made—out of sheer desperation—one of the smartest decisions I have ever made. I would go to Nashville. Looking back, I have no idea now what was so exciting about that, because I really didn't know anyone in Nashville, but I felt that city would be better for me than Los Angeles.

So now I had to undertake a scenario I hated most—driving alone cross-country at night. I had actually never done this, but I knew I wasn't going to be happy. I had driven long distances, but Mickey Jones had always been along to tell me stories and keep me company. Before I hit the Arizona border, in the middle of the desert and nothing but straight, boring roads, I started to really miss him. I had nothing to do but drive and no one to talk to.

I was approaching the city of Winona, Arizona, when I suddenly realized that I was driving "Route 66," the old Bobby Troup jazz number that I had sung a thousand times with the Bobby Doyle Three. That kept me singing to myself until I reached Oklahoma, where I started wondering if this was really a good idea. I was headed for a city where I knew no one and had no reason to think my job skills were wanted or needed. But there was no turning back now; I had a commitment to make my music work and Nashville was the next stop. I thought this might be my last chance—I was thirty-seven at the time—and I knew that success can only follow true commitment.

I had been to Nashville before but mostly just passing through. As I look back on that time, I'd say there was a much older, more tradition-bound, less outgoing group of people running things in Nashville in 1975. They loved their country music, loved their stars, and were suspicious of anyone outside the country music family, especially pop or rock stars trying to edge into their territory. From their perspective, that is exactly who I was.

During that transitional year of 1975, I spent some time in Nashville, living at the Spence Manor Hotel. Like L.A., Nashville was a place where new music contacts could be made, so I thought I could at least look around for some possibilities there. After a short time there, I was introduced to a guy named "Shug" Baggott. I never knew his real name. Everyone just called him Shug, so I did, too. Shug was managing George Jones, and he was interested in managing me.

However my career might unfold, I would certainly need a backup band to replace the First Edition musicians. Shug took me down to Printers Alley, where music was king in Nashville. There were bands everywhere—good bands—but Shug had seen one group that he thought would be perfect for me. They specialized in "big" vocals and full music sounds. We went into a little club called the Starlight. The piano player in the trio was Steve Glassmeyer, who is still with me today; the drummer was Bobby Daniels; and Gene Golden played a Hammond B3 organ and the foot pedals for the bass line. They were extremely versatile in their choice of music. I don't remember negotiating with them, but they agreed to work with me. The group was called Turning Point, and it was—for all of us.

Not long after we had put a show together, and God only knows where this offer came from, we were invited to do two weeks in Saudi Arabia. Now, who wouldn't take that offer no matter what it paid? So off we go to Saudi Arabia, courtesy of Aramco Oil Company for two weeks. We assumed we would be performing for English-speaking Americans who wanted to enjoy "a little piece of home." It was a surprise, to say the least, that our audience was all men, mostly Pakistanis who spoke no English and had never heard "Ruby, Don't Take Your Love to Town." We knew this would be a conundrum of the biggest nature.

I have to paint this picture for you. First, it wasn't just our group. The duo who opened for us were traveling with us. So there were seven or eight of us in a minivan traveling across the desert in the middle of what the Saudis call a shamal. These are heavy winds that blow and create large sandstorms that come several times a year. We were just lucky enough to be there during a major sandstorm. Our interpreter, Muhammad, was also in the van with us.

Now we learned pretty quickly the laws of the road in Saudi traffic. If the car or truck to your left honks once, it means he would like to come over. If he honks twice, it means he is coming over. That's very literal.

So picture a small Toyota pickup truck with at least twelve Pakistani oil field workers in front of us on this very bumpy highway. The truck had a one-inch steel bar that wrapped around the bed of the truck, a little above head high, for the workers to hold on to, so as not to fall out.

We're probably doing sixty or seventy miles an hour when this big tanker truck pulls up to us on the left, then pulls alongside the little white pickup truck in front of us. We had just commented on the fact that the workers didn't appear to be talking to each other, just bobbing heads, with arms extended, on a rough road. That in itself was funny enough, but when we heard one blast of the horn from the tanker and the little truck didn't move, then two long blasts of this air horn . . . we knew the rules. This gigantic truck, with no further warning, just turned sharp right. With no place else to go, and I promise you without anyone so much as changing expressions, the pickup turned right and disappeared over some sand dunes. It literally vanished into the desert. Twenty seconds later, out of nowhere, like some choreographed dance, the little truck with the bobbing heads reappeared in front. It had never broken stride. No one was angry, no one was offended. They were back in the flow of traffic, and the heads never stopped bobbing. It was a thing of beauty to watch. This was Saudi culture right in front of us.

Then it was "Showtime in the Desert." After some fifty miles or so of harrowing traffic experiences, we arrived at an oil field and the building we were to perform in. The place we worked seated literally thirty-five people, no more. The stage was maybe at the most eighteen inches high. There were no "set" decorations, no frills, no fancy moving lights. Just us . . . We were all set up and ready to go. We had been assured by the people of Aramco Oil this was a very enthusiastic group and they very much looked forward to these nights of music.

The opening act was a couple, as I mentioned earlier. I never knew if they were married or just dating, but I knew they were very good. They did some Carpenters songs and a couple of Beach Boys songs. I don't remember their names and I wish I did, but the girl was quite a bit overweight at this point in her life. Still, to these guys who hadn't seen a girl of any kind for, in some cases, years, this girl was *hot*.

There were about twenty-five Pakistanis, maybe five Americans, and five Englishmen or Germans in the audience every night, so the odds of them speaking fluent English were pretty slim. Basically, for the first few nights, they were polite but not impressed. I finally figured out if I threw them tambourines and did mostly fast songs, they would love us. It worked. Getting the tambourines back, however, proved to be a nightly challenge.

Here comes that culture thing again—not wrong, just different. In the United States, if people don't want to stay for the end of the show, they'll usually wait for a dark moment, or at least the end of a song, so as not to be too obvious when they leave. Not in Saudi Arabia. When people there are ready to go, they're ready to go. Instead of just slipping out, they would literally come stand right in front of us, almost nose to nose, then turn and walk out. That one took a while to get used to.

One of the really great customs we observed was in an alley in a little town. Muhammad was walking in front of us when we passed beside an older man, who kept motioning for us to come into his house. We went in, and he served all of us tea and watermelon. As we were leaving, we asked Muhammad why he had invited us in. Muhammad said the old man had quoted a scripture from the Koran: "If you pass my house, even if you are my enemy, I must invite you in." It was one of the nicest customs I have ever been a part of, and a great memory for all of us.

At the end of our tour, full of the wonder and beauty of Arabic customs, we started to leave, but Muhammad wouldn't return our passports until we all paid him $100 each.

Back in the States, my pending management deal with Shug Baggott didn't work out, and all I can say is, thank goodness for things that don't work out. I kept my base in Los Angeles and continued to be managed by Ken Kragen. It felt good to have a band again and a fresh start.

We started out by doing three shows a night for three weeks at Harrah's in Reno. Then I didn't have any work coming up, so I had to cut the band guys loose. It was strange. I had always been part of the group, not responsible for employing the group.

Then, however, we got a slot opening for Captain and Tennille. As the opening act, we were not treated well. I called Ken and told him that the situation was not what I had in mind for the next stage of my career. I swore that if I ever got back to being the headliner, I would never treat an opening act the way we were treated. They were flying city to city, but we were all packed up in a station wagon driving city to city. We would take turns driving to be able to drive straight through. It was a lot like the early days of the First Edition. Keith Bugos, my sound guy/roadie who started with me with the First Edition and is still with me to this day, can attest to that.

We also opened for Steve Martin. At the end of my show, for as long as I can remember, I'd throw out tambourines during the last song. That's fine if you are the closing act. It didn't work well with Steve Martin following you and the crowd banging on my tambourines throughout his whole act. He actually did a whole bit racing up and down the aisle screaming "The tambourines, the tambourines! They are driving me insane!!!" Fortunately, Steve didn't hold it against me. We remained good friends, and he would always come to play in my charity baseball game for the Special Olympics that I hosted in Las Vegas.

On our own, we were playing lounges and doing guest spots on TV music shows like *The Midnight Special.* On one of those shows, we followed Bob Marley and I remember being introduced as Kenny Rankin.

One person who didn't write me off during this painful stretch was hotel owner Steve Wynn. Steve booked me and the band into the Golden Nugget in Las Vegas. Even though I was playing a little three-hundred-seat lounge, Steve gave me star treatment. I had a suite, a Rolls, and star billing. It was amazing, and it gave me plenty of confidence to keep on going strong. There's nothing like having your name in lights and a Rolls in the parking lot to give you a boost.

Gigs like that aside, I was pretty much broke or actually less than broke—I owed $3,500 and had no idea where to get it.

Being $3,500 in debt while getting a divorce might have been a big deal to me if I hadn't been there before. When I first moved to L.A. from Houston to join the New Christy Minstrels in 1966, I had about the same amount of debt with no visible way of getting it. But at that time, once I got to L.A., I remembered that I had written a song called "Please Don't Laugh at My Love" in 1960 for an Eddy Arnold album. I didn't write all that many songs, so I tended to remember the ones I did. And in this case, I had never been paid any royalties.

The publisher was Henry Mancini and his office in 1966 was in downtown Los Angeles. Never having received a royalty statement from these people, I had no idea what to expect. It could have been thousands, it could have been millions, or it could have been nothing. I quickly looked up Henry Mancini Publishing in the Yellow Pages. When someone answered the phone, I meekly volunteered my name and a short explanation of my dilemma.

The lady on the phone shocked me when she said, "Mr. Rogers, we've been looking for you for a couple of years! You didn't leave a forwarding address when you moved last time in Houston, and we had no way of reaching you. We have a check for you for $2,875 in accumulated royalties."

I literally couldn't speak.

She could tell I was thrilled but couldn't respond. "Would you like to give us your current address? I can send it to you," she said. "I'll be right there," I replied, and I was.

I know this was only $2,875, but when you have nothing and you're in a new city, it might as well have been two million dollars. It was a godsend. There I was, a "hundredaire" in Los Angeles with a new job and a thirty-five-dollar-a-night hotel room in Hollywood. Tomorrow would be the beginning of the rest of my life. I kept thinking all the way over there, *I need to write more songs.*

Unfortunately, my dilemma in 1976 was a different story. The First Edition was over, I was in the throes of a death match with my ex-wife, and once again I had $3,500 in credit card debt. I told myself the first time that I would never be broke like that again, but I was. The difference was, I couldn't go back to Henry Mancini for a quick royalty check. I had to find a new miracle. I was now staying in a sixty-dollar-a-night hotel room at the Holiday Inn—which I obviously couldn't afford for long—just down the road from that $35 room I had in 1966. I had some pocket money with what was left of my last check from the First Edition, but it wasn't much. As Yogi Berra would say, "This was déjà vu all over again."

I was in bad shape in every way, but I wasn't exactly alone or without some options. I still had the faith and the guiding hand of Ken Kragen as my manager, and even at what I felt was my advanced age of thirty-eight, I still had the firm belief that I was heading up and not down.

CHAPTER ELEVEN

Lucille

During this difficult period, Ken Kragen remained solidly behind me. He never considered that I wouldn't emerge on top. He was always the voice of reason in that chaotic time, and he always had a plan. His plan for this transitional time in my life was to keep my name and face before the public.

With that in mind, and also seeing the possibilities of Nashville, he booked me to appear on *Hee Haw,* probably the most popular country-oriented TV show at the time. It was there I met the woman who was soon to be my fourth wife, Marianne Gordon Trikilis. Marianne was in the middle of an amicable divorce from a producer at Hugh Hefner's Playboy Productions, Michael Trikilis, and against immeasurable odds, I had finally survived my divorce with Margo. Over time Michael and I became good friends, and he ultimately produced the only actual theatrical movie I have ever starred in, *Six Pack.* He was a joy to work with.

Neither Marianne nor I was in any hurry to get married again after what we had just been through, but there was no doubt there was an immediate attraction between us. During our courtship, I was visiting Marianne in her hotel room one night. The then girlfriend of Hugh Hefner, Barbi Benton, had become a regular on *Hee Haw* and had just gotten a record contract with Playboy Records. Barbi, who had connecting rooms with Marianne in the hotel, innocently asked if I would write her a song for her new album. I said "sure," like I did that every day, and went next door to her room with my guitar and proceeded to write a song called "Sweet Music Man," which may be the most personal song I've ever written.

The song was rooted in a conversation I had had on an airplane the day before with Jessi Colter, Waylon Jennings's wife. She had been telling me about Waylon's band and how they would never say no to him, so they were always working, and how worried she was that something would happen to him on the road. But no matter what problems they may have had, she said, "When he starts to sing, he is still my sweet music man." I thought there was something so special about that concept and their relationship.

The first half of the song was written about Waylon, but the more I got into it, the more I started writing about myself and my own career.

> So sing your song, sweet music man.
> You're makin' your livin' doin' one-night stands.
> They're through with you, they don't need you.
> You try to stay young but the songs you've sung
> Have all begun to come back on you.

Not long after, I sang the song on *The Tonight Show*. John Davidson was guest hosting and somehow the conversation got around to my rose-tinted glasses. It really made me start thinking about my image. If you are afraid to change your image in this business, your time is limited. Less than a week after writing that song, I had cut my long hair, gotten rid of the glasses, and removed the earring from my ear. I felt so much more like me and less like that guy who wanted to be with the First Edition. In a sense, I was shedding a costume of an earlier era and becoming "Kenny Rogers" again. It was transformative, to say the least.

Back to Marianne: she was a true blessing. At a time in my life that I didn't have a penny to my name, along came a woman who did not seem to care about any of that. Marianne even ended up loaning me money for child support payments. Not many women would do such a thing. I, of course, now had a double reason to get back on my feet and prove to the musical community that Kenny Rogers wasn't done yet—not by a long shot.

Despite my bad experience with Shug, country kept calling. After all, my earliest exposure to music was country music. My dad and brothers played guitar and fiddle on the front porch like true country musicians. That singing prize I won at age ten where I got to meet country star Eddy Arnold was for my rendition of "Lovesick Blues," a Hank Williams song.

Sometimes, I guess, it takes a while—and any number of detours—to end up where we should have been in the first place. And we don't really know it until we get there. In my case, it took almost half a lifetime to locate my natural musical terrain. There were no guarantees that I'd be welcomed there with open arms, but at least it felt like the right direction home.

My objective, once again but with even more determination, was to leave L.A., get back to Nashville, and see if Ken and I could turn my country-rock successes like "Ruby" into a solid country career.

I was about to take off for Nashville when a strange thing happened. Remember those hip black-and-white leather outfits the First Edition had worn and been so proud of? Well, someone broke into the trunk of my car in the Holiday Inn parking lot and stole all six of mine the night before I was to leave.

At first I was furious that someone would take my memories from me. That is, until the hotel offered me $8,000 to settle the matter. Memories or not, that one was a no-brainer. I took the money. There was a God, and just as with that Henry Mancini song years before, I had witnessed my second miracle.

My first experience in Nashville on that fateful trip was walking into the Ryman Auditorium—the legendary home of the Grand Ole Opry and a country music shrine—late on my first night in town, not knowing anyone, and hearing this country band I had never heard of performing onstage. When they finished, the roar was deafening. The announcer said, "How about a nice round of applause for Tommy [Somebody] and Family; they had a hit back in 1943."

I had never heard that kind of appreciation for a group that hadn't had a hit record for thirty years. I remember saying, "Wow . . . this is where I want to be." Country music just felt so right.

The next day Ken and I had a meeting with a producer named Larry Butler. Unbeknownst to me, Larry, then head of United Artists Records in Nashville, had been following me since my days in the Christy Minstrels. He was a child prodigy pianist and a multigenre artist who performed with the Harry James Orchestra at age six and sang with Red Foley at age ten. Moving to Nashville in the early 1960s, Larry soon was playing piano on hit records like Conway Twitty's "Hello Darlin'," and he so impressed Johnny Cash that Johnny hired him as a studio manager, producer, and pianist.

I didn't realize it at the time but this one man, Larry Butler, would be responsible for some of the most successful years of my life. Larry became not just a friend but a champion of my talent.

He not only believed in me; he put his career on the line for me. I didn't know until recently how hard he fought the record company to keep my chances alive.

As I mentioned earlier, the executives at United Artists Records thought I was too old, creeping up on forty, and too pop to have much success in country at this stage of my life. The Nashville music establishment has traditionally been something of a closed society. Not just anyone can march in and announce that he or she is a country singer. They were leery of "outlaws" like Waylon Jennings and are still tentative about artists who might bridge the gap between country and pop or rock. I was one of those potential crossover performers, and it made them nervous. Fortunately, Larry had his own power with the label, and between Larry and Ken, the executives finally caved and let Larry try to make me into a country star.

Our first year together was pretty much uneventful. We had some success but nothing you would remember. My first album for United Artists Records, *Love Lifted Me,* did okay, thanks primarily to the title song and another song called "While the Feeling's Good." It was not much but enough to keep going, and that's all we needed.

Then in 1977, lightning struck. Larry had found a song that was both tender and tragic at the same time. It was called "Lucille." The backstory of the song was simple: songwriter Hal Bynum was sitting in a bar near the Greyhound Bus Station in Toledo, Ohio, one night, when he heard a couple nearby arguing. No names were spoken, as he remembered, just one haunting line: "You picked a fine time to leave me." The song spent its first year scribbled on a bar napkin, until Hal got together with a songwriter named Roger Bowling and they finished it. Then Roger pitched it to Larry.

"Lucille" is a classic example of the story-song form that I referred to earlier. First, in these kinds of ballads, you know exactly where you are from the first line.

In a bar in Toledo across from the depot

Then the song takes you on a journey and drops you off at the end with a powerful feeling, something "Lucille" certainly did.

You picked a fine time to leave me, Lucille,
With four hungry children and a crop in the field.
I've had some bad times, lived through some sad times,
But this time the hurtin' won't heal.
You picked a fine time to leave me, Lucille.

What a great song. And what a start for my country music career.

United Artists felt the same way about "Lucille" that they'd felt about Larry signing me in the first place. They worried that the audiences wouldn't accept it. They had finally gotten excited with the music I was making with the more pop-flavored country. Now here came "Lucille," deep in stone country territory, too deep as far as they were concerned. What was Kenny Rogers doing singing about "four hungry children and a crop in the field"? He didn't grow up on a dirt farm in East Tennessee. He's "countrypolitan," not old-school country.

Larry thought they were wrong. Whatever my past styles, he thought I had nailed this sad country ballad and that he should roll the dice with the release. He went to the wall for it. Ken did the same, and the executives caved.

Out of nowhere, "Lucille" sprang from the album and started

something none of us could have ever imagined. This was going to be huge and we knew it. The single ended up selling five million copies and created a whole new acceptance for me on the radio. It was the beginning of a country career we could only have dreamed of.

Once we made the story song a viable country art form for me, the songs just poured in. Every songwriter with a story song sent it to me. There must have been thousands to pick through. Most were stupid and not well written, but boy, when you found a good one, it made it all worthwhile.

My life was suddenly spinning fast. I was soon operating on a whole other plane. I had real money. Marianne and I, having spent a year together, got married in 1977 in Los Angeles. No one can ever say I have a fear of commitment. We were married at the first of many homes I would buy in L.A. The wedding guest list included many dear friends from the L.A. music and entertainment community whom I had met in the First Edition days and before: Ken Kragen, Chuck Woolery, John Denver, John Davidson, and Don Henley.

Back on tour, I hired more band members to complement the guys who had stuck with me through the hard, pre-"Lucille" times. They included Edgar Struble, Randy Dorman, and Chuck Jacobs. Edgar stayed through the 1980s and then went on to become a top-rated musical director. Randy and Chuck are still with me today. I also doubled my crew by adding a road manager, Garth Shaw, who would stay with me through the next ten years.

I now also had a record label that was solidly behind me. Jim Mazza was the head at EMI, which had taken over United Artists. Ken and I scheduled a meeting with him, and Ken was going to ask him to allocate $63,000 as a promotional budget for our new album; Mazza looked at us like we were out of our minds. "Sixty-three thousand?" he said. "I'm going to put a million dollars into promoting Kenny Rogers." I immediately knew there was something I liked about that guy.

As the bookings piled up and the royalties began to pour in, my financial status reached new and amazing heights. It was hard to imagine that only two years earlier, I was living in the Holiday Inn with a negative net worth. That's what an international hit single—including hitting the top of the UK singles charts—and a hit album and a nonstop concert schedule can do to a bank account.

Because of the relentless touring schedule, I finally did something that I had never thought possible. I bought my own plane to move from venue to venue. It was a British-made BAC 111 jet that belonged to Las Vegas businessman Kirk Kerkorian and, as I found out later, had once belonged to Elvis. In fact, we were actually in the air when Marianne told me in 1981 she was pregnant. It just took all my whiplash success that much higher. Life was hectic but it was good.

After "Lucille" in 1977, songs and projects seemed to come out of the woodwork, but I just want to pause a moment and talk about one very important person in my life and our work together.

At my very first recording session with Larry Butler, I walked into a dark recording studio and sat down next to him, and it was there, for the first time, I heard Dottie West sing:

You want things your way
And I want them mine.
And now we don't know
Just where to draw the line.

How can love survive
If we keep choosing sides?
And who picks up the pieces
Every time two fools collide?

"Larry," she said, shielding her eyes from the glare of the studio lights. "Is that Kenny Rogers there?"

"Yeah," Butler answered. "Come on over and say hello."

That simple invitation was the beginning of a great musical and personal friendship between Dottie West and me. I had heard a lot about Dottie but had never actually heard her sing live until then. She was special in so many ways, to so many people. She was, at this time, a single mom with three kids and getting it done for her family. That alone was a great credential. But equally as impressive was her voice. You believed everything she sang. That was her gift.

To me, Dottie represented everything good about country music, and as I would come to learn, she had, in one form or another, lived or would one day live most of the things she sang about. I had often heard the expression "Dottie doesn't sing her music, she lives it." It didn't take me long to realize how true that was.

The first thing she said when she came in the control booth, even before saying hello, was "I want to sing with you!"

What made this meeting such a twist of fate was that Larry was producing both Dottie and me in the same studio, virtually at the same time. Her session was supposed to have ended at eight P.M. and mine was to start at nine.

After she sat down, she said, "Larry, we have to find a song we can sing together." I was more than flattered. No one had ever come out and said anything like that to me before. That's a usual invitation in this business. But then managers, agents, record companies, or someone else get involved and screw things up. More creativity is lost with technicalities than you can imagine. Sometimes you've just got to do it and let the chips fall where they may.

Of course in this case, Larry had a lot of juice with the company, and I was starting to have some of my own. I had loved so much hearing what she sang that while I was sitting there, I had subconsciously begun singing along with her. So without fear of repercussion and convinced I could sing in that key, I suggested: "How about *this* song?"

Dottie and Larry were shocked, as was I, at my eagerness to hear us together. I brazenly walked into the studio, put on her headphones, and started singing:

You lay the blame on me
And I the blame on you.
Why do we keep finding fault
With everything we do?
How long can we keep right and wrong
So cut and dry?
And who picks up the pieces
Every time two fools collide?

You have no idea how great that felt. Here were two people who had never met before, knew nothing about each other's personal lives, and yet were about to sing a song that wasn't actually written as a duet. But it was a perfect duet: each of us could understand the pain of the couple from our own perspective and experience.

My session was put on hold for the night so we could finish the song. This was less like doing a song than sharing an experience with a new friend.

I want to tell you the history of that song, because it is a good story—and I love hearing about how songs come about. "Every Time Two Fools Collide" was written by Jan Dyer and Jeff Tweel and was one of those accidental cowrites, where luck or magic shows up and takes charge. Jan was working as a secretary at United Artists Publishing, typing up song contracts and handling general office duties. But like so many people with day jobs in Nashville, Jan was also a songwriter. On one particular day when a lot of the company writers were standing around in the office, someone knocked over a little cactus plant on Jan's desk, spilling dirt all over the contracts and lyrics Jan had just finished.

"See what happens"—she laughed, looking at Jeff Tweel— "when two fools collide?"

It was a line of Jan's that she had used for years, but somehow she hadn't used it in a room filled with songwriters. Jan remembers a hush coming over the room, the same kind of hush that happens when a hook line is spoken. You could hear a pin drop as the writers snapped to attention. Every writer glanced at the next one, but Jeff spoke first.

"That is Jan's and mine!" Jeff announced. The other writers moaned and wandered back to their desks. Jan and Jeff worked on the song all that afternoon and evening, then polished it up and took it to UA's publisher, Jimmy Gilmer. Jimmy, in turn, took it to Larry Butler.

Can you imagine? A cactus gets knocked over and gives Dottie West and me a No. 1 hit!

Dottie and I went on in that post-"Lucille" period to have several huge records: "What Are We Doin' in Love?," written by Randy Goodrum; "All I Ever Need Is You," written by Jimmy Holiday and Eddie Reeves; and "Anyone Who Isn't Me Tonight," written by Julie

Didier and Casey Kelly. Along with our buddies the Oak Ridge Boys, we did—for three years in a row—the highest-grossing tours in the music business.

Dottie and I just had this great connection. Part of it might have been that we were both raised in a poor family and yearned for something more. Dottie was raised in Tennessee, the oldest of ten kids. Although we both were raised in poverty, there was one big difference in our upbringing. Dottie was sexually abused by her father until she was seventeen years old. He used fists on her and the rest of the family on a regular basis. Finally, at age seventeen, she reported the abuse to the sheriff. Her father was sentenced to forty years in prison, giving Dottie and her family a respite from years of terror and pain.

She wanted success and she deserved success. She had something to prove, to herself, if no one else.

Jump forward to backstage at the Country Music Association Awards in 1978. That young girl who had endured so much at the hands of her father was now standing beside me, looking like a million bucks, waiting to see if the announcer called our names. Dottie and I were nominated for Duo of the Year and she wanted it so badly. She couldn't get over the fact that I was so nonchalant about it. Finally she turned to me and said, "I gotta have you want this as bad as I do, because I *really* want it!"

She was a nervous wreck, and I found myself now wanting it just as much for her as for me. When we did, in fact, win, I have never seen anyone so excited. I think her feet were two feet off the ground. And I have to say, I saw no sign of the scared seventeen-year-old girl in the woman who graciously thanked the CMA for her award that night.

Dottie was unique in her kindness and generosity. We would

go out on tour and get back into Nashville at four o'clock in the morning and she would insist that everybody, crew and all, come into her house so that she could serve up breakfast. She would put out a spread of biscuits and gravy and just about anything else you could possibly want. But that was Dottie—simply one of the sweetest ladies you could ever hope to meet.

I loved performing the song "Anyone Who Isn't Me Tonight" with her onstage. This is a really sexy song and was a favorite of ours to sing together. I would start out by singing to her:

You've got the kind of body
That was made to give a man a lot of pleasure.

As we sang, Dottie would start on one side of the stage and I would start on the other. Then we'd finally come together in the middle. Her lines to me were equally sexy.

When you made love to me tonight
I felt as if I'd died and gone to heaven . . .

And Dottie knew how to sell a song, let me tell you. I would often joke to the audience after we finished that song: "Look for this in the *Enquirer* next week!"

Nineteen seventy-nine proved to be a banner year for Dottie and me, and for me personally. I was hosting the CMA Awards that year and was nominated in five categories, including Duo of the Year again with Dottie. We won, and once again Dottie was beside herself with excitement. I was nominated for Entertainer of the Year, but that award went to some guy named Willie Nelson! Of course, Dottie and I got a kick out of it when the newspapers started calling us "the hottest country duo around, closing in on Waylon and Willie." Notice they said, "Closing in."

Dottie had made more money on those tours than she had in years. She had rekindled her career, and she and her very talented family were doing well. Everyone in country music was happy for her. Shelly West, her daughter, had an outstanding career in country music. She had Dottie's unmistakable beautiful red hair and looked and sounded so much like her mom. And then there was her son, Mo West, who was a brilliant musician and engineer.

Dottie lived the life of a sad country ballad to the end. Many years after our record-breaking tours, she came to the attention of the IRS. Due to some shady bookkeeping by her (and Larry Butler's) business manager, she didn't have the money to pay her tax bill. She *thought* she did. She thought it had been paid. But it hadn't.

As usual, to the IRS none of that mattered. Agency bureaucrats didn't care how happy she had been and how hard she was trying. They wanted their money, and they wanted it now. If Dottie didn't have it, they would take her house, her car, her bus—anything of value, or, what seemed to be a new standard, whatever made her comfortable or brought her joy.

Dottie told me IRS agents would show up at any time of the day or night, stripping her house. Right in front of her, they took her awards and broke them down, throwing the statues in one box, and the bases in another. I think they even took her platinum records and auctioned them off. But the worst thing they did, the thing that really broke Dottie's heart, was they took her mother's old china dishes. They were all she had left from her mother, and though they probably weren't worth much monetarily, she treasured those dishes. She begged the guys to let her keep them, but they literally ripped them from her hands. It was ugly.

I love this early family photo. It takes me back to my family roots in Houston. I'm second from the left, with my father beside me and my mother leaning in front of me. You can see what a big family I came from and how it was always an adventure. *Courtesy of Sandy Rogers*

This picture from grade school is the one that Mary Gwynne Davidson Ridout mentioned in her very kind letter. I'm the one in the second row from the back, second from the right in the white shirt, and she's the brunette two people to my right. *Courtesy of Mary Gwynne Davidson Ridout*

I was proud to be the first person in my family to graduate from high school. *Courtesy of the author*

The group I was a part of as a teenager, the Scholars, gave me my first taste of the music industry and helped me discover my passion for music. *Courtesy of the author*

Imperial Records sent the Scholars to Los Angeles to record, and our experience there turned out to be a major turning point for me. I realized that L.A. was where I needed to be to truly pursue my music career. *Courtesy of the author*

I am particularly fond of my sisters' hair in this shot from a family reunion in the '70s, and my brother Billy's pants were always a big hit. In the photo are *(from left to right)* Billy Rogers, Randy Rogers, Geraldine Rogers Houston, Roy Rogers, Lucille Rogers, me, Edward Floyd Rogers, Leland Rogers, Barbara (Rogers) Thumann, and Sandy Rogers. *Courtesy of Sandy Rogers*

The First Edition played our last scheduled shows in Las Vegas in the fall of 1975. The breakup was more of an evolution than a falling apart. At that time I never could have imagined the wild ride that awaited me as a solo artist. *Michael Ochs Archives/Getty Images*

The First Edition was a big part of my life. The success we enjoyed for nearly a decade was a good thing, and so was the opportunity to grow as an artist, but what I cherish most from that time are the great laughs, good friendships, and incredible experiences we had together. *Dick Barnatt/Redferns/Getty Images*

Following the success of hits like "Something's Burning" and "Tell It All Brother," the First Edition performed live in 1971 on NBC's *Make Your Own Kind of Music*, just one of the countless television performances we gave. *NBC/ NBCUniversal/Getty Images*

I performed "The Gambler" on *The Tonight Show Starring Johnny Carson* on November 16, 1978, the day after the song was released as a single. Soon after, it shot to the top of the charts. It was a thrill to receive a Grammy for Best Male Country Vocal Performance. "The Gambler" is more than just a song about gambling; it's a philosophy of life, which I think we can all follow. *NBC/NBCUniversal/Getty Images*

I saw Ray Charles perform when I was twelve, and it changed my life. I knew then what I wanted to do. To meet him and perform together later in life was truly an honor, because I was such a big fan. Ray brought that "feel good" with him everywhere he went, and it was contagious. *CBS Photo Archive/CBS/ Getty Images*

I love the character Brady Hawkes and enjoyed playing him in the *Gambler* movies. *Photo by Kelly Junkermann*

Two women, Susan Bradley and Sharman Pirkle, have been to over one thousand of my shows and always hand me roses onstage. *Photo by Kelly Junkermann.*

Lionel Richie is a master of making songs out of conversations, and "Lady" is no exception. Recording that song took things to a whole new level for me. *Photo by Kelly Junkermann*

My earliest exposure to music was to country, and I've always had an ear for it. *Photo by Kelly Junkermann*

Here I am at a backstage rehearsal going over a song. *Photo by Kelly Junkermann*

I've grown to love large crowds like this one. When they cheer for every song and laugh at my jokes, I know I'm doing my job right. *Photo by Kelly Junkermann*

Embarking on a solo career was a new and exciting challenge for me. These gold and platinum albums represent some of my successes as a solo artist. I feel so fortunate to have enjoyed such a long and fulfilling career that continues today. *Photo by Kelly Junkermann*

I've known Dolly for the better part of forty years, and I have yet to see her when she hasn't been all dolled up. Even the one time I saw her dressed as an old lady so she could be incognito, she had a lot of makeup on. *Photo by Kelly Junkermann*

In my First Edition days I wore rose-tinted glasses and an earring, but here I'm back to being Kenny Rogers. *Photo by Kelly Junkermann*

I love to sing songs with lyrics that every man would like to say and every woman would like to hear. *Photo by Kelly Junkermann.*

There is always the danger of being so closely associated with someone that you lose your own identity. If I'm going to lose mine, I want to lose it with Dolly. *Photo by Kelly Junkermann*

Here I am with my friends Willie Nelson and Dolly rehearsing for a show in 1989. *Photo by Kelly Junkermann*

Lionel Richie is like a brother to me. Our friendship goes way beyond music. When the two of us get together, you never know what is going to happen. *Photo by Kelly Junkermann*

I don't care how many people ask, "Where's Dolly?" I can only say, "Well, I don't know, but like you, I wish she was here!" *Photo by Kelly Junkermann*

I think downtime with family and friends is important. My brothers, Billy, Roy, and Randy, and my longtime friend Kelly Junkermann enjoyed this fishing outing with me. *Courtesy of Kelly Junkermann*

My mother, Lucille, has been a source of strength and wisdom for me throughout my life. *Courtesy of the author*

My mother always knew how to say a lot in a few words, and much of her wisdom was drawn from Biblical proverbs and everyday axioms. *Courtesy of the author*

I am so proud of the men my sons Kenny Jr. *(left)* and Chris *(right)* have become. *Photo by Randy Dorman*

A great shot with the one and only Lionel Richie from the Bonnaroo Music and Arts Festival in 2012. *Photo by Romero*

"IT ALL STARTS AT HOME"

This is a family photo we took for Habitat for Humanity's project "It All Starts at Home." We loved the concept, we liked the picture, and we enjoyed being a part of this. There is nothing like spending quality time at home with Wanda, Justin, and Jordan. *Courtesy of the author*

In all fairness, it wasn't just the IRS. It was everybody—her ex-husband, a couple of ex-managers—who seemed to want a piece of Dottie West's soul. Eventually, though, Dottie pulled herself together and planned a comeback. Some of her friends were going to do an album with her, people like Roger Miller, Tanya Tucker, Tammy Wynette, and me. It was in the works, but we never got to do that album.

Dottie had just been in a car wreck in her Corvette, and because of all the injunctions, she couldn't buy or own anything of value for fear of losing it. I had a car at my house in Athens, Georgia, that was not being used, a 1985 Chrysler New Yorker, so I loaned it to her. That way she would have some form of transportation the debtors couldn't touch. It was the car she was to drive to her appearance on the Grand Ole Opry on August 30, 1991.

For whatever reason, on August 30, 1991, the Chrysler wouldn't start, and once it did, it apparently stalled en route to the Opry. Dottie, the ultimate professional, hated to be late and asked for a ride from her eighty-one-year-old neighbor who just happened to be passing by on the freeway. In an effort to get her there on time, he was speeding. He lost control of his vehicle on the Briley Parkway exit in Nashville and became airborne, hitting the middle divider.

Dottie survived and didn't originally think she was hurt that bad. She insisted her elderly friend be treated first. It turned out that Dottie had a ruptured spleen and a lacerated liver.

I hurried to the hospital from Athens, Georgia, to be with my friend, having no idea how badly she was hurt. When I got there, she had just gotten out of surgery, and I swear, she was virtually unrecognizable. Her eyes were swollen shut. They had put what looked like swimming goggles on her eyes to contain the pressure. It broke my heart to see her like this. She had gone from being this incredibly vibrant, joyful person who could fill the room with her "country sunshine" to someone struggling with every breath she took to survive. When I went in to see her, her family had advised me not to be shocked and said she hadn't spoken for some time.

As I stood by her bed holding her hand, I told her: "When you get out of here, we need to do another duet."

They say when someone is dying, you can read a lot of false information from things you think they say or do, so who really knows, but I swear she smiled and squeezed my hand. Even if it's not true, I choose to believe it was. She was my dear, dear friend and I couldn't help but remember all the good times we had had together, and how innocently it had all started: "I want to sing with you!"

Looking back on this period, I guess I could map my life by the stuff that happened between hits. "Lucille" was released in January 1977. My first hit with Dottie, "Every Time Two Fools Collide," came out in January 1978. "Sweet Music Man" was released in October 1977, between "Lucille" and "Every Time Two Fools Collide." During those first two "country" years, I was constantly on the road, and in many ways, those road adventures were as memorable to me as the songs I was singing onstage. You meet a lot of interesting and strange people on the road.

I now had a lot of opening acts for my shows, and probably the ones I liked best were the comedians. I love comedians—there is no greater gift in this world than the gift of making people laugh. I have, in my career, worked with some of the funniest people in the business, like my friend of thirty years, Lonnie Shorr, a comedian who would go onstage having no idea what he was going to say. "I'll just go out and talk about things that make me laugh. That should work," he would say—and it did.

Lonnie was a bit of a dichotomy. He was this little Jewish guy from, of all places, North Carolina. He had a thick southern accent, which sounded strange coming from his body. But he was genuinely funny. Between Glen Campbell and me, we kept him working every night, and he kept us and our audiences laughing for the better part of five years. He made us both feel and look better. As I've said before, and I don't think you can appreciate this until you've tried and failed, people will clap to be nice but they will not laugh to be nice; trying and failing at comedy is a process worse than death.

At one time, at different stages of their careers, I have worked with the likes of Andy Andrews, Jerry Seinfeld, Steve Martin, Harry Anderson, and Gallagher. All are totally different in their approach, and all are truly funny.

Jerry Seinfeld was managed by the same managers who booked Lonnie Shorr, so that was a natural transition for us.

Jerry's first concert with us was to be in Florida at the Sunrise Theatre. There was a sold-out audience of about fifteen thousand people. Jerry would open the show, followed by the Oak Ridge Boys and then me.

It was an eight o'clock show and I would go on at about nine thirty. My brother Lelan, who was my road manager at that time, and I came down from our hotel rooms to head over to the venue at about seven thirty and there was Jerry waiting in the lobby. "What are you doing here?" we asked.

"Waiting for my ride?" he said.

"There's only one road into that place. You were supposed to be over there with the band two hours ago," Lelan told him.

He jumped into the car with us. The arena was only a few miles away, but traffic was bumper to bumper. Keith Bugos called from the arena and kept checking on our progress. There was dead silence in the car. We were stuck on the one road in. At about 8:15 we were still all in the car inching along. We waited as long as we could and then the Oaks had to go on. Jerry had missed his first show.

You can see how much that mistake hurt his career. Someday I would honestly love to hear his side of the story. I bet it's really different from mine.

I had another rendezvous with Jerry about fifteen years later. Actually it wasn't me. It was some of my chicken. Let me back up a little to tell the story.

With celebrity comes opportunity. The most difficult part is deciding what to lend your name to, so when I was approached for a chicken franchise, I was a bit skeptical. I had visions of them putting my head on a chicken. That just didn't feel right. So you can imagine my surprise when I agreed and the franchise turned out to be a very respectable chain of restaurants. It was called Kenny Rogers Roasters.

The former governor of Kentucky, John Y. Brown, one of the main forces in Kentucky Fried Chicken and a good friend, brought the idea to me. It was actually one of the first health-driven restaurants. We all know how much I love health food. I start each morning with a Diet Coke and an Egg McMuffin. But it is great when healthy food tastes good.

The food was right up my alley, with entries like mac and cheese, string beans, garlic potatoes, and wood-grilled chicken roasted on a rotisserie right at the restaurant. Who wouldn't love that? For about three years the chain was extremely successful and appeared to have a very bright future. To this day, it is one of the most successful international fast-food franchises in parts of the world.

One time when I was in Greece, I saw a Kenny Rogers Roasters and decided to go in. I opted not to say who I was, but just stand in line and buy my food. The cups had my picture on them and I noticed that behind the counter and down the way the manager was holding one. He was really curious. He kept looking at me, then the cup, then back at me, and finally decided it wasn't me! When I told him it was me, he didn't believe it. Anyway I assume that's what he said in Greek. He made me pay for my meal.

Roasters had a very high visibility based on its acceptance by the people and the publicity that came from unsolicited sources. One night when I was doing *The Tonight Show*, Jay Leno took the cameras and crew and went to the Roasters across the street from the studio in Burbank and brought back chicken to the audience.

So I decided that I could play the promotion game, too, and I went on *Late Night with Conan O'Brien* to talk about Roasters chicken. Conan put a blindfold over my eyes and put three pieces of chicken in front of me and dared me to pick the best chicken. My God, it was Roasters and I had a 33 percent chance at being right. Unfortunately, the chicken I picked was wrong. I honestly believe everyone thought it was a gag and thought we were good sports to do that.

Then Jerry Seinfeld dedicated a whole show to Kenny Rogers Roasters chicken. In the show, a Roasters opened next to his apartment building. He and Kramer detested the smell of chicken roasting at ten in the morning. The light from the Roasters neon sign was also keeping Kramer awake at night. They schemed to shut the restaurant down, but Kramer, with the help of Jerry's nemesis, Newman, became hopelessly addicted to the chicken. After eventually closing us down at the end of the episode, Kramer, with his head out the window, screamed, "Kenny, come back!" We wouldn't. We had our pride.

It was a great episode. I think most people appreciate self-deprecating humor. Maybe the *Seinfeld* episode had more effect than we had anticipated. We went out of business about a year later.

I also worked for a year or two with Gallagher. I found this guy to be one of the most engaging, thought-provoking people I've ever met. He had a line in his show that to this day makes me stop and try to visualize what he was saying. His question: "What would a chair look like if our legs bent the other way?" I strongly urge you not to spend a lot of time trying to figure that out.

Gallagher's showstopper was the smashing of a large watermelon in the middle of the stage with a sledgehammer. Every night I watched people laugh and be amazed at the audacity of someone doing this. It has great shock value.

One night at the Riviera, just before Gallagher went onstage, I noticed a man in a completely white suit in the front row, only a few feet from the soon-to-be-exploding melon. I pleaded with Gallagher to cancel the watermelon for the show. His response: "Kenny, that's my hit song, my 'Gambler.' Would you close without that song?"

Well, the moment onstage came, the watermelon was smashed to bits, and the man in the white suit, along with half the audience, was covered with chunks of it. At the intermission before I went on, I had the chance to go out and apologize to the guy and offer to replace the suit, no matter the cost. I sheepishly approached with my heartfelt apology and offer. He said, "Are you kidding? That's the most fun I've had in twenty years." All he wanted to do was to meet Gallagher in person. That was easily arranged and the man went home looking a mess, but happy.

CHAPTER TWELVE

The Gambler

Starting with the release of "Lucille" in 1977, my life would never be the same. If I were looking for my niche in my life and career, I had found it. I showed up in Nashville at the right time; had the love and support of my new wife, Marianne; had the right people like Jim Mazza, Ken Kragen, and Larry Butler guiding the way; and was almost divinely fortunate to find the right songs that fit me, the times, and the listening public. Every artist prays for that one song that defines them when the public hears it. "The Gambler" was mine.

I have to admit that things moved so fast during such a short period of time that parts of it are like a blur to me. I may be jumping back and forth a little here, but I'll do my best to keep things straight.

If "Lucille" launched this rocket, and my work with Dottie helped fuel it, "The Gambler" sent it even higher. "The Gambler" is a story song written by veteran, Grammy-winning writer Don Schlitz, a Songwriters Hall of Fame inductee, who later wrote No. 1 hits for Randy Travis and Keith Whitley, among others. Don—a nongambler—thought it was as much a concept about how to live your life as a song about gambling. He had already pitched this song to many artists who passed on it. Bobby Bare did a recording and Don even recorded it himself, but in both cases, it hadn't gone anywhere. No offense, but

I thought those who passed on it had to be nuts. It was a great song, and I knew right away that we had another hit.

Don's story in itself is pretty great. Not only is he a nongambler, he was a twenty-two-year-old computer programmer on the day "The Gambler" came to him. He was walking to work when he wrote the song in his head, beginning, in order, from the first line, "On a warm summer's evenin' on a train bound for nowhere . . ." By the time he showed up at the office, he had finished it. Like many songs, country or otherwise, the whole enterprise was a burst of pure inspiration, including these now-classic lyrics:

> *You got to know when to hold 'em,*
> *Know when to fold 'em,*
> *Know when to walk away, know when to run.*
> *You never count your money*
> *When you're sittin' at the table.*
> *There'll be time enough for countin'*
> *When the dealin's done.*

The minute I heard the sing-along chorus I knew we had a shot at something big. Audiences love to sing along. Don Schlitz and I would give them something to sing along to.

"The Gambler," Don's first No. 1 hit, soared from the very beginning. The song earned almost every award there was, including, for Don, the Grammy Award for Best Country Song and the CMA Song of the Year, and for me, the Grammy Award for Best Male Country Vocal Performance, CMA Male Vocalist of the Year, the American Music Award for Favorite Country Male Artist, and for all of us, CMA Album of the Year and the American Music Award for Favorite Country Album for two years running.

I remember so well when Don ambled to the microphone to accept his awards in front of an audience not used to seeing this man on a country music stage. He took a moment to take it all in, then said, "You know, I find all of this . . . very encouraging."

I didn't know at the time we recorded the song that Johnny Cash had also recorded it the same weekend we did. In fact, when the song was first reviewed in the *New York Times*, it was about Johnny's version and not mine. But, for whatever reason, mine is the one that lasted.

After the "Gambler" single and album hit, we soon came out with another album, in 1979, simply called *Kenny*. The songs most remembered from that record were "You Decorated My Life," the lead single, and another story song, "Coward of the County." Then, in that narrative spirit, we produced a concept album, similar to the form of the First Edition concept album, *The Ballad of Calico*. Called *Gideon*, it was a song narrative of a cowboy looking back on his life. My old friend from the New Christy Minstrels days, Kim Carnes, was reunited with me by my friend and president of the record company, Jim Mazza. Kim and her husband, David Ellingson, wrote and produced the album. She had already had a huge hit with the song "Bette Davis Eyes," and together as a duet, we produced another one with "Don't Fall in Love with a Dreamer." Again, as with Dottie and later with Dolly Parton and others, I had the great fortune of finding a partner to sing with in perfect harmony, both musically and emotionally.

Although Kim and I had been friends for several years, I don't think that we had ever sang a duet together. In the Christys, there were nine of us, and we all sang all the time. So when Kim wrote the album *Gideon* and we started singing "Don't Fall in Love with a Dreamer" together, we knew we had found something special.

We both sounded like we were hemorrhaging when we sang hard. As hard as it is to believe, that was appealing. I've always felt that I sang so much better in duets than I do by myself. Singing is a little like running the hundred-yard dash. Someone tells you to run it as fast as you can, so you run it as fast as you think you can. But the minute you put someone beside you who runs faster, you can bet your ass you will run faster. That's what happens to me with duets. I sing it as well as I think I can, but when I sing with partners like Kim, I inevitably sing it better.

One of my most memorable duets was never even released on a record. Steve Glassmeyer and I had written a song called "Lady Luck," and I performed it on one of my television specials with my idol, Ray Charles. Ray played the piano and we sang it together. I knew once we started, it was an unfair race. He was going to run away from me, but I was going to do everything I could to keep up. The difference between Ray Charles and everyone else is that his music comes from a special place in his heart. Some people sing songs the way they learn them. The greats sing the way they feel. I remember asking him at one time, "How do you know when to do those soulful licks?" As only Ray Charles could put it, "If you have to think about them, they're wrong."

I didn't know it then, but the same year, 1980, that *Gideon* was released, "The Gambler" became a permanent part of my life. The song had been out there for a while, but in the wake of the song, the whole concept and story line quickly generated its own separate business and grew to be an iconic image for me.

Again, it all began with Ken Kragen. Ken lived in Los Angeles and was connected to all the major studios for music and television.

He was like Jimmy Bowen—he had the knack of making other people see his vision. To expand upon the reach of "The Gambler," Ken hired the famous L.A. concept photographer, Reid Miles, to shoot the cover for *The Gambler*. Reid spent the better part of two days setting the shot and arranged for hair, makeup, and wardrobe as well as locating this incredible cast of characters to fill out the frame before he even brought us in.

Once I got there and wardrobe put me in a classic western gambler outfit, the shot took only about an hour to finish, but it certainly did set people in the business talking. There was no doubt this needed to be a TV movie. The album cover looked like a still shot from the movie itself.

But again, Ken left nothing to chance. He attended an awards program, found two CBS executives backstage, and cornered them. He had made up a big poster of me as "The Gambler" and unfurled it for them to see. He had a one-line pitch.

"Don't you think this guy needs to be in a movie?" he asked them.

The executives apparently agreed to a movie deal on the spot, sticking out their hands and saying, "Done!" As incredible as it sounds, that's how simple it was! Ken is one of the best.

So here we go, making a western movie, with no idea how to do it or even where to start. You couldn't find a greener actor than me. This was my first acting gig since my high school glee club production of the Gilbert and Sullivan musical *H.M.S. Pinafore*. The scriptwriters—script by Jim Byrnes, story by Jim Byrnes and Cort Casady—were smart enough to give me a bumbling partner, played by Bruce Boxleitner, to distract from my rudimentary acting skills.

My theory of acting, for what it's worth, is that there are broadly two kinds of actors. First there are people who can act. You give them some unbelievable dialogue in an unbelievable situation, and they can make it totally believable. And they can embody a thousand different characters. And then there are actors like me. Give me believable dialogue in a believable situation and I can keep it believable.

I think that my talent in this area is that I'm good at being me in different clothes. I've been me in cowboy clothes, me in detective clothes, me as a racecar driver, and in *Dr. Quinn, Medicine Woman,* I was me as a landscape photographer losing my eyesight from diabetes.

I am a really versatile, mediocre actor.

I was told, prior to shooting the first *Gambler,* that acting is really creating a character in your mind who has qualities and flaws that make him relatable to the audience. We decided that my character, Brady Hawkes, would have a limp and a cane that he could use for self-defense if necessary. The problem was that, greenhorn that I was, I would limp with my left leg one day and my right foot the next. On the fourth day, director Dick Lowry pointed out this inconsistency. Since I couldn't remember which leg was bad, I hit upon the idea of putting a small stone in the boot of the bad leg as a reminder. I ended up creating a stone bruise on that foot for the duration of the production.

I won't be using that technique again.

I think what the writers did so well was to make Brady Hawkes a part of true American history, with abundant references to real-life figures like Sitting Bull and Buffalo Bill and real-life events like the San Francisco earthquake. On the day that history was actually made, Brady would be somewhere else in his journey, which is why you never saw his name in the history books. That was all part of the believability factor that allowed me to pull off the role.

The poster that Ken concocted turned into a critical and ratings smash TV movie, expertly directed by Lowry. On its first airing on CBS, it got a 50 percent share of everyone watching TV in America, becoming the highest-rated TV movie of all time. It went on to win two Emmys and set the stage for four sequels. Taken as a whole, it was the longest-running miniseries of television movies ever produced, spanning close to twenty years in time. *The Gambler,* for me, was the start of a long story-song movie era.

In 1981, coming off the first *Gambler* movie, we decided to convert another No. 1 hit, "Coward of the County," into a movie. The song I recorded, written by Roger Bowling and Billy Ed Wheeler, told the germ of a powerful story. It profiled a young man named Tommy, who earns the reputation as the "coward of the county" since he never stood up for himself and fought.

The movie, also directed by Lowry, by now the go-to guy for every one of my movie projects, expanded on that essential story line. Set during World War II, I played a preacher in a southern town, the uncle of the "coward" and the brother of his dad in prison who had made his son promise not to make the same mistakes he had made—namely, fighting his way out of every situation. Tommy refused to fight until forced to defend the honor of his girlfriend against some local thugs, the Gatlin brothers, who had raped her. After locking the door to the bar and kicking the shit out of the Gatlin brothers, in true Clint Eastwood style, Tommy explains to his dad: "Sometimes you gotta fight when you're a man."

About this time I started to worry that we were beginning to repeat ourselves musically, especially in the vein of country sagas like "The Gambler" and "Coward of the County." Every new song submitted tried to mine the same lyrical and musical territory, and they all sounded the same. I needed to break the pattern.

One of the strengths of my eclectic musical history, perhaps dating all the way back to that day as a child when I heard gospel music pouring out of the little church in Houston, is that I never felt hamstrung by one form, even if I had been successful with it. During the First Edition days, for instance, I was perfectly comfortable going from a drug-culture song, "Just Dropped In," to a country-tinged story song like "Ruby." Having been exposed to and well versed in all kinds of music before Nashville, I saw no reason to limit the range of songs I could do after getting there.

Over the previous few years, I had developed a true appreciation of the R&B group the Commodores, which hit gold in 1978 with "Three Times a Lady." I loved their music. The more I listened to them, the more it felt like, to me, they were writing what could have been country lyrics and singing them to R&B tracks. This is just the reverse of what Ray Charles had done when he took a country standard like "Georgia on My Mind" and gave it a soulful R&B makeover. I wondered what it would sound like for me to sing a country rendition of an R&B-flavored song.

Jim Mazza told me that a Commodores song had actually charted on the *Billboard* Country Top 100 and agreed that it would be a great idea to reach out to them to see if they would like to do something together. He said he would talk to the main writer for the group, Lionel Richie.

He called to arrange a meeting with Lionel and said he would send him a first-class ticket to meet me in Las Vegas where I was performing. Lionel hesitated. He told Jim that his songs were like his children and that he didn't want to give any of them away. Jim told him the song would go on my greatest hits album, which would probably sell in the neighborhood of six million records. Lionel then asked, "Could I get two tickets?"

At the time I was working the Riviera Hotel in Las Vegas. I had just finished the show when Jim brought Lionel backstage. After a few minutes spent getting to know each other, we got around to the subject of music. I asked if he had something specific in mind to play me.

This is exactly how the conversation went down: "I have a song I've been working on for a while and the Commodores passed on it. Would you like to hear it?"

With a setup like that, how could I say no? Lionel sits down at this old upright piano in the dressing room that looked like it hadn't been played since the days of vaudeville and proceeds to play and sing.

"Lady—la la la la la la la la la la la la—you have made me what I am and I am yours."

I waited and waited. Then he said, "That's all I have so far. What do you think?"

I swear to you, having heard only that much, I said jokingly: "I can't believe the Commodores turned that *word* down."

Actually, I loved what I had heard—a highly romantic and soulful love song that was so universal in its feel that it transcended commercial music pigeonholes. And it felt like something I could sing. I was quick to say, "Let's do it."

"Who's going to produce it?" Lionel asked.

"You are," I said. "It's your song, you produce it."

"When?" he asked.

"Next week," I said. "In my studio in Los Angeles. I'll see you there."

Little did I know, going in, that Lionel had never actually produced a song before. It was quite a session—unlike any I've ever done. I really didn't know Lionel personally or musically, so I didn't know what to expect. But I can promise you, I didn't expect what I got either. At one point, I noticed that while I was singing into the microphone, I couldn't see Lionel. I finished singing what was written and realized there was another verse to come, but there were no more words left to sing. So I asked James Carmichael, Lionel's co-producer, and he said, "Here's how it goes . . . when you go in to sing, you get what is written so far." I said, "Well, what do we do now?" James said, "Lionel is actually in the toilet writing the second verse."

I think a lot of the song was being written as I was singing it. Lionel would disappear and come back with more lyrics. I guess it's a true testament to a songwriter's talent to be able to write under that kind of pressure. Plus, Lionel is a master of making music out of conversation. I hear his songs and invariably I say, "I could have written that," but in truth, I couldn't have.

And with that, we set off to record a song that scored big on every chart. "Lady" became the first record of the 1980s to chart on four *Billboard* singles charts—Country, Hot 100, Adult Contemporary, and Top Black Singles. It went to No. 1 on three of the four.

"Lady" came out in 1980, and our feeling that it would cross all the usual categories of popular music was proven true. The audiences of the four categories in the singles charts where "Lady" rose to the top heard their own music in that song. A black guy from R&B and a white guy from country had created a color-blind hit.

It was the launch of both a classic love song and a thirty-year friendship. Lionel produced "Lady" for my *Greatest Hits* album. On the album, *Share Your Love*, released in 1981, he produced the record in its entirety, including the No. 1 hits, "I Don't Need You" and "Through the Years." It was a marriage made in Vegas.

I can't move on before telling my favorite Lionel story in at least an abbreviated form. At the time, the *Greatest Hits* album with "Lady" on it was huge, selling 250,000 copies a week and heading toward platinum status. I had purchased a big boat called, naturally, *The Gambler's Lady,* and along with Jim Mazza and our wives had planned a boat trip to the Bahamas. We asked Lionel to come along. His response: "I don't care anything about going out on a boat."

My response to that: "Oh, come on. You'll have a great time!"

We finally convinced him to come along. As we headed out to sea, the water was like glass and Lionel, the breeze in his face, was exclaiming, "Wow, I think I could really like this." Then, as often happens on the ocean, we turned a corner and things got ugly. Suddenly fifteen-foot waves were pitching the boat around like a toy in a bathtub. Lionel proceeded to toss up everything in his stomach, including the Ritz Crackers I thought would save him.

After a few hours of this, we got to the Bahamas and Lionel was feeling good again. So I suggested that we try a little scuba diving.

"Wait a minute!" he said. "Let me get this straight. You want to put weights on a black man and throw him into the water? I'm sorry, I don't see me doing that!"

But he did, out of pride or whatever, and in his own words: "Suddenly I went straight down! My feet hit the bottom of the ocean and I couldn't get back up. I was sure I was going to drown. I would try to push up and then go right back down again. I finally found the anchor rope and pulled myself back up, still thinking I was dying, when I broke the surface of the water. And there's Kenny, leaning over the side of the boat with a big smile on his face . . ."

"Now, wasn't that fun!!!"

Coming back, we hit the big swells again and now everyone on board was sick. By the time we sighted land, we were sharing high-fives. We had cheated death. Just then, the Coast Guard pulls up, guns drawn, ready to haul us in for running drugs. We obviously looked suspicious. I mean, who else would be out in this ridiculous weather?

As they were corralling us in the middle of the boat, one of them recognized Lionel, and all was instantly forgiven. Now they all wanted autographs and pictures with each of us. After one of the worst experiences of his life, Lionel had saved the day. Was it worth it? You'll have to ask him. For me, that trip was a journey I wouldn't have missed for the world.

"Lady" came only three years after Larry Butler and I walked into the studio to record "Lucille." You see what I mean by crazy? The first half of the 1980s represented, without question, the pinnacle of my professional and financial career. Between 1977 and 1985, we managed to turn out fifteen No. 1 country hits, each of them a story of its own. Some not mentioned before, but just as memorable, included: "Love or Something Like It," "She Believes in Me," "Love Will Turn You Around," and "Morning Desire." On top of that, we released twelve studio albums plus the first two *Gambler* movies, the *Coward of the County* movie, another TV movie, *Wild Horses*, the theatrical movie release *Six Pack*, and an untold number of videos, TV specials, tour dates, and special appearances. I know this list-making can get a little boring after a while, but it's the fastest way I know to underscore how much was going on in my professional life in such a compact period. I can't explain it—hell, I still don't quite understand it to this day—but I can only say that it was the perfect storm of success for a fortysomething singer from the projects of Houston with a prematurely gray beard and what some might call a gravelly voice.

During this insane period, I had sold an unimaginable fifty million albums and set concert attendance records everywhere. And I had many of the material things that go with that kind of success. I had the boat that almost killed Lionel, I lived in a big house in Bel Air, I owned a nine-story office building on Sunset Boulevard, and I had bought a state-of-the-art recording studio on Beverly Drive in Beverly Hills. It seemed, at that time, every record we cut went multiplatinum. My albums had stayed at No. 1 for an unprecedented 119 weeks on the country charts. One would rise and fall, only to be replaced by another one.

Here's a perfect example of the craziness of it all. In 1982, Jim Mazza suggested I record a duet with Sheena Easton of a great Bob Seger song, "We've Got Tonight," and made it the title track on an album of the same name. David Foster, winner of sixteen Grammys and producer of scores of artists, produced the duet on a Wednesday. By the following Monday, it was playing on the radio all over the country. Before you could blink, the single was on top at No. 1 and the album made it to No. 3. Sometimes I thought I was more of a bystander watching this stuff go on than the person actually in the middle of it.

In 1983, my contract with Liberty Records (formerly United Artists Records) was coming to an end. I had just met Bob Summer, the president of RCA Records, and he wanted me to meet with them and discuss a "groundbreaking" record deal. I wasn't sure what he meant by "groundbreaking," but that word got my attention, so I showed up for the meeting.

I was offered a twenty-one-million-dollar deal for signing for five years. I doubt seriously if I even stopped to think about what that meant, but somehow we got around to yes. I have always been a tough negotiator. This was supposed to be the beginning of something really big and special. I say supposed to, because within about a year Bob Summer was fired, for something completely unrelated to my deal.

So I go into RCA and meet the new president. I'm excited to say hello and let him know I'm ready to do whatever the record company would like to keep this momentum going. I honestly don't remember the new guy's name, but his exact words were "You need to enjoy your twenty million because that's the last money you'll ever get from us." When I said, "I don't get it," he proceeded to explain how the music business—and maybe all big business—really works.

"If I continue to make you successful," he said, "then I make Bob Summer look good and someone may question why they fired him. If I find my own act to sign, then *I* look good."

I never understood such twisted logic, but I knew one thing: I had no hope at RCA, and I got the message loud and clear.

But the party was far from over. In 1983, before the genius executive told me he wasn't going to lift a finger on my behalf, one of the most amazing events of my long career happened—I sang a song with Dolly Parton.

Not a night goes by that someone in my audience doesn't yell, "Hey, Kenny, where's Dolly?" If this continues, I plan on giving everyone who asks her home phone number and they can ask Dolly herself where the hell she is. The answer to the question is, I have no idea.

What an incredible career the two of us have had, and what a joy she was and is to work with. I've known Dolly the better part of forty years. And I have yet to see her when she's not dressed beautifully—hair, makeup, and clothes.

Well, that's not entirely true. There was one time when Dolly and I were on tour and Rob Pincus, my son Christopher, and I were standing in front of some hotel. We had asked Dolly to go sightseeing with us and she had gracefully declined. Standing there, we saw Dolly's assistant, Judy, and asked, "Where's Dolly?" Without saying a word, Judy smiled and motioned to her left, and there was Dolly five feet away, in full makeup but dressed like an old lady. She was going out on her own, incognito. I swear she could have said hello and I would have never recognized her.

The first time I met Dolly Parton was in the 1970s. I was asked to perform on her television show in Nashville, simply called *Dolly*. I remember she had an eight- or nine-foot-high butterfly as her logo. I would like to say that we became immediate friends, but we didn't. I was just another guest in the mix of her very hectic schedule.

Now I must bring Barry Gibb into the story of Dolly and me. It was now 1983. I'm not sure who suggested Barry to produce my next album, but he certainly represented a style of music I had never performed. I knew he wrote hit songs and that the Bee Gees' tracks were always a little slick but, without exception, exciting. The fact that Barry was going to produce an album for me made the project that much more intriguing. I had never analyzed what it was that made Barry Gibb songs so different, but when I started singing, his style of music did not come natural to me, as they say. His lyrics tend to all be on the upbeat, which is totally different from what everybody else does. We worked for hours to get things just right. I knew one thing for sure—I could never have been the fourth Bee Gee.

This was clearly a new direction for me. As Ken Kragen said years later, "Kenny is the master of retreating and attacking from another direction. And that's different from reinventing yourself. Madonna reinvents herself. Kenny circles the wagons, comes in at a different angle, and comes up with something different."

Well, I surely needed a different angle about now. Barry and I were working on a solo version of "Islands in the Stream," written by three of the Gibb brothers, Barry, Robin, and Maurice. I had worked on this song with Barry for at least four days, something I was not used to doing. I finally told him I didn't even like the song anymore. Pondering this for a split second, Barry had an epiphany. Without breaking stride he raised one finger in the air and said, "What we need is Dolly Parton."

So I guess "Where's Dolly?" started way back then. What are the chances that Barry, recording in L.A. and not Nashville, says "Dolly Parton," and forty-five minutes later, probably via Ken Kragen, Dolly marches through the door and changes my life forever? She happened to be in town and in pure Dolly fashion, just signed on to the idea without a lot of hemming and hawing. The minute she started singing, we all knew this was going to be special. In a matter of hours, we did have something special. Who could have known how that song would take off around the world? Who could have known that a fateful recording session in L.A. would lead Dolly and me, over the next five years, into producing four television specials and three albums, doing two world tours together, and creating another No. 1 hit, "Real Love" and a lifetime of memories?

I've lived through earthquakes in California, twisters in Kansas, and hurricanes in Georgia, but nothing prepared me for working with Dolly. Before we started touring, we rehearsed for a week or so. I was sure I could hold my own, but quickly learned, when Dolly comes marching out onstage, I don't care who you are, you might as well stand back.

Our first night together, I almost started clapping for her myself when she came out. We were working in the round and when we began singing, we were to enter from opposite sides of the stage and meet in the middle. By the time I got to the top of the stairs, she was already on my side of the stage, at which point she announced, "Come on up here, Kenny! What's keeping you? You're not that old!" Remember, this was our very first show together.

I think we just got each other right then and there. And I think we made each other sing better each time we performed. She was, and still is, one of the sexiest women I've ever met, and there was always a tremendous electricity between us. At least for me, every night was a thrill.

Dolly, as the world knows, is a world-class kidder. She often liked to sum me up with a line like this: "Kenny, if Johnny Mathis and Willie Nelson ever had a child, he would sound just like you!"

I'll leave this next story for Dolly to tell in her own words, because I'll never do it justice.

One of my most precious and funniest memories was in Arkansas when Kenny and I were doing a big show at a stadium where they had evidently just had a big Razorback ballgame. I found a big Razorback pig mask backstage. I was dressed in my beautiful sequin gown, and the meanness in me took over. It was about time for me to go onstage. At the end of his show, Kenny would introduce me and we would finish the show with duets. I would be at the top of a set of stairs, and the spotlight would hit me. I would go into the Bob Seger song "We've Got Tonight." I thought, "I don't care, I have to do this just to make Kenny laugh." So I put on the big ugly hog snout mask, and when the lights hit me, there I was with a big pig head on. I started singing the song. Of course the crowd went wild, because they were Razorback fans. Kenny couldn't hold his composure, but I refused to take it off until we had finished that whole song. Needless to say, the song wasn't very good, but the laugh was worth millions to me.

After a hundred stunts like that, I learned something from Dolly. We can joke pretty hard with each other and we never take it personally because she knows as I do, whatever is said between us comes from love. The two of us have a very special friendship, and nobody can explain it better than Dolly can:

> *We are as close as two people can be without being blood kin or romantically involved, which we are neither. We are what you call soul mates, or kindred spirits might be more accurate. We can't fool each other in ways that we might pull the wool over someone else's eyes. And we nail each other to the wall at times, which makes for some very deep emotional and meaningful laughs, almost as if we are looking in a mirror. Often we will say to each other if we forget who we're talking to, "Hey, it's me so cut the crap!"*

Dolly has been and continues to be a great friend.

After "Islands," we were asked to do a Kenny-Dolly Christmas album and television special. At this point I told her that I would like to coproduce the album with David Foster. She readily agreed if I allowed her to write the music. I had no idea what a talent she was. Within two weeks she had written five of the six original songs on the album. Each one was individually spectacular. I found that to be one of my better trade-offs.

What I remember most about the television special is the two of us standing in separate windows but side by side, singing Christmas songs. In between takes Dolly was telling me some of the dirtiest jokes I have ever heard. The director, Bob Giraldi, asked us if we would like to take a break. Dolly said, "No, thank you, I'm out of jokes anyway." That's the kind of relationship it's been since day one. We say things to each other that to someone else might sound offensive, but what we both learned is that anything that's said from love shouldn't be hurtful.

But if recording and acting with her was special, boy, touring was a whole new world. One of my favorite tours ever was a trip to Australia with Dolly in 1987. We both had previously had successful tours there but wanted to go back together. The concerts were huge and the response greater than either of us anticipated.

Our tour coincided with the America's Cup sailing competition off the coast of Fremantle, Western Australia, the first time it had ever been held outside of the United States. After our show in Sydney, Dolly and I were both invited by Dennis Conner, the American captain and a four-time winner of the Cup, to go for a sail on the U.S. entry, the *Stars & Stripes*. Dennis had just won the 1987 competition. It was a proud day for America. I can only assume Dennis wanted to meet Dolly and I was invited along for the ride.

I couldn't wait to go out, but Dolly passed. We all assumed that she might be afraid of the ocean, but that wasn't going to stop me. The seas can get rough, for sure. At one point Dennis let me take the helm for ten minutes and I felt like it must have felt on the *Titanic*. I was standing there with the wind and salty breeze in my face and for the first time saw how people could get hooked on sailing.

Later that same afternoon, Dolly and I were asked to do an interview on the *Stars & Stripes* with Bryant Gumbel. That's when I found out the real reason she didn't want to go sailing. She was afraid the wind would blow away her hairpiece! She did the interview anyway and held on to her hair the whole time.

At sea, it's every man for himself—hairpieces be damned.

It didn't matter what I did or where we were, when Dolly walked

out onstage, it was always magic. I love Dolly's spirit and was reminded of it once again as I read over a few more words she wrote
reflecting on the times we've shared:

> *I love Kenny Rogers, always have, always will. I always
> look forward to seeing Kenny or working with him. I never
> get tired of hearing him sing. I've always been a fan, since
> long before I met him, and I'm an even bigger one now that I
> know him.*
>
> *I loved touring with Kenny. We had a lot of fun and a
> lot of laughs. Kenny has a wonderful crew and a wonderful
> band. I made lifetime friends with many of them. We are
> alike in that way also. We are very loyal and devoted to the
> people we work with.*
>
> *Kenny has always been very generous with his time and
> talent with me. He even appeared on my very first Dolly TV
> show back in the '70s. He was also on my Dolly variety show
> in the '80s. Then we toured in the '90s. And we're still doing
> things together. I'd do anything for Kenny. Any time he says
> "jump," I say, "at what?" We both jump at any chance to be
> together, and I'm sure it will be that way forever.*
>
> *Kenny Rogers, I will always love you.*

And I will always love her. There is always the danger of being
so closely associated with someone that you lose your own identity.
If I'm going to lose it, I want to lose it with Dolly. I don't care how
many people ask me "Where's Dolly?" I can only say "Well, I don't
know, but like you, I wish she was here!"

CHAPTER THIRTEEN

The Good Life

With the success of those records, and movies, and concerts, and all the rest of it, I was making more money than I had ever dreamed of, and I couldn't wait to enjoy it. Very early on, as I mentioned, my mentor, Kirby Stone, gave me some very valuable advice about how to survive as a professional musician: find other interests and creative outlets as a respite from the constant pressure, travel, and exhaustion of a music career. Even though I was as busy as I'd ever been during this period, I still carved out the time to take Kirby's cue and pursue some private passions. These included a passion for tennis, a passion for photography, and a passion for buying houses and driving myself crazy remodeling them.

My love of tennis began long before I hit it big in Nashville. One thing you can be sure of: when I was growing up in the projects of Houston, tennis was nonexistent. For most of my childhood, I had never even seen the sport played. Tennis balls were for hitting with a broomstick in a baseball game.

I didn't even know what to wear on the court. Early on, I remember prepping for a match with Marianne and some lady friends of hers. I showed up in a brand-new all-white outfit: white shorts, white shirt, a white headband, white shoes, and long white socks that came up to my knees. I thought that was the required attire. Needless to say, I looked like a complete dork, instantly recognized as "the idiot who looks like he was dressed by his mother."

In any case, I had a desire to learn the game, with or without the kneesocks. About a year before Marianne and I were married, we took a trip to Florida, staying at the Amelia Island Plantation. Marianne was a great tennis player, having played in college at the University of Georgia, and since I was still a novice, I looked around for a teaching pro. The guy everyone seemed to fight over was Kelly Junkermann, a seasoned player who had been on the ATP tour for three years and worked with a lot of great players, not the least of which was tennis legend Chris Evert. Kelly and I hit it off, and in a week, I learned a hell of a lot of tennis from him. By the way, this was before the success of "Lucille," so I was no star in his eyes. He knew a couple of the songs from the First Edition, but that was about it.

I left him with these words: "Listen, if you ever get out to L.A., give me a call and we can play a little."

Two years later, after "Lucille," I got a call one day from Kelly in L.A. He said he was in Manhattan Beach, and I invited him to our house in Westwood. Dropped off by a friend, Kelly first noticed twin Rolls-Royce cars in the driveway. Not one, but two. He was impressed.

Once we got past that, we headed for the home of one of my friends, Ron Samuels. He was managing some of the most beautiful actresses in the world and was married to Lynda Carter. He also had a great tennis court and was an excellent player.

"You mean," Kelly asked, "we're going to play tennis at Wonder Woman's house?"

We played and he could see that I had taken his lessons to heart and was much improved. By then I was playing almost every day and quickly realized how much fun it would be to have Kelly as my full-time coach. He was itching to get back on the pro tour, and I said I'd sponsor him. Before the day was done, he had agreed to relocate in L.A.

I then asked him how he was going to get back to Manhattan Beach, and he said he would have to call his friend.

"Just take one of the cars in the driveway," I said. He looked at me like I was crazy.

"One of those Rolls? I can't take one of your Rolls!"

To this day, Kelly still laughs at my answer.

"You know what? It's just a car."

What Kelly would soon learn about me was that I preferred driving a Chrysler minivan anyway. I could get in and out of it easily, there was room for my friends, and no one ever paid the slightest attention to me when I was driving around town.

That began both a friendship and a working relationship that has lasted right up to today. Kelly was certainly a tennis pro, but also much more. He clearly had both creative instincts and organizational skills that I sorely needed. Half the projects I would do over the next thirty years—everything from movies and TV specials to videos and custom-made stage shows—simply wouldn't have gotten done without Kelly. He was, and continues to be, the best friend a guy could have.

And did we ever play tennis! Sometimes eight or ten hours a day when time allowed. My tennis game continued to improve under his tutelage. When Kelly wasn't on his tennis tour, he started going with me when I was on tour with "Lucille." He would get all of us, band and all, out playing tennis. It was great because it helped everyone stay in shape and gave us some downtime away from the stage.

Kelly and I got pretty obsessive about tennis. We'd pull into a city for a concert and before you knew it, Kelly had lined up a match with a local pro and his assistant, and nine times out of ten, we would beat them. We made a good doubles team. We each knew what shots the other would take before he took them. It was actually during one of those weekend tennis tournaments in Reno that Steve Glassmeyer, my keyboard player, and I wrote the song, "Love or Something Like It," another No. 1 song for me.

Kelly loved the fact that our opponents always underestimated me because I was a singer and didn't exactly *look* like a tennis player.

"They see you comin', Kenny, and they think you won't be much of a challenge. If they knew how strong your legs and lungs were, they might not be so complacent."

As Kelly would later explain, "Kenny is a student of the game. That is just his nature. Whatever he gets interested in, he goes at it full bore. His stamina is amazing."

I think Kelly is right about this. My stamina is, I think, beyond the norm. I don't know if it is just good genes or the fact that I have led a pretty clean life. I don't smoke or drink, and with the exception of three or four times in my younger days, have never done drugs. Furthermore, I am active. I always have to be doing something—keeping busy.

My stamina has a lot to do with my general outlook. I do the best I can in any situation, and then don't worry about it—a lesson from my mother. I think worry adds a lot of stress to a person's body and doesn't have one redeeming feature. Worry won't solve anything.

Tennis soon became an even larger part of my life. When Marianne and I learned that there was no collegiate tennis hall of fame, we donated the money to build one at her alma mater, the University of Georgia. Tennis also became a way for me to get involved in all kinds of charities. I have played in hundreds of charity tennis matches over the years.

Some of my celebrity matches were so intense that I do remember the outcome. Another tennis pro friend of mine, Doug Dean, traveled with me when Kelly was on tour. He had been playing a lot with Robert Duvall. Robert lived in Malibu at the time and had just won the Academy Award for *Tender Mercies*. He was nice enough to come to my house to play Kelly and me. Now in all fairness they had beaten us once before, but on this day we beat them 6–0, 6–0. All I remember about the end of the match was Robert slamming his racket to the ground and screaming at Doug, "I drove all the way from the beach for this shit?" I don't think we ever played him again.

Berry Gordy, the Motown president, was a favorite competitor of mine and one of the few singles players I played regularly. I have never known anyone so driven in my life. To Berry, winning was everything. We must have played fifty singles matches and truthfully, he beat me like a drum for two years. He knew he could beat me, so he never shied away from the chance to put another notch in his belt.

Just before I moved from Beverly Hills to Athens, Georgia, Berry and I had a match scheduled. I realized he would have never let me leave that city without one more shot at humiliating me. Unfortunately, I won. He was shocked. He hadn't counted on that, and he wanted to play a second match immediately afterward. He continued to tell me how lucky I was and how I would never beat him again. All this time I was packing my rackets and explaining how I would never play him again. He kept asking,

"Why? Why?" I explained, in the future, if anyone asked me how well he played, I would simply say, "I don't really know. All I know is I beat him the last time we played." He insisted our mutual friend Doug Dean arrange another match before I left. It never happened. So if you ask me how well Berry Gordy plays, you know my answer.

Doug had been a roommate of Bobby Riggs for a while. Bobby was the number one player in the world in his younger days and was then known as a tennis hustler. As an exhibition in 1984, Doug arranged for me to play Bobby one set of singles for ten thousand dollars. They called it, "War of the Stars: The Gambler vs. The Hustler." This was televised and it was big. The money would go to the charity of our choice. I must admit I was extremely flattered, and really scared at the same time.

Bobby is the only person to ever win the men's singles, doubles, and mixed doubles at Wimbledon all in the same year. Okay, so when we played our match he was probably sixty-five and I was maybe forty-five, but this was still Bobby Riggs. I felt a little of what Kelly must have felt when he realized he was playing against Wonder Woman.

Bobby agreed to give me one game and five points to use anywhere in the set when I needed them. All I wanted was to get out alive and not embarrass myself. Believe it or not, there was a moment when I checked the score and it hit me, *Oh my God, I could win this!* If I remember correctly, we were at four games all. I started doing the math and realized, I was serving at 30–15. All I had to do was win the next two points, then I could use my "gift" game and win this match and a $100 side bet Bobby had made me just before the game started. I was two points from the biggest win of my tennis life.

First of all, I was never a singles player; I specialized in doubles. I didn't start playing tennis until I was thirty-five years old. So here I am, now forty-five and playing singles against one of the best players who ever played the game. And about to beat him [in my mind]. It would be a daunting task, but if I could pull it off, this would make history. This was something I could tell my grandkids about. I think it was about here that Bobby did some math of his own and decided that wasn't going to happen. He had no concern for my grandkids.

We made it to a tiebreaker, and once there, to everyone's surprise, Bobby changed the rules. He claimed the five points he had given me were for the set only, not a tiebreaker. Once we got there it was every man for himself.

Bobby won the tiebreaker 9–7, as he should have. It was a great event. The crowd had been thoroughly entertained, the charity had gotten its money, I hadn't embarrassed myself, and Bobby had won. I thought it was really classy of him to play me in the first place.

In most of the indoor tennis courts in Las Vegas, there are what they called "walk bridges" that surround every court, so spectators can watch their friends play, and can walk or run laps.

Kelly and I were hitting on one of those courts one day when we noticed a young boy and an older man watching us. I was flattered that they would want to watch me play.

They seemed very impressed and walked from side to side looking from every angle, watching us play and commenting on our skills. It was exciting for me. I immediately stepped up my game.

After our match, as we packed up our rackets and started from the court, they came out of nowhere and approached us. The man said, "Hey, buddy. You're pretty good. How long have you been playing? You've got a great game."

I looked at Kelly, then back to the man, and said, "Thanks, I haven't been playing long, but I love the game." I just assumed he was a fan.

"Not you," he said. "The blond guy."

So now I'm slightly embarrassed and really pissed off. Kelly said, "I wouldn't say I'm great. Why do you ask?" The man said, with a great deal of sarcasm, "I have a fourteen-year-old son here who I think can kick your ass. In fact, I'll bet you $100 you can't get a set."

I said to Kelly, "Go ahead, I'll back you. Teach this guy a lesson. Don't let him talk to me like that."

So Kelly played the kid. It went back and forth for the first couple of games, a couple of ads, and couple of deuces, back and forth. This kid was really good, but once Kelly decided to play, he beat the kid, 6–3. While the two of them were in the middle of their match, the older man turned to me and asked, "Who is this guy?" I told him he was a touring pro who traveled and hit with me. He looked at me and said, "And . . . who are you?" I told him "Kenny Rogers." There was nothing. It didn't even register with him. It was like the old comedy bit.

He looked at me and said, "Nope . . . never heard of you."

When it came time to pay, the man refused, saying Kelly hadn't told him he was a pro. Kelly reminded him he hadn't asked. He still never paid.

The man's son was Andre Agassi. At fourteen, Andre was already being hustled around Vegas for money. Maybe that kind of pressure is what made him such a fierce competitor. That's also probably why Andre ended up hating the game so much.

Kelly swears every time I tell this story, Andre gets younger and younger. One time I told it and Andre was nine.

Kelly and I actually had a ranking on the ATP tour. We had played two pro tournaments in 1979. We lost to Wimbledon finalist Chris Lewis and U.S. Open finalist Van Winitsky. Later that year in Green Bay, Wisconsin, in another ATP tournament, we lost to NCAA champ Bruce Nichols and Wimbledon mixed doubles winner John Austin, Tracy's brother. The singles winner of that tournament was Vince Van Patten. It was his first pro title, and later that year he went on to beat John McEnroe and Jimmy Connors. Believe it or not, I was actually ranked ahead of Björn Borg in doubles when he was number one in the world singles rankings. (He had played only one tournament.) Kelly showed me the ATP ranking list and there it was, Kenny Rogers, and a few spots down—Björn Borg.

There comes a time in the life of every "superstar" when they need "people." Thinkers need doers, just like doers need thinkers. I was a thinker, so I needed doers. I can't "do" anything but sing, as my mom used to say.

At this point, I had been doing some appearances with the likes of Luther Vandross, Aretha Franklin, and Diana Ross—now, Diana Ross had "people." She had security, makeup, family, and she had friends. There must have been twelve to fourteen people around her wherever she went. You didn't get close to Diana unless Diana wanted you close to her. She was a superstar. On the other hand, I had me and Kelly, my tennis pro. No offense to Kelly, but I felt so unimportant in the grand scale of things. So now I'm making a lot of money, and I immediately start looking around for an entourage. Where do you start? You don't just add for the sake of adding. Everyone has to have a purpose. It was then I realized there must be someone out there who would want to hurt me. Surely I needed security.

Kelly and I were in Atlantic City working at the Golden Nugget, Steve Wynn's casino, when we met an undercover cop named Rob Pincus. I think the word *undercover* carries its own status and air of professionalism, plus we both really liked this guy. By the time we left Atlantic City, I had hired Rob away from the A.C. police department. I immediately felt twice as important. I now had *two* "people." By the way, you're not allowed to count wives in your entourage.

Kelly, Rob, and I set out to increase our posse, but the only people I knew were entertainers who worked as much as I did and certainly didn't want to be one of my followers. Everyone Kelly knew was either a tennis pro or had been a tennis pro. I knew that wouldn't work. After all, how much tennis could I play? Diana Ross would never surround herself with tennis pros, so, okay, I wouldn't either.

We turned to Rob. The only people he knew were policemen or other undercover cops, and God knows we didn't need another cop. We hadn't even figured out *who* it was that might want to hurt me, so I didn't need more security until we did.

Rob also came up with the theory that the more people we had in our group, the more obvious we would be. "Really, Rob?" We now realized he had no clue what he was doing in the way of private security, but I had hired him and we were stuck with him. The good news is, we liked him a lot, and his personality fit us perfectly.

About six months later, we were finishing a long, pretty intense tour and had a couple of days off before starting back again. Kelly and I decided we would go to Athens, Georgia, play some golf, and see my family. Rob would go back to Atlantic City for some needed time with his family as well and wait for us. We were coincidentally working in Atlantic City next.

I don't think there's any question we were still impressed with some of the stories Rob would tell, and needless to say, we believed everything. It was great theater. As an undercover cop, he'd had a life of adventure compared to ours, so it was exciting. We hung on every word.

One night on the tour, almost in a moment of shame and confession, Rob admitted to us that he had been kicked out of a casino in Las Vegas for card counting. Kelly and I saw this as both a virtue and an opportunity to make money.

Don't ask me where Kelly got his share, but the two of us gave Rob $5,000 each and sent him ahead to Atlantic City to win big for us. With his illicit skills, if he didn't get caught in the process, this would be brilliant.

We would follow in the next couple of days. With a $10,000 bank he should be able to rack up some huge money for me and Kelly to pocket and probably lose back when we got there. That was our game plan.

As we left Athens, the excitement was growing about our plan. We were on my plane so we could use the phone to get the play by play from him. The first time we called, he said it was going slower than he had hoped, but this was a process and he had to be careful. It was his arms and legs they would break if they caught him. Wow, we hadn't thought of that. It was just like the movies.

Card counting wasn't illegal, but we knew the casinos frowned on it. So we called him again; he was down a little, he said, but feeling good. "How far down?" we asked. "About three thousand." We still had almost two hours of flying time before getting to Atlantic City.

We were new at this, but Rob didn't seem worried, so we chose not to be either. He said he was uncomfortable taking phone calls while he was playing, so we agreed not to call him again. Rob said he would meet us at the airport. We would know then how much he had won. Let the games begin. It was hard, but we didn't call back.

As my plane touched down, we didn't see Rob anywhere. We waited a short time, then called him. Rob was uncharacteristically quiet. He finally said we had lost some of our money.

"How much?" we asked.

"All of it."

In the time it took us to fly from Athens, Georgia, to Atlantic City, New Jersey, our card-counting undercover cop had lost it all. We didn't get to play one hand and we were out $10,000. In all fairness, he said he had been kicked out of Vegas for counting cards, not for winning . . . big difference.

Through the years there would be many more things done out of our friendship. These were my people.

Meanwhile, when I wasn't working or fooling around with Kelly and Rob, Marianne and I were building a very solid marriage. I was bound and determined not to make the same mistakes I had made earlier on. It took three marriages to show me that the person you are going to share your life with needs to be an active part of that life.

We did everything together, right from the start. She toured with me when it was possible, she was in the audience for television appearances, and she was even onstage with me. When we set up our charities, it was always the two of us, never me alone. Marianne was right there being interviewed alongside me at food drives or hospital openings. I talked about her all the time during my interviews. This time I was going to get it right.

And that started with a home. My dream growing up in the San Felipe Courts was to have a house big enough to have automatic sprinklers. Well, with the means at hand, I kept looking for the perfect home, and after a couple of nice places, I thought I had found it. The movie director Dino De Laurentiis owned a house that had been built by the Doheny family, a legendary L.A. oil family, and wanted to sell the place for a whopping $11 million. This house was so big it had a name: "The Knoll." At the time, it was on record as being the largest house in L.A., and for whatever reason, that sounded like a dream to me. The place was huge. It was thirteen acres in the middle of Bel Air, had twelve bedrooms in fifty thousand square feet, and even included a couple of guesthouses bigger than most people's main house.

This was my lucky day. I would like to say I negotiated it down to a cut-rate $9 million, but Dino says I paid full price for it. It allowed me to indulge another one of my passions, home design and remodeling. Before it was all done, I probably put another $4 million into "fixing it up," so now I was into the place for $13 million to $15 million. Thank you "Lucille," "Lady," and all those other hits. Speaking of "Lady": Lionel and his wife, Brenda, lived in one of the guesthouses for two years.

When Marianne and I got married in 1977, we had decided not to have children right away. We were traveling so much and had such an incredible lifestyle that wasn't really conducive to children, but we both knew the time would come. Flying back home from a concert one night, Marianne sat down on the arm of a seat across from me and asked if she looked different. I said, "No, why do you ask?"

"Well," she said, "I will in about eight months." She was pregnant. On December 4, 1981, our son, Christopher Cody Rogers, was born at Cedars-Sinai Hospital in Beverly Hills. We had no problem finding space for young Christopher at the Knoll. He was special then and still is a very special part of my life.

Christopher started school in L.A., but the older he got, the more we became convinced that we didn't want to raise him in Los Angeles. Marianne's mom lived in Athens, Georgia, and her brother lived in Dalton, Georgia. This was a much healthier environment for our son, plus I think Marianne wanted to be closer to her family when I was out of town. Even after all that remodeling work, we decided to sell the Knoll and move to Athens for a more livable existence for all of us.

I had met oilman Marvin Davis and his wife, Barbara, at several L.A. functions and we had become good friends. The Davises were renowned for their generous charitable giving, but when their youngest daughter was diagnosed with juvenile diabetes, they knew they couldn't buy her a cure. They set about creating a foundation to help underwrite the years of research needed, and today it is still a leading source of JD fund-raising.

Marvin heard I was interested in selling the Knoll, so he and Barbara came by for a tour. They absolutely loved the house and wanted to make an offer, that day—no broker, all cash, sixty-day closing. That's how wildcat oilmen do things. I told him I wanted $22 million for the place and it was not really open to negotiation. "I don't have to sell," I said. "I *want* to sell." I probably had the lyrics of "The Gambler" rattling around in my head at the time.

My guess is that Marvin Davis had never paid full price for anything in his life, so he graciously offered me $20 million, in cash. "Thanks," I said, "but no thanks." He was shocked, and quite honestly so was I. He had made the fatal mistake of telling me how much he loved the place early on. We finally settled on $20 million cash and I would carry $2 million in paper for two years. I guess he had to get something in the negotiation. And I wasn't taking a big risk carrying paper for one of the richest men in America.

In a matter of about an hour, Marianne and I had sold our "dream" house and were headed for Athens, Georgia. I forgot to tell Marvin that Lionel and Brenda went with the house. They continued to live there for at least another year. One more thing about the Knoll: Aaron Spelling, an occasional golfing partner of ours, soon built an even bigger, 55,000-square-foot house. Was he just trying to top his old friend Marvin?

The next move for the family was to our new place, Beaver Dam Farms in Athens. Around this time in the '80s, we made the only theatrical feature in which I was the star, *Six Pack*. Produced by Marianne's ex-husband, Michael Trikilis, it was a movie about a washed-up race car driver who couldn't afford a pit crew and conspired with a group of orphan kids to "borrow" parts for his rig. If you look really hard, you can see Chris in his mother's arms in a crowd scene. Future stars Diane Lane and Anthony Michael Hall were two of my pint-sized pit crew.

Again, acting in this movie reminded me of one of my favorite stories about okay actors like me. Randolph Scott, a very successful star in Westerns, applied for membership at the L.A. Country Club, a place notorious for rejecting actors. When he was told this by the membership board, he reportedly replied, "I'm no actor—and I have fifty-one movies to prove it!"

That's kind of how I've always felt about the profession.

The same year that Marianne and I got married, 1977, I did four concerts in Sikeston, Missouri, for the twenty-fifth anniversary four-day Sikeston Jaycees Bootheel Rodeo. During my visit there, I was approached by a couple of guys who were local Jaycees who had to be ten years younger than me. They told me how passionate the Jaycees were about doing something special for their city and their kids, and that they wanted to build a children's therapy center that would provide care for children with special needs. It's hard not to get caught up in that kind of emotion about such an incredible cause.

At the time, I was raising Arabian horses, and I had this beautiful stallion named Borraabby. Realizing I was about at the end of my horse-raising era, I donated Borraabby to help them raise money for the center. He raised $75,000 at auction. This apparently was more than they needed to break ground on a new center and get their dreams started. It was shortly after this donation that the Jaycees informed me the therapy board wanted to name the new center after me. Obviously, I was very flattered and wholeheartedly agreed.

The Kenny Rogers United Cerebral Palsy Center started off as a relatively small operation in the '70s, treating around twenty kids, but it has blossomed into the Kenny Rogers Children's Center, providing physical, occupational, and speech therapy to children with all types of special needs. Today the center treats well over four hundred children (with more than one hundred on the waiting list) and helps them function more independently, attend public school, and gain the confidence they need to lead more active and productive lives. Amazingly, no family has ever been charged anything for the services they've received. A third expansion of the center was recently completed—a 7,000-square-foot, state-of-the-art, million dollar addition—with a plan to provide treatment well into the future at no charge to the children served.

I've had the pleasure of going back to Sikeston periodically over the years—first with my friend Dottie West in 1978 and 1979—to do fund-raising concerts to benefit the center. It never ceases to amaze me how a few young men with a dream—the Jaycees, and in this case, the great people of Sikeston and the surrounding communities—can make such incredible things happen. I am so proud of my friends in Sikeston and thrilled to be associated with this amazing project.

One thing I've learned is the more successful you are, the more you can accomplish with just a little effort.

Back home in Athens, always antsy to do something between recording, touring, and playing tennis, I decided to undertake the construction of an eighteen-hole golf course on the property. I might not have had good sense, but as Kelly said, I had stamina. I liked to play golf, and the idea of a whole course came gradually. I started by adding a couple of short greens for fun, then spotted a great place across a lake for another hole. I brought in a landscape designer, Joe Gayle, my brother-in-law, Don Thumann, and probably thirty University of Georgia students, including football great Herschel Walker, and we set out planting and moving trees, digging sand traps, and laying sod.

I would be out on tour and play a golf course, see something I like, and come back and build it. One of the problems was that part of the farm had no trees on it, so I bought a thing called a tree spade. It was a huge truck with a big claw on the back that could dig up a tree, roots and all, so that the tree could be replanted. And, boy, did I dig them up. I was going all over town and thinning out overcrowded trees from people's homes and moving them to the farm. In fact, I even got the Athens Airport to give me some of their trees in exchange for some of my photographs! In all, I planted five thousand yaupons and transplanted three hundred trees. The golf course was really taking shape.

Some three years later, when National Amateur Left-Handed Championship winner and local golfer Stan Kanavage and I were playing, he cut across a dogleg hole that I had designed and hit straight at a green. That was not supposed to be the way the hole was played. I got my trusty tree spade and planted a few trees in that path. A few days later he came over and we played again. It was great to see the look on his face when he couldn't take the shortcut. When he double-bogeyed the hole, I knew I had a golf course.

Chris loved the course, naturally, and at seven was just starting to drive a golf cart, usually recklessly. We were building a lake bridge one day and Chris came over the hill full speed; when he saw us, he slammed on the brakes and slid fifteen feet on the grass to the very edge of the lake. Frightened to death, he looked up and said, "Sorry, Daddy, I don't think I was in complete control." That struck me as all the punishment he needed.

Marianne had found her place in Athens. She had her mom, her brother, her girlfriends, and most important, she had Christopher living a free, country life.

My dad once told me, "If you have five friends when you grow up . . . even with no money . . . you are a very wealthy man. Be friendly to everyone, but friends with only a few." I think I was finally getting old enough to understand what he meant. My friendships have always been very important to me . . . not a lot of friends, just enough that we could all be there for each other when we needed someone. I had my friends: Jim Mazza, Kelly Junkermann, Rob Pincus, Ken Kragen, and Steve Wynn. They were there for me, and I would be there for them.

I had gone to great lengths to learn as much about landscaping as

I could while Joe and I were building the golf course. I will tell you I think Joe Gayle is one of the most creative people I have ever met. He has worked with me on every project I've done in the last twenty years, and I have been proud of everything we have done. We studied, to me, the Rolls-Royce of golf courses, the Masters course—the Augusta National Golf Club—in Augusta, Georgia, and did as much as we could to reach that standard of detail and beauty at Beaver Dam.

Having finished the course, we wondered not about the aesthetics, but about the degree of difficulty for an accomplished player. That's the final test. Kelly and I were playing one day and we started talking about testing the course. I casually asked him, "How well do you think a professional golfer would enjoy this course?"

He said, "I don't know. Let's have a Gambler's Invitational here and find out. We can invite a bunch of pros to play, sell tickets to the public, and give it to a local charity."

I had held what we called a Gambler's Invitational tennis tournament when I lived in Beverly Hills. That one was just for sport, but very competitive. I had built what Jimmy Connors called his favorite tennis court to play on because of the acoustics. The idea in the tournament was to invite six of my friends and their respective pros.

My friends the first year were Johnny Carson, who lived three houses down; Lionel Richie, who had played on the tennis team at Tuskegee University; Bert Convy, the game show host; actor Robert Duvall; Bruce Jenner, the world's greatest athlete; and me. We all had about the same level of game, which made it really competitive.

Everyone put up $500. The winning celebrity's pro got all the money. We had no trouble getting pros to play, and the competition was fierce and we had a lot of fun. So that was the premise we started with.

In Beaver Dam, I had also built two green clay tennis courts, and we realized the barn was big enough to have a half-court basketball court. So now we're on the back nine and we have this grand scheme to invite a group of high-profile athletes to come and stay at my house and compete in both their own sport and other sports as well. We'd round up four professional golfers, four professional basketball players, four professional tennis players, and four well-known celebrities and create mixed teams. A pro golfer, for instance, wouldn't just compete at golf. He'd have to compete at basketball and tennis as well.

By the end of the round, we had it almost all figured out. Our good friend Larry Levinson, another of the pros from the Gambler's Invitational, joined us in fine-tuning the event. To pay for it, we turned to Steve Wynn. The Golden Nugget was the perfect sponsor for the Gambler's Invitational and now this. Steve, as always, was quick to say yes and agreed to put up $500,000. So now we had the money, the place, and the concept, but no athletes.

Kelly and I decided if we could get Michael Jordan, whom we had already met, everyone else would fall into place. We first called Michael and told him we had John McEnroe set up, then we called John and told him we had Michael set. Now we had agreements from both. From there this event just took off.

In our first year, 1988, the basketball players were Michael Jordan, Larry Bird, Isiah Thomas, and Dominique Wilkins. Our tennis players were John McEnroe, Vitas Gerulaitis, Jimmy Connors, and Mikael Pernfors. The golfers: Ray Floyd, Payne Stewart, Tim Simpson, and Lanny Wadkins. The celebs: Lorenzo Lamas, Kris Kristofferson, Mark Harmon, and me. I'm sure most of these pros came just for the opportunity to meet one another.

With the additional help of the production company Guber-Peters, we added two additional components to the contest, including fishing, and found just the right charity. We would take all the money and create an Athens Area Homeless Shelter. Guber-Peters agreed to produce the TV version and lined up a network immediately. The only hitch is that gambling had a bad connotation in sports TV, so we decided to call it what it was—"The Classic Weekend."

What made the event unique was getting athletes to compete in something they did not excel in. Adding fishing may have seemed inconsequential at the time, but it became one of our favorite events. We had offered $5,000 to the person who caught the biggest fish and an additional $5,000 to the person catching the most fish.

What we didn't know was Michael Jordan was deathly afraid of the water and really wanted no part of this. I explained to him that as tall as he was he could probably stand up anywhere in the lake. So after we agreed to have everyone wear life preservers so he wouldn't look silly, he said yes.

Now picture, if you can, a ten-acre lake with three thousand people sitting on the banks watching sixteen of the most recognizable people in the world get in their boats with their partners and, at the sound of whistle, spread out over the lake and fish. Lines were going everywhere—on the shore, over other boats, and into the spectators. It was a mess, but a fun one.

The irony is that Michael, who didn't want to do this at all, caught the biggest fish. After realizing he had just won $5,000 dollars, he offered his boat partner Ray Floyd $2,500 to take the fish off the line for him. That's just the kind of event this was, pure fun from day one.

At the end of each day's competition, everyone was exhausted and would retire to their rooms on the property for the night. That's when the games really began. I don't want to mention any names, but his initials are Isiah Thomas, and he was holding court in the corner, on the floor of the main guesthouse. It seems someone had inadvertently left a pair of dice and Isaiah had stumbled on to them. All I know is someone came up to the main house and told me to "Come quick, there is a game going on in the guesthouse and people are losing all their money." By the time I got there it was obvious this was not Isiah's first rodeo. He had literally cleaned everybody out. When I walked in it, I was fresh blood. Now I've never considered myself a real gambler, but I saw an opportunity to shine. I was going to ride in like a knight in shining armor and show him a thing or two about dice. I started with $1,000—and was broke in three minutes flat.

Yep . . . I showed him.

The third year, things got even more competitive. Larry Bird woke up every morning before everybody else to find the best fishing spots. Charles Barkley was bound and determined to master golf like his good pal Michael Jordan. Jimmy Connors, John McEnroe, and golf great Payne Stewart turned out to be excellent basketball players. When Woody Harrelson sank a five-foot putt on the final hole to win the golf event for his team, he and his teammates, including Michael Jordan, hugged and shouted and sprayed the champagne around like they had just won the NBA championship. Good pal Bruce Boxleitner's team won one of the years as well.

It was a family event, too. I woke up one morning to find all the kids in Christopher's room huddled around Michael Jordan as he played the Michael Jordan video game.

The next year JCPenney, with whom I had a clothing deal, stepped up for the next two years and put up $1,000,000 to keep the event alive. The entire event was put together in less than two months with a small staff, all under the command of tournament director Phil Kramer. The proceeds single-handedly built the Athens Area Homeless Shelter.

The amazing part is it all started with two friends walking around a golf course and wondering . . .

CHAPTER FOURTEEN

A Life of Photography

During this great bubble of success in the 1980s, I indulged in one other grand passion that's become grander by the year—photography. It was a big part of my life from early on, but it really became a pre-occupation after Marianne and I moved to Beaver Dam Farms.

As I said, artists need outside interests to help balance the unreal lives they are living. There is no question that photography has been an extension of my creative self, but it has also offered me an escape from the scrutiny of the public eye and the craziness of a concert tour.

When my old mentor Kirby Stone saw that I was interested in photography, he introduced me to Milton Greene, the famous high-fashion photographer whose subjects included Marilyn Monroe, Frank Sinatra, and Judy Garland. Kirby's exact words: "Milton, give him some pointers. He wants to do photography."

I had a whole bunch of equipment by then, so I started by listing off all my lenses. I don't think Milton was too impressed. He told me, "Pick one and throw the rest away. All great photographers see in one plane. Some guys see landscapes wide, some people like to shoot on the table, but you have to figure out what your eye tends to compose."

I thought it was a great piece of advice, but I still have twelve lenses and I've tried to learn how to use them all. I think Milton was talking about taking a certain type of picture where one lens will usually suffice. And he was certainly right that having only one lens teaches you to perfect a certain kind of composition.

During the early '80s, I was doing 150 shows a year. It was a great opportunity to see the country and, as the great French photographer Henri Cartier-Bresson said, "capture a moment in time." I had always built a darkroom for developing and printing in the house I was living in, and if I was shooting a movie, we would transform the bathroom in the hotel room into a darkroom.

One of the greatest gifts I have ever received was Marianne giving me a week in the darkroom with John Sexton, the assistant of famed photographer Ansel Adams. John came to my house in Beverly Hills and spent a week teaching me the style of Ansel Adams.

There was now so much more for me to do than just take a picture. I enlisted Kelly as my production and creative copartner and we went everywhere, including up in the air in planes and helicopters, which always made Kelly a little more nervous than me.

One time we were in British Columbia and had hired a couple of helicopter pilots to take us into the wild, where we might be able to catch a few unique photographic opportunities. We are flying through gorges, zooming in and out, and all at once, through an open mike, we hear our pilot talking to the copilot.

"Yeah, I used to be a Vietnam helicopter pilot." Well, okay. That's a good thing. Clearly a guy who knows his business. His next line: "Yeah, my wife left me and I don't have that much to live for anymore."

Right then we were starting up the steep side of a mountain.

Kelly looked at me, took a deep breath, and said one word, dragging it out for about ten seconds. "Soooooooo . . ."

On another occasion that Kelly hasn't forgotten, we chartered a little single-engine Cessna to take us over the Grand Canyon. Rob Pincus was with us, and it was a little harrowing. The turbulence over the Grand Canyon is always edgy. That day it went from bad to terribly bad. When we went over the lip of the canyon, the wind took us and just threw us sideways. I was still trying to take pictures from the window, but by now Kelly was flat on the floor, trying to get a few shots that way. I ordered the pilot to take us back, and when we landed, Kelly kissed the ground!

A day or two later, another single-engine plane crashed in the canyon, and they made a new ruling—no more single-engine planes would be allowed to fly over the canyon. I have to say that, judging from our ride that day, it was a good ruling.

Photography opened a whole new door for me, and I embraced it. My daily routine changed dramatically. I would fly into a city, get a rental car, and set off to find the treasure that city had to offer. I was armed with the same type of camera that Ansel had used, called a 4 x 5 camera. With Kelly and Rob as my sherpas, we'd often get lost looking for something interesting to shoot. I'd do my show, then fly back home to L.A. or the farm in Athens, and jump right into developing the film. To hurry things along I would dry the negative with a hair dryer, then make the print. This was not the digital age. Sometimes to get a print that I was satisfied with, I would spend hours printing and reprinting. A lot of those sessions went until the early hours of the morning.

The next morning would be more of the same: fly to the next concert, have an Egg McMuffin and a Diet Coke for breakfast, and be off in search of my next great photograph.

Because of touring, I was always on location. I have come to know the sometimes haunting faces of men out of work, the homeless, sheepherders, and wealthy cattlemen, whose deeply lined faces indicate exactly how they attained their riches. I've seen the charm in an old tombstone or broken-down shed, a massive ridge of granite in the Sierra Nevada, a rushing mountain stream, or that old standard, the Maine lighthouse. Our country became alive for me in a way I had never known.

If you really want to see America, take up photography. You don't have to start out with a fancy camera—just take what you have and start shooting. You will never regret it.

In 1986, I selected the best of my travel photos and published them in a book called *Kenny Rogers' America.*

It was during this time that the hours spent in the darkroom began to affect my throat. I was probably spending a minimum of four hours a night in the darkroom, and doctors advised this probably was not a good idea for a guy who had to depend on his throat to make a living.

My days on the road today are a lot like they were twenty years ago. My road manager, Gene Roy, is now my right-hand man, but the day starts the same.

One day, after *America* had come out in the '80s, Ken Kragen stopped by my studio on Sunset Boulevard and noticed some of the portraits I had been shooting for several years and asked why I didn't put out another book with only portraits. The idea started germinating. I came up with the idea of shooting well-known people, the ones who are familiar to all of us, and calling the book *Your Friends and Mine.*

My young son, Chris, was the one who actually got the ball rolling. He was a big Michael Jackson fan, and one night after I had hosted the Grammy Awards, Chris found Michael, introduced himself, and gave him a little plastic Grammy that had been attached to the flowers his mom, Marianne, had given me. The upshot of that meeting was Michael asking if I would like to take some pictures of him and Chris. By this time, most people knew I was heavily into photography. The day he came for those shots, I told Michael my idea for a book. He loved it.

"Why don't you start with me?" he said. "I would love to do a photo shoot with my chimp, Bubbles."

So Michael Jackson and Bubbles were my first subjects. They came and stayed eight hours. They changed clothes about six times. I have pictures of him that have never been seen. I took the first pictures of him in a hat he had brought with him. I think he was about to have plastic surgery and was trying to hide his face. I ended up with some really cool pictures of Michael and found him shy, thoughtful, and willing to give his best at anything he did.

Yousuf Karsh, arguably the most famous and accomplished portrait photographer of all time, came down from Canada and spent time teaching me portrait photography. Yousuf shot the famous, almost growling portrait of Winston Churchill that is said to be the most reproduced portrait in history. I was also honored when he wrote the foreword for my book *Kenny Rogers' America*.

When I was going through the photos of Michael Jackson and Bubbles, Yousuf happened to be at my studio. He looked through them and announced: "That one!"

"Why?" I asked.

Yousuf said, "Because *this* is the star, and *this* is the monkey!"

And he was right. You want to see Michael first, then discover the chimpanzee.

With the idea now firmly fixed in my mind, I went back to Little, Brown and Company, the company that had published *Kenny Rogers' America*. They loved the idea and gave me a year to complete the task. In the beginning, I thought that would be plenty of time. Toward the end, I wasn't so sure.

Kelly wasn't so sure I could pull it off at all. "Kenny," he said, "you aren't a celebrity type of guy. You eat breakfast every day at McDonald's. You're a jeans and warm-up suit type of guy and you drive a minivan! You've never even met half these celebrities—how are you going to get them in here?"

I started by calling people I knew to see if they would let me shoot them for the book. Two friends, Linda Evans and Linda Gray, agreed right away. Elizabeth Taylor knew me only in passing—from when Lionel Richie and I had sung at one of her birthday parties—yet she was so sweet about coming, didn't hesitate for a minute. I think it was Ken Kragen who contacted her.

She was the only person who was two hours late, but it was more than worth it when she got there. Her photographs turned out beautifully, and I used one on the cover of the book. After I had photographed Michael, Linda, Linda, and Elizabeth, the word got out. People began to know what I wanted when I reached them on the phone. Or I should say when *someone* reached them. I discovered right away that if I knew someone who knew someone, it was better to have that person do the contacting.

The early photo sessions were taking up to five or six hours, so I decided to go with only one setup per person, taking only six black-and-white photos and three in color. That became my selling point: in and out in thirty minutes, and if I don't come up with a great photo, I won't use it. And it worked.

Shooting with an 8 x 10 camera, I quickly learned that studio photography can be complex and complicated, with multiple types of lighting at variable levels. Through Mario Casilli, the famous *Playboy* photographer, I met and hired his assistant, Bernie Boudreau. Bernie has now been my friend and assistant for thirty years. He also has multiple levels of wisdom. Since he has it, I don't need it.

The great comic Jonathan Winters came in wearing a Cincinnati Reds baseball outfit and a cap and wanted to mimic Babe Ruth pointing to the bleachers. I asked Ray Charles to sway like he was onstage. He refused. Then I told him the dirtiest joke I knew and at the punch line, he started swaying. It was perfect.

George Burns just walked in off the street with his cigar. I said: "Stand right over there." I took two shots and said, "Thanks, George."

"That's it?" he asked. And that was it.

The best story came from President Reagan. He was at the Century Plaza Hotel, so I went there and got all set up. The Secret Service came into the room and asked what my plan was. I answered, "Well, I thought I'd shoot the president over by the window."

"Find another word!" the agent said.

"Okay," I said. "I'll take a *picture* of President Reagan over by the window."

"Then give me two hours and let me move all my snipers," he said. I quickly threw in the towel. "Let me sit him at the desk, take his picture, and we'll be done."

And that's exactly what happened. But the president was so engaging. He really wanted to chitchat with me. I realized that perhaps a president doesn't have anybody to just chitchat with very often. I started getting antsy because I was supposed to be on my way to Hawaii, but I also didn't want to be rude to the president of the United States. Finally I said, "Mr. President, I really have to be going. My family is on the airplane waiting for me at the airport."

"Well, just let me tell you this dirty joke," he answered.

He gets about halfway through it and a lady walks in and he says, "I'll tell you later, Kenny," just like we see each other every other day. He was so sweet.

When I photographed celebrities, I tried to do one of two things. Shoot them as the public sees them or shoot them as they want to be known. Most were photographed in my studio, but I also went wherever I needed to go to get someone to shoot with me. I shot backstage at a Phil Collins concert, went up to get Hef at the Playboy Mansion, and went over to Bob Hope's house. In typical Bob Hope fashion, he asked as he watched Bernie setting up the huge 8 x 10 camera, "Really, Kenny, how much money can you make going door to door with that thing?"

Another president I really enjoyed meeting was Gerald Ford. A friend of mine, Finn Moller, was having a party at his house and President Ford was coming. I asked Finn if the president would mind me taking his picture. Finn asked, and he said he wouldn't. That evening I set President Ford up at the end of a long dining room table and took his photo. Very nice guy, but quiet. We mainly discussed golf. We even talked a little about getting together to play, but we both agreed that together we might put the spectators in real peril and cause a national scandal.

I managed to bring the book in on schedule, but I never worked so hard in my life. In all, *Your Friends and Mine* had eighty photographs of well-known people. Each one was a story, and I was touched by each and every individual in one way or another. The dedication was an easy choice. I made it to the person who was responsible for getting me started on this incredible journey, my son Chris.

I'll round up my life in photography with a quick trip to the White House. I've been to the White House many times and it's never the same. Every president puts his own stamp, his own feel on it during his stay. My first meeting with President Clinton was almost accidental. I was part of a TV special called *A Day in the Life of Country Music,* written and directed by Kelly. The premise of the show was to have different cameras follow country artists around for a day to see what their lives were like.

Thanks to Ken Kragen, again, I was to take a photograph of First Lady Hillary Clinton in the White House. At the same time, the president was doing what I learned were called "shuttle" interviews. He would do an interview at one end of the hall and then move to the other end of the hall for another interview, then back to the original end again, back and forth, on and on. As President Clinton passed the area where I was taking Hillary's photo, he saw all the people and a lot of commotion and asked his Secret Service agent: "What's going on in there?"

The agent explained to him what I was up to. Still new to the office, the president asked: "Can I go in there?"

"Of course you can, sir," the agent said. "You're the *president.*"

He came in as I was wrapping up my shoot with the first lady. I had brought a copy of my photography book *Your Friends and Mine* to sign for Hillary as gratitude for her time. Now that the president was there, I thought I would sign it for both of them. Not wanting to presume to know how to address an inscription to a president of the United States, I asked, "How would you like for me to sign this?"

You could see it all over his face. He had no idea. Finally he said, "To President Bill Clinton, I guess. I haven't got this protocol down yet."

With photography or anything else, really, I don't have to be number one. Just get me in the top of the group and let me hang around for a while. It *is* important to me that I have the respect of the professionals in the field. When I started playing tennis, for example, it became important to me to be able to hit with pros like Chris Evert or Jimmy Connors. I didn't need to beat them, but just to have them say, "He's put in his time. He does it well." With photography, I'll never be John Sexton or Yousuf Karsh, but I want their respect.

Several years ago I had to have throat surgery and the doctor was concerned I might not be able to sing anymore. He couldn't understand why I was not terrified at that prospect. I said, "Doc, I don't get too upset over things I have no control over. And if I do lose my voice, I'll just spend more time on my photography, be more broke, and be perfectly happy."

CHAPTER FIFTEEN

Around the World

My connection to the world outside of the United States came not only with personal appearances. It also came with an increased consciousness of global problems brought to me largely by other artists. That sounds kind of lofty, a little bit out of the league of a country singer from Houston, but it's really not. A compassion for suffering everywhere is as down to earth and human as a simple phrase: We are the world.

In the 1980s, Ken Kragen was managing Harry Belafonte, Kim Carnes, Lionel Richie, and me. It was a good, well-rounded roster of talent. We were all friends who ascribed to the idea that "Success without sharing is unacceptable." Because of that, when Harry started talking to Ken about an awareness-raising anthem about the plight of starvation and the need for famine relief in Ethiopia and other parts of Africa—the anthem that came to be known as "We Are the World"—Ken contacted his other clients and me and we all jumped on board immediately. If I'm correct, the original intent was for Lionel and Stevie Wonder to write the song. Stevie, however, was unavailable to help because of prior commitments but did appear vocally on the record and as always was great.

Lionel presented the idea to his friend Michael Jackson, who understood both the concept and the need for this song right away. This put the two of them on a mission to write a "global" song that would make people all over the world acutely aware of the tremendous crisis of poverty that existed in Africa.

After Lionel and Michael wrote the song, only finishing it a night before the actual recording in 1985, the job of bringing it to life and creating the historic recording went to Quincy Jones and Michael Omartian, another highly respected music producer. Originally, I was told, Ken thought that only Michael and Lionel would sing the song, which in itself would have been quite an event, but once Quincy got involved, the concept grew into something much bigger.

Quincy quickly realized the American Music Awards ceremony was coming up, and a who's who of stars in the music business would be in attendance, meaning they would all be in L.A. at the same time. Things got very exciting right away. A list of performers was put together and selected. I don't know how the selections were made, but everyone involved was sworn to secrecy as to the time and location of the recording. The mere thought of a throng of fans outside a studio when these stars showed up was scary and might have sabotaged the whole event. This was about allowing big stars to come together and share their gift of music without the hassle they would normally go through in their everyday life.

Ken helped with about every aspect of the project but the singing. When the number of artists agreeing to come reached twenty-eight, Harry and Ken decided they had to cut it off. A few people were a little angry with Ken because they wanted to participate, but Ken held firm. Then at the last minute, Michael asked if some of his brothers and sisters could come. No one had the heart to say no because of all the work Michael had done for the project, so the number went a little higher.

At that time, I owned my own recording studio, which was called Lion Share, and I agreed to donate all the studio time they needed. In addition, Lionel and I agreed to put up $200,000 for related video and audio costs. We wanted all the proceeds to go for their intended purpose, not expenses.

Lionel held a "staging" rehearsal at his home the night before to determine the placement of everyone in the studio. If he hadn't thought of that, the whole thing could have been a disaster. The original tracking of the music was done at my studio. Michael and Lionel did a vocal guide for everyone's part—kind of a musical blueprint.

Quincy's group had printed sheet music that notated all the parts and their exact sequence. Thanks to the respect everyone had for Quincy, his now-famous CHECK YOUR EGO AT THE DOOR sign, boldly displayed above the studio door, was pretty much followed. There was a lot of talent in this room and the potential for ego flare-ups was enormous, but I think this group of people, in itself, was too intimidating as a whole for any one performer to dare to ask for or expect special treatment.

The truth is, everyone was given special treatment. Thanks to the vocal arrangers, Tom and John Bähler, the parts were given out not on the basis of how big of a star you were but according to who sounded best on each particular part of the song. I didn't hear one person complain about what they were singing or when they sang. The magnitude of this event was truly humbling for all of us.

I've been involved in a lot of big things, but nothing in my life has ever come close to this. Here you have more than thirty of the biggest and best singers in the world standing side by side on little risers. It looked like a high school choir getting ready for a Friday-night recital. Everyone was humming or singing their parts to themselves in preparation for the start of the music.

The adrenaline was pumping everywhere in that room. I was standing next to Paul Simon and Diana Ross, with Lionel and Michael Jackson next to us. Once I had finished singing my lines, I was awestruck to listen down the line to these great singers all with different styles, different backgrounds, and different timbres to their voices, singing this incredible piece of music as if it were written especially for each one of them. We had completed about six takes when Quincy announced: "Last one. This is it—show me what you've got."

And we did. In the end, it didn't sound like a free-for-all group sing that you might hear at a big all-star concert. It came together, as music, better than anyone had hoped.

Once the last note was sung, there was dead silence in the room. Everybody there knew that not only had we done something good for humanity, we had been a part of something that could never be repeated. In our hearts, this was our moment.

Now try to imagine this. I decided to ask Diana Ross to sign my "We Are the World" sheet music. She then in turn asked someone next to her to do the same. From then on, there was complete chaos in the room—any organizational structure that may have been there before was gone. It was everybody in the room, pencils and sheet music in hand, going from star to star trying to commemorate this singular moment with autographs and perhaps extend the night as long as we could.

Over ten million copies of that single, under the supergroup name USA for Africa, were sold worldwide and more than $63 million was raised for African famine relief. It also won four Grammys. Harry and Ken's dream had come true, and for everyone in that room that night, we realized, many for the first time, that "we are the world."

As a side note to that momentous event, I was later given an award that is dear to me. Sometimes it's easy to underestimate the power and strength of someone you know really well. An example would be my friend Tom Johnson, publisher of the *Dallas Times Herald* and the *Los Angeles Times,* who also ran CNN for a few years. How could I not know he was powerful? He was simply my friend. But at some point along the way he submitted me for one of my most prestigious awards, and one that I think that I appreciate as much or more than any other: the Horatio Alger Award. It is an award given to those who rose from humble beginnings who achieved success and give back to the community. I think he based my submission on having been involved with Harry Chapin and his work with world hunger, which was the lead-up to Hands Across America and ultimately to my involvement with "We Are the World" and USA for Africa. Tom saw much more in me than I did, and I thank him for that.

The constant touring in the 1980s, however exhausting and mind-numbing it was at times, covered the physical world, too. Nashville hits became worldwide hits. I'd like to think that in some small way my music helped introduce the art form of country music to areas that had never heard it. Songs like "The Gambler," "Lucille," and "Coward of the County" were surprisingly well received in most major foreign countries.

In Shanghai, China, while dining in a restaurant, I listened to a young musician playing a traditional Chinese instrument, the pipa. She came up to me at the end of her set with four of my albums that she happened to have in her car. She had no way of knowing I would be there that night. I always found it interesting that I'd go to some countries and could not carry on a conversation, but they would know all the words to my songs.

While traveling through Jamaica with Jim Mazza and our families, Jim and I ended up in a little Jamaican bar. We sat there thinking about how lucky we were to have this lifestyle and enjoy these incredibly beautiful places. After about twenty minutes, we noticed in the corner a group of Rastafarians, dreadlocks and all. Now I know this is profiling, but the way they looked at us scared me to death. Jim and I both agreed that we should not just leave, we should get the hell out of there. As we started to the door the entire table started singing "You got to know when to hold them, mon . . ." We spent the better part of an hour talking and laughing with our new Jamaican friends. The music may have begun in Nashville and L.A., but it played everywhere. "Islands in the Stream," for example, was at one point the biggest hit around the world.

As I continued to tour in the United States as well as around the world, I began to expand my stage performances beyond simply a standard concert of my best songs. Somewhere in the middle of the '80s I was performing at the Fox Theatre in Detroit. It was the middle of December and I was cruising through my greatest hits when, from the back of the auditorium, someone yelled, "Hey, Kenny. It's Christmastime! You gonna do any Christmas music?"

"Sure," I replied. After about thirty seconds with the band to establish a key I could sing in, we decided on "O Holy Night." I was actually shocked at how good it sounded without rehearsal. The audience response, perhaps because of the spontaneity of the moment, was amazing.

I had done Christmas music before, but not onstage like that. As I mentioned earlier, Dolly and I had done a CBS Christmas special in 1984 that did really well—*Kenny & Dolly: A Christmas to Remember.* Our Christmas album, *Once Upon a Christmas,* included music from the special and went on to sell seven million copies. Ironically, we shot the show in L.A. during the hottest part of the summer.

So the next year, after my Fox Theatre experience, without any prompting from the audience, I did two Christmas songs to an even better reaction than the year before. After two years, I got it: people want to hear Christmas music at Christmastime. Who would have thought?

Now, having done my thorough and exhaustive scientific research, I was ready to honor the audiences' request. This was creatively very inspiring and provided me a chance to sing great Christmas songs and give the hits a break. My goal now was to make every year bigger, better, and more spectacular than the last.

It was somewhere in here I realized this was too big for me to do alone. It was no longer just seasonal music. We needed production value. So what did I do? I brought in my tennis pro, Kelly Junkermann.

Actually Kelly had become my right-hand man and a damn good producer in the time we had known each other. When I discussed my Christmas tour goals, he told me about seeing Sting when we were on tour in Australia. He had used a choir in his show and it was truly majestic. Kelly thought he could line up local choirs in every city to sing with us when we got to their town. I mean, isn't that what choirs did? He had another idea. His cousin Becky was a music teacher. He thought he could have her contact local music teachers and we would use local kids in the show as well. It would be perfect, he said—Kenny, kids, choirs, Christmas! It would really have a family feel to it.

Every year we would come up with a different concept or theme for the show. We had been doing a lot of the shows at Chicago's Pheasant Run Theater. The director, Diana Martinez, was great helping Kelly and me cast as well as tweak the staging for each of the shows. One year we decided we would start the show off with a bunch of elves decorating the stage. They would break into a medley of songs before I would come on. We cast the elves at Diana's theater.

Little did we know that two of those elves would move on to Los Angeles and star in their own television series. Sean Hayes, from *Will & Grace*, would go on to win an Emmy. Not only did he open the show for us, he played the piano for the auditions as well! Another of the elves, Rosa Blasi, went on to star in the Lifetime series *Strong Medicine*. What are the odds of two people from our Christmas show going on to star in their own series?

Kelly had another idea for involving the local towns that we would be in. Why not have puppies in our show? He reasoned that each year parents went out and bought their kids puppies for Christmas. Why not do some good and contact the local Humane Society and have them provide us with puppies that could be adopted? The puppies would fly onto the stage in a wrapped Christmas present and land under a tree. The kids would then unwrap the gift and cuddle up with the puppy. It all worked just as planned. That is, until unfortunately someone forgot to "walk" a puppy. When we opened the box, the smell was not pleasant and kids scattered everywhere. Nobody onstage tried to hide his or her reaction to the "accident." Ah . . . live production. It doesn't get any better than that. But we did do some good. In one city alone we had fifty puppies adopted by people in our audience. That was pretty impressive.

We soon noticed an interesting thing. Very few artists toured at Christmas, so we had some great talent to choose from each year. It was a chance to have some fun and make new friends as well.

Garth Brooks's first tour was with me on my Christmas tour. You could tell early on that he was going to be something special. It was also a really fun tour. He and his guys loved to play basketball, and every town that we played we found the local gym and battled his band and crew against mine. I will go on record—at least until Garth's autobiography comes out—as saying we beat them every time we played.

I think the Forester Sisters with their amazing harmonies were the first act to be on the Christmas tour. Trisha Yearwood, Faith Hill (who wanted a puppy from the show), Emmylou Harris, Shelby Lynne, Linda Davis, Sawyer Brown, Mark Chesnutt, Little Texas, and Rebecca Lynn Howard are a few of the others who have joined me.

Suzy Bogguss is one of my favorite visual memories of the Christmas tour. The two of us were sitting on stools, cozying up to each other, singing, "Baby, It's Cold Outside" while she was seven months pregnant, and as big as a barn. It added a whole new dimension to the song.

For the past few years, it's been my pal Billy Dean who has joined the kids and choirs to make Christmas a special time.

I've always been a very trusting person, so when someone tells me they can train doves to fly from the back of a theater to the top of a Christmas tree onstage, that struck me as a great idea. A magician told me just that, so I set her up with Kelly and we came up with our theme "The Magic of the Season." Off she went to train the birds.

During the first day of rehearsal, she put some kind of special dove food on the top of the Christmas tree, went to the top of the theater, and released two birds. They flew in circles to the top of the building and were retrieved only after someone put bigger portions of dove food on the rail halfway down. Four stagehands and two cast members finally captured them.

"Tomorrow would be better," she assured us, and it was. This time they made it all the way to the stage, but they didn't land. They just circled . . . and circled . . . and circled until finally they were retrieved. The magician explained that it was probably the loud noise of the music that they weren't used to. I reminded her this was going to be the grand finale of the show. There would not only be loud music but a thirty-voice choir, seven kids, me, and whoever was working with us in that show.

"We'll have them there by showtime!" she responded reassuringly.

The third time would be the charm. It was our dress rehearsal and she would start them from a few rows at the front of the stage. They would get to the tree and it would be no problem on opening night. We all waited anxiously to see what would happen, and much to everyone's surprise, some headed straight for the tree, right on cue, and then headed backstage; others ended up in the front row. They would have been fluttering in somebody's Christmas hairdo. It was not going to be a pretty picture. That was it for me.

To her credit she would not give up. Opening night, I looked over during the finale and there she was with a dove in each hand, throwing them like darts at the Christmas tree. They circled the tree, then flew off together to the ceiling of the theater—and circled and circled and circled. I told Kelly, "Fire the magician."

After about ten years of touring with the "Christmas only"

show, we returned to the Fox Theatre in Detroit. In the middle of "Away in a Manger," someone from the back of the theater (I would swear it was the same guy who started this mess years earlier) yelled out, "Hey! Kenny, do 'Ruby, Don't Take Your Love to Town.' We wanna hear some hits!"

I know you can't please all the people all the time, but God knows I try. In the last five years or so, I have been doing half hits and half Christmas. As you can tell, I stay right on the cutting edge of audience research.

As we were traveling the world and in the midst of all these memorable days on the road, my "real" life was taking a very sharp turn for the worse. After living without my father since 1975, my mother was starting to fade.

When my dad died, it really crushed my mom. Even with all his drinking, and his reluctance to travel more than fifty miles from home, she had loved him more than any of us realized. He had been her anchor through so much pain and joy. They had been married since they were kids and then he was gone, and it had happened so quickly. She hadn't had the time to get prepared to be alone.

Mother started trying to get out a little and go on vacations with my sister Geraldine and her family, who traveled every summer to somewhere new and different. They had always been great about taking the younger kids on vacation with them when we were young, including me.

For Mom, though, summer and summer travel just didn't come often enough. She was a woman who was ready to go at the drop of a hat. At one point after my dad died, I took her in my airplane to see one of my shows. The show was in Huntsville, Texas, only about 160 miles from the Crawford area. She hated flying, but she wanted to go. She was so proud of my success, not because of the money, but because she saw how happy it made me.

Knowing her hunger to travel, I came up with a great compromise for her and a chance to pay her back for my not being there to help the family when Janice and I had to get married. I had not forgotten the looks on their faces and the financial drain on the family I had caused back then. This would be my chance to make amends.

I called a friend of mine named Alan Hill who had worked with a number of big country stars, and together, we showed up in Crockett, Texas, in a big, shiny black-and-brown Prevost bus with the name Lucille on the scroll in front. My mom thought I had rented it just to come see her and was thrilled. When I told her it was a gift to her from me, I thought she was going to faint. She now had her own private coach, and Alan signed on as her own personal driver. This may be the only time I ever heard Kenneth Ray used as a term of endearment, when she said, teary-eyed, "Oh, Kenneth Ray . . . You shouldn't have."

I was about to call my pilot to come and pick me up when she announced, "Oh, no, wait. Alan and I will take you home on the bus." I reminded her it was about a thousand miles to my home in Atlanta and she said, "Is that one way or round trip?" She had made up her mind that she was going somewhere that day. "Alan doesn't care, do you, Alan?"

She adjusted to this personal driver concept very well and very quickly. They took me home to Atlanta in "Lucille." I think I enjoyed it more than she did.

I kept thinking, what a shame it was that my dad wasn't there to see all of this. Then I remembered how much he hated to travel. It was probably good I had waited. No question, they would have gotten a divorce over this bus.

I can promise you this, Alan had no idea what he was signing on for when he agreed to drive Lucille. They were a perfect pair. He didn't need to talk, and she couldn't stop. I had given her wings, and his job was to keep her flying. In the first year alone, she and Alan put several hundred thousand miles on that bus. He was a perfect choice as her driver. He was about the same age as my older brother, Lelan, so she looked at Alan as she did her sons, and I think he must have looked at her as he did his mother. Rumor has it, she never went to the back part of the bus to cool out. She wanted to sit up front in the passenger seat next to Alan and wanted to travel only during the day and never at night. She didn't want to miss anything. I could probably have just bought them a car to drive and accomplished the same thing.

Was it from my mother that I got my very early impulse to move around, way back in the day of the Bobby Doyle Three? Probably so.

My mom had two passions in life: traveling and fishing. I have never known a woman who loved to fish as much as she did. Everywhere that bus went, my mom carried along fishing equipment. It wasn't a fancy rod and reel. It was a cane fishing pole with a bobber on the end.

Just so you have a visual image of my mother: she was very striking for her age. At that point she would have been between sixty-eight and seventy years old, and she stood about five feet, eight inches. Pretty tall for a woman. She had that beautiful silver hair that women her age like to have done once a week at the local beauty shop. She wore glasses and had a gold cap on one of her front teeth. Not for style, I think, but simply because gold was cheaper in those days than whatever the other option might have been.

I have no idea how many identical matching outfits she had, but her favorite was a pink pantsuit with a small plastic corsage that she pretty much wore all the time. There was also an orange jumpsuit on the bus that she could throw on over her pink pantsuit for emergency fishing opportunities along the road.

She didn't need a formal invitation to go fishing. Alan said that time and again she would ask him to pull over as they were driving down a road in some strange town. She would sling her orange jumpsuit on over her pantsuit and corsage and climb the fence of some perfect stranger's property. She'd go to a corner of his lake with her little portable chair she had underneath the bus and just start fishing like she owned the place. When she was finished, she'd lose the jumpsuit, return to her seat, and say, "That was fun. . . . We can go now."

Alan said she looked like an escaped convict from a distance in that orange jumpsuit. He warned her over and over that someone was going to be upset if they ever caught her. No one ever said a word to her in the two years he drove for her. She fished some of the best lakes and small ponds in this country.

My mother began to take her bus and show up at my concerts almost every night with Alan. They would sit in front-row seats with "Alan and Lucille" written on them. It was great that I also had two of my brothers, Lelan and Roy, working with me at the time, so they were always around to take good care of her. This was what she wanted, and this was what she loved.

In 1986, my mom was at Beaver Dam Farms—my place in Athens, Georgia—visiting my family and had spent the day out fishing in one of our lakes. I was sitting in front of the TV in the den area when she walked by. She asked if I needed anything and I told her no. After a few minutes without seeing or hearing from her, I went to the kitchen. She was sitting at the table. She had a strange look . . . kind of glazed over. I asked if everything was okay, and she said something to the effect of "Bayou Bay." I repeatedly asked her different questions but no matter what I asked, her answer was always the same: "Bayou Bay."

She had apparently had a massive stroke between the time she walked by me and the time I went in the kitchen to her. She was rushed to the hospital, but the only thing she ever said for the rest of her life was "Bayou Bay." No one in the family had any idea what she was referring to or if she even knew what she was saying.

My mom lived another six years in a hospital in Houston on life support with my sister Sandy by her side every day taking care of her. We just couldn't pull the plug. It's interesting to me that the last words she said to me were: "Do you need anything, Kenneth Ray?"

CHAPTER SIXTEEN

After the Gold Rush

Success is never everlasting, and mine was no exception. At some point, inevitably, this parade of hits had to end, and that point came halfway through the 1980s. Except for the Barry Gibb album *Eyes That See in the Dark,* which included the duet "Islands in the Stream" with Dolly and sold more than five million albums, and the *Once Upon a Christmas* album, again with Dolly, also selling more than seven million albums, my success as a hit maker first gradually tapered off and then came to a standstill.

Actually the last No. 1 song I had for many years was a Grammy Award–winning duet with Ronnie Milsap in 1987 called "Make No Mistake, She's Mine." After that I couldn't buy a hit.

I kept performing, of course, and people came out to hear my litany of hits. Remember, this is country music, where fans are much more loyal and long-lasting. But by the early '90s, it was getting tougher and tougher to even get my songs played on the radio. Garth Brooks was starting to come into his own, and in his wake, a whole new generation of country performers emerged. "Young Country" was the new marketing phrase. At that point, I must not have been, in the eyes of the record executives or radio programmers, either country enough or young enough. Once again, just as in the days of the

First Edition, I was "too old" to play in this young man's game, and I couldn't grow my hair long and put on rose-tinted glasses to solve this problem.

I have always been fortunate to have a presence on television, and during this very painful and drawn-out recording drought, TV is what saved me. It had started back in the First Edition days when we headlined the *Rollin' on the River* show that we shot in Canada. Then in the '80s, the *Gambler* movies came along and, together with *Coward of the County*, were network ratings successes and made a lasting impression with a whole generation of television execs.

It was around 1990 when we had finished our third year of the Classic Weekend and Kelly had written a treatment, which is basically a short story, for a new *Gambler* movie. There hadn't been one since *The Gambler, Part III: The Legend Continues,* in 1987. Kelly, like the rest of us of that age, had grown up watching all the classic Western TV shows like *Bonanza, The Rifleman, Wyatt Earp,* and *Bat Masterson.* How clever would it be, he thought, if my character, Brady Hawkes from the *Gambler* series, knew all of them. After all, they had all lived during the same great Western era from the end of the Civil War until the early twentieth century. In a new movie, Brady Hawkes would travel across the Plains in search of the last great poker game in the Old West and run into all these classic Western heroes.

Ken Kragen got Kelly's treatment to the networks on a Friday, and on the following Monday morning we had a deal. It kind of happened like that with the very first *Gambler* movie. For it to happen again—the instant network buy—was extremely rare. In the truest sense, we realized, you have to be careful what you wish for.

We wished, we received, and now we had to deliver. We had to find these actors from the old TV shows and talk them into reprising their youthful roles one more time. One of the great things about having success is you can cut through a lot of red tape to get to people. It became Kelly's job to track these guys down. My theory was: your idea, your responsibility.

Interestingly enough, this task turned out to be easier than we thought. Written well, this was going back to the glory years for these legendary performers. They wanted to be a part of it. We quickly signed Hugh O'Brian as Wyatt Earp and Gene Barry as Bat Masterson. They still had the wardrobe that they had worn in their original series. Sure, they were a bit older, but they were every bit the heroes they had portrayed in their original series. Kelly was like a bloodhound. He kept on tracking them down, one by one—*The Virginian,* the cast of *Wagon Train, Kung Fu,* and *The Rifleman*—all the big boys. It would be like a class reunion for Western stars, and they all agreed this was going to be a lot of fun.

They also wanted to stay as true to their characters as they could and bring their own sense of what their character might contribute to the scene. Brian Keith, for instance, had played a crusty old character in Sam Peckinpah's television series *The Westerner.* He took a look at the script and gave Kelly a call back. "Sam Peckinpah would roll over in his grave if he saw this crap!" Brian's language was a bit more Peckinpah-ish, so needless to say, Kelly used Brian's guidance to rewrite the dialogue. Brian's final line was: "The end of the West is near." It was a perfect line to advance the concept of the dying days of a lifestyle that everyone knew was coming. The writing was on the wall for the Old West, and all these mythical TV characters had known it.

We ended up with pretty much everyone we went after, except for one we really wanted—James Garner, that is, Maverick. I had seen him playing golf at the Bel Air County Club almost daily with my friend Mac Davis, the writer of the First Edition song "Something's Burning."

Kelly suggested that maybe I could ask him one day while he was in the middle of his game. We thought he might just say yes to get rid of me, and we were not proud at this point. We wanted Maverick. I started with "You may not want to do this, but I have to ask anyway . . ." and laid out the entire scenario for him.

And surprisingly he said no. I make his response sound cold and disrespectful, but it really wasn't. He just had his doubts we could pull it off. It was a concept he didn't feel comfortable with, plus he was up about six shots over Mac in their golf game and that had to take precedence over our dream. We would later learn why he said no. He appeared as Mel Gibson's father in the theatrical release of *Maverick* later the next year.

We didn't get Brett Maverick, but we did get his brother Bart, Jack Kelly. He was more than happy to be part of it. He would represent the Maverick family at the final poker game in the Old West before gambling would be illegal.

The woman who cast our movie, Junie Lowry, had started out by casting the extras for the original *Gambler* movies. Her brother, Dick Lowry, had directed all my movies up to that point. He had a real love for the Old West. Dick, Kelly, and I had a great working relationship. He was pretty gracious about listening to my ideas and trying to work them into the story. Junie, his sister, has now become one of the top casting agents in Hollywood and has since won several Emmys. She suggested using Reba McEntire to play the female lead opposite me for this movie, *The Gambler Returns: The Luck of the Draw.*

Reba's success in country music, her Oklahoma roots, and her great riding ability were a perfect fit for us. I had ridden a lot as a kid, but I had never been a particularly good rider.

That would all change as we started shooting and riding eight hours a day. I had learned there is a lot of riding in a Western. Reba was right at home in the saddle and welcomed the chance to show her ability. She had been a barrel rider in some Oklahoma rodeos when she was younger and still had all her skills.

What a trip through time it was. Every day on the set I was acting with some of television's most iconic figures.

You could still sense the competition between Bat Masterson and Wyatt Earp. Twenty years ago they had battled each other for ratings. This was not about ratings for them. It was a bigger goal, keeping the story alive at the end of an era. The classic Old West was at stake. These were the guys who had laid the groundwork for the way Western television history had evolved.

Mark McCain, the kid from *The Rifleman,* was reunited with his father, Chuck Connors. They could still cock and fire their rifles just as they did on their show twenty years ago, and we were all counting on everyone else doing just that. And they all delivered. We had defied all the odds and done something original and exciting.

Although Westerns had been out of vogue for a while by then, the movie won, and won big, helping to win sweeps for NBC. That's all the network executives asked. That's all they needed and we delivered.

The network exposure kept me in front of the public. We had brought Westerns back to television and we were, if nothing else, opportunistic. Several of the actors got renewed series.

We had just helped win the sweeps for NBC, but I think they thought it was a lucky one-off for us. While we were shooting *The Gambler Returns,* Kelly had gotten his hands on another script that had been around for years. The main character was Quentin Leech, a bounty hunter. He was dirty, dusty, not particularly friendly, and would shoot first and ask questions later. He was the opposite of Brady Hawkes.

NBC said no thank you: "Nobody wants to see Kenny Rogers like that."

Kelly, who refused to give up, believed this would not only be a different role for me, but a chance for me to grow as an actor, and he knew how much I loved the character. Undaunted, he marched directly over to CBS and ran it by the network guys there. Their reaction was what we had hoped for. They said, "Hell, yes. You kicked our asses with that damn *Gambler* movie, and we'd rather have you with us than against us."

We now had a new home—the network where it all began with the first *Gambler*—for our next movie, *Rio Diablo*.

Junie again cast it and put together an amazing cast. Ken Kragen was managing an up-and-coming country artist, Travis Tritt, and we fought to make him my sidekick. The chemistry really worked, as it wasn't that much of a stretch to play the mentor to this emerging star. We looked to country music for another of my costars, casting Naomi Judd as my love interest. Naomi had actually started her career by auditioning as an actress and appearing in the Dick Lowry movie *The Hank Williams Story*.

Naomi and I did have a romantic scene together. She was supposed to be giving me a bath after a long ride to her place. It all sounded good on paper, but sitting in a bathtub all day surrounded by the entire crew was not my idea of a romantic moment.

The movie was shot in the hottest place I have ever worked, and I've worked in Saudi Arabia. Terlingua, Texas, is a remote part of Texas on the Mexican border. The movie had a great authentic

Western look and feel—it was as dirty and dusty as we were. The young production designer who was now working with us, Jerry Wanek, had helped on my photography book and would go on to get many Emmy nominations in his career. The whole thing just felt like we were living back in the Old West, bad teeth and all.

It was a great role for me and fun not to have to be a good guy all the time. Maybe it brought out my dark side, as I got to shoot people at the drop of a hat. It was also a lot of fun to be more authentic, grittier and nastier.

As we were finishing up the last days of the shoot, we realized we had apparently not thought through the ending of the movie. I was supposed to die, God forbid. What a shock that was going to be for the audience. The network said, "You can't kill Kenny Rogers!"

"But what a great surprise ending," we argued. We had already broken every other rule that we were told wouldn't work. Why stop now? Why not, for the fun of it, stay with the script as written?

We found a compromise. I would get shot by Stacy Keach, fall off a cliff, and drop three hundred feet into a raging river. We had saved our shock ending yet left enough doubt about whether I was dead or alive.

It was genius. That way, in case the movie was a hit, I could have floated downriver and been rescued by Indians. But we had another problem. The network did not like the title. We shouldn't call it *Rio Diablo,* they said. No one will know what that means. We should call it by its English translation, *Devil's River.*

That didn't sound like the movie we had just made, so we argued for the purity of our trade. Like I knew what that was. The execs all finally decided to stay true to the original name and let people figure it out for themselves. It would be *Rio Diablo.*

The headline in *Variety* read, "*Rio Diablo* wins sweeps for CBS!"

I have to admit there was a certain satisfaction in doing something that had been totally against what was my norm and being successful.

It's amazing what helping networks win a couple of sweeps will do. NBC was now calling and wanting to do a series of movies with me. At that point I actually thought, *Who needs music, anyway?*

For as long as I could remember I had been married. I have to admit I was pretty good at it, as I had been married four times. There are reasons marriages end, but I'm not sure what happened between Marianne and me. We were the American dream couple, or so *People* magazine and the Hollywood tabloids kept telling us. It was something we had never promoted or asked for. We were two people who had enjoyed making my career together and raising our young son, Christopher. I enjoyed the years spent with her family, and I believe she enjoyed the time spent with mine. During the early and mid-1980s Marianne and Christopher traveled everywhere with me. We were constantly put in the public eye. When we moved to Georgia to be closer to her family and to raise Christopher in a more stable environment, it seemed like the perfect move. Marianne was close to her Georgia roots, and I enjoyed building Beaver Dam Farms. As Christopher started school, they were able to travel on tour less and less; still, I was so busy at the farm with my photography and building that I flew in and out of Athens, Georgia, for most of my concerts. But something was changing—as I say, it's hard to explain—and we were growing apart by 1992.

Did you ever do something in your life and look back on it later and say, "How could I have ever thought that would have ended well?"

I was separated and going through my divorce with Marianne, and for one fleeting moment, I had an epiphany. I realized I could do things now that I had not done nor had wanted to do for fifteen years or longer. I could date women and have some wild times without feeling guilty. Being married so many times, I probably had an urge for adventure that had been pent up as I spent every waking moment crafting a career. This seemed very attractive and enticing to me at the time. It was never really about having sex with other women, as much as it was that I could now think about it with a clear conscience and no guilt. That was very exciting to me.

At that point in my life, I enjoyed talking to beautiful, alluring women on the phone. I would have to equate it to today's online chat rooms, but these were private conversations, intended only for me and whomever I invited in. To do this, I used, in what now sounds like something from the Ice Age, a restricted phone number that only this group and I had access to and that required a code to access.

Let's start with this. I have a friend in Dallas, Texas, who was the ultimate single guy at this point. He had access to all the party girls in his area. So very quickly, I established a relationship with two of his "friends." I met them in person while in Dallas one weekend and developed a long-distance telephone relationship with both of them.

I mean, this was to be the ultimate "safe sex" for me. This was never about physical contact, just erotic and sexually explicit messages left on a limited-access phone line that was always solicited by the other parties, and remember, I wasn't doing this with random people I had met. These were my friend's friends and I trusted them. So I felt comfortable that this was happening with consenting adults.

It didn't take me long to get right in the middle of the fast track in the Dallas nightlife. But no matter how much fun I thought I was having, I couldn't shake the fact that I wasn't completely divorced and my guilt kept nagging at me. This was all new. I rationalized it by thinking this activity would be far enough from home that it was safe and at the very least, if it went as planned, respectful to my soon-to-be ex-wife, who theoretically should never know about it.

I must admit in retrospect, I think the problem was I saw these girls as my friends and they saw me as their opportunity.

I will tell you the one thing a public person treasures most, of all his or her possessions, is his or her public image; these girls either knew that when this started or figured it out very quickly. They knew that this would be my Achilles heel—something I would protect at all costs.

So recordings made in the privacy of this little group were then recorded by them and distributed to the *National Enquirer* for money.

This was devastating, and they knew it would be. In the context of tabloid exploitation, no matter what I intended, I came off as sleazy.

I refuse to play the guilt card on anyone. I was a grown man, and I knew what I was doing. These conversations were sexually explicit and designed to arouse the listener.

The plot unfolded with the *Enquirer* in full front-page banner mode. The women hired lawyers who went for the throat. They wanted money, lots of it, claiming I had sexually harassed these obviously young pure women (in their thirties) to the point of damaging them beyond repair, even though the way this worked, they didn't have to call the number and retrieve the message if they were offended. They also asked me to do this for them.

Whatever damage I had done to them, I figured, could be solved by money.

In all honesty, I did settle this lawsuit, but for nowhere near the amount of money they wanted. It was over then, and I was thrilled to have it behind me.

The press was following me everywhere. If I checked into a hotel, they knew I was there, and somehow they got on the movie sets. To see where I'd been the last week, all I had to do was pick up an *Enquirer*.

In 1993, I was Lindsay Lohan for the tabloids, kind of the celebrity du jour whose every dirty secret the tabloid press could either dig up or invent. I sold a lot of magazines and they wanted a piece of me and everything I did. There were hungry young would-be journalists around every corner, in the bushes, behind garbage cans—everywhere I turned—and while it may seem flattering to someone who's never been through it, I can assure you, it is not a pretty thing. These guys were everywhere, and the worse the picture, the more money they made.

Honestly, looking at it in retrospect, I don't think it was as bad then as it is now. There is a take-no-prisoners attitude now. Tabloid photographers have absolutely no concern for what you feel or what people think of you when your fifteen minutes are over, and they smell blood.

The good news in all of this bad-news period—the flat career, the failure of yet another marriage, all the tabloid character assassination—is that while this was going on, I met my wife, Wanda.

CHAPTER SEVENTEEN

Wanda

So I was on my own again, not a common experience for me but one that I could see could open new possibilities. I had been dating around Atlanta aimlessly and was on a date with a girl I had met through a friend of mine, Charlie Minor, the national promotion man for Capitol Records, when I bumped into my future wife, Wanda.

We had chosen a little Italian restaurant called Pricci and were in the middle of our "getting to know each other" banter when the hostess walked by our table. I'm honestly not sure she even looked at me, but I saw her. I don't know what and I don't know why, but there was just something incredibly different about her from the minute I saw her. She had a smile, not a hostess smile, but something more genuine, and believe it or not, it rocked me to my core.

Bear with me for this next part, because I know how shallow it might make me sound, but it's exactly how it went down. If things hadn't turned out this well, I probably would never be telling this story. I honestly don't remember how my date ended, but it did. I would like to believe I was nice and courteous to her, but early on, we both knew the food was great but the relationship wasn't going anywhere. I dropped her off at her apartment and went back to the hotel where I was staying.

I had no clue what I would do next. I didn't want to go back to the restaurant, but I couldn't miss this opportunity, if there was one. My friend Charlie had been at the restaurant that night, at a table not far from me. I also knew this was a restaurant he frequented. Maybe he even knew this girl. So I decided to enlist his help.

This was 1992, long before everyone had pocket cell phones. If anything, people had those *big* spy-looking cell phones. I called the restaurant and asked for Charlie. I knew he was well known there. When he got on the phone, I asked him if he happened to know the hostess on duty. He said he didn't know her, but he did know she had an identical twin sister. My exact thought was *How can you not know someone and yet know she has a twin?*, but I didn't ask. I was just happy that he knew who I was speaking about. He suggested I speak with the manager, a friend of his named Jesse, if I wanted to meet her.

Having never done anything like this before, I was very uncomfortable asking a restaurant manager about one of his employees, but I did it anyway.

Jesse said her name was Wanda Miller. He went on to tell me she hadn't been working there long but that she was a really sweet girl. He asked if I would like to meet her. For some reason I was taken aback by the suddenness of it all. I knew she was young, so I felt compelled to ask him how young. Jesse said, "I'm not sure, but I think she's maybe twenty-one." My heart sank. I told him that as much as I would love to, "I can't do twenty-one," and thanked him. I was fifty-four at the time, so that was way too young for me. We hung up, and I assumed that was the end of it. As disappointed as I was, I couldn't imagine what we could have had in common. So I had to let it go.

Then the phone rang. It was Jesse. "She's not twenty-one," he said. "She's twenty-six." I don't know what I thought the difference was, but I remember saying, "Well, I can do twenty-six." He said he had spoken with her and she had given him permission to give me her phone number.

To say our first date was awkward is an understatement. Wanda had the same smile I had been drawn to the night before, but I swear she now looked like she was twelve years old. She was wearing a simple black dress with the biggest yellow bow I have ever seen in my life on the front. I felt like I was having dinner with my granddaughter. But she was beautiful and incredibly interesting, so as awkward as it was, it was fun.

She had chosen a little Russian restaurant on Roswell Road in Atlanta to have dinner. I have no idea why she chose this place. I can only surmise it was because it was two hundred yards from the safety of her apartment, her sister, and her friends. Just so you know, I have never eaten in a Russian restaurant before or since. But we got through the Russian restaurant, her yellow bow, and my age just fine, and we actually had a great time.

We decided after dinner that, in the future, I would dress a little younger and she would dress a little older and we'd meet somewhere in the middle. We agreed to get together the next day for lunch at Houston's and she would bring her sister with her. I had never dated an identical twin before, but having spent that little bit of personal time with Wanda the night before, I was comfortable I would be able to tell them apart.

One thing I hadn't counted on: twins like being twins and they often dress alike. So here they come, and the entire Houston's restaurant watched them as they came in. Individually they were beautiful, but together they were stunning.

I was maybe twenty yards from the front door when they arrived, and from that far away I'm embarrassed to say I couldn't tell them apart. They were both extremely beautiful girls and seemed to walk in lockstep. I made the snap decision that I didn't care who was who, and since I didn't know, I would gladly accept whichever one sat next to me. Tonia, Wanda's sister, had that same unmistakable Miller smile, and in all fairness was equally as beautiful, but Wanda and I had made a connection the night before that somehow made her different.

So Wanda and I began dating, but in those early months, we kept a low profile. At this point her parents didn't know what we were doing, so out of respect for them and for Wanda's safety, we avoided the public eye.

Wanda was with me while I was doing a concert in Chicago that still brings back such great memories for me. I had Ray Charles and George Burns, of all people, opening for me. George had a hot new single on the radio called "I Wish I Was Eighteen Again." At the age of ninety-six, he was still working. So I pulled him aside and asked him, "George, how do you keep working at ninety-six?" In typical George Burns fashion, without even breaking stride, he said, "You stay booked." As simple as it sounded, it was profound. You must have a purpose in your life, a reason to get up in the morning, a reason to keep pushing forward.

George and I had met years before and become friends when I took his photograph for my book of celebrity portraits, *Your Friends and Mine*. He was truly amazing that night in Chicago. He came down the aisle, walked up the stairs to the in-the-round stage, walked all around the stage, acknowledged all sides of the audience, did about twenty minutes of his sly, witty comedy, then sang his song with my band playing for him. He got the longest standing ovation I have ever seen. The audience stood the entire time it took him to walk back down the aisle and into the dressing room area.

As if that wasn't enough for one night, my idol, Ray, came out after that and completely dismantled that group of people just by being Ray Charles. I have never in my life, before or since, witnessed how such simplicity could create the kind of emotional response those two guys received that night.

I was not looking forward to walking out on that stage after they finished. I do think the audience appreciated me making this night available to them, so things went well for me, too.

All this proves a theory I have long had about performing: the audience expects to be entertained 100 percent for their ticket dollar. If the opening acts give them only 10 percent, I have to give them 90. If the opening acts give them 90 percent, I have to give them only 10 and they'll be satisfied. All I had to give was 10 percent that night, and we were all happy.

The night before that concert, the Chicago Bulls were playing the Phoenix Suns for the NBA Championship. I tried to reach Michael Jordan to see about getting tickets for Wanda and me as well as for Kelly and Rob, who were acting as our foils for the tabloids. The magazines would have loved to have gotten a picture of me with a beautiful twenty-six-year-old girl. That would have added fire to what they were already saying about me, and I didn't need that.

After attempting to reach Michael and having no success, I had just about given up when we ran into the Phoenix Suns star player Charles Barkley at our hotel. Charles had come to my farm for the Classic Weekend and was happy to help us out. He said, "You don't need Michael Jordan, man. I can get you tickets," and he did.

The four of us went to the game, making sure Wanda and I were never standing together. They were great seats, however, two on one side of the arena and two on the opposite side. So Rob and I sat on one side, and Kelly and Wanda sat on the opposite side. We waved at each other a couple of times but had no personal contact during the game, so there were no pictures of us for the tabloids. What a game it was. Chicago went on to win their second of three consecutive NBA Championships.

It never dawned on me that Wanda was just there to see the game and didn't care where she sat. She was just impressed that I knew Charles Barkley but not totally sure I really knew Michael Jordan.

It was on a trip down to Mexico during this period that I realized how crazy this press stuff was getting. Wanda and I checked into our room and there was a photographer for one of the tabloids actually in our room, ready to catch us in our "secret Mexican getaway." The hotel arrested him. Down in the lobby, the Mexican authorities showed up and were ready to take him off to jail. I didn't want to see that happen and did not press charges, so they let him off. The next week, the pictures and story of the trip were on the front page of the tabloids.

Wanda and I dated for almost six months before she worked up the nerve to tell her parents about me. Actually, I'm not sure whether she told them or they read it in the tabloids. Either way, it was not pleasant. The fact that I was two years older than her parents put an awkward slant on things right from the start. Not for me, but I'm sure it would be troublesome to any caring parent, and I understood that.

The timing of this could not have been worse. This was at the end of the "phone sex" issue in the magazines, and her family did not deserve to be put through that. Even I knew how bad it looked for all of us. But as wrong as it may have looked, I also knew this—my relationship with Wanda felt right to me. After allowing her mother and father to explain their concerns in a phone call, I assured them that I respected their feelings. I made them a promise that I would never lie to Wanda, and I would never lie to them. We reached a shaky understanding that as long as "I gave respect, I would get respect." That was good enough for me, and for Wanda.

After Wanda and I had been together for the better part of a year, we were living in a house I bought in Las Vegas. Her sister, Tonia, was a flight attendant for Southwest Airlines and stayed with us on her Las Vegas layovers, so the two of them got a chance to catch up every now and then. Things could not have been better for us.

However, we had one small hurdle to get over—Wanda's parents still had not met me. Her father, Charles, decided he needed to see this man who had taken his daughter and moved her in with him in, of all places, Las Vegas, Nevada. His mind was racing as he imagined what her life must be like. Our arrangement, on the surface, was against everything both he and her mother believed in.

To his credit, I believe that when Charles came to Vegas, he saw that we had a respectable life. We didn't drink, we didn't smoke, and we weren't doing drugs, so I'm sure he felt that he could relax a bit. I'm also sure he had no idea what Wanda saw in a man my age, but he trusted and respected his daughter enough to allow her to make her own decisions. That took a lot of strength for a father, I know.

I also knew that since he didn't gamble and had very little use for Vegas as a city, we had to find some other way to entertain him for three days. Fortunately I had the perfect answer. About three months prior to her dad's visit, Wanda and I had purchased a fifty-foot houseboat on Lake Powell, unquestionably one of the most beautiful places in the world. It's basically the Grand Canyon with water in it. By anyone's standards it is breathtaking.

Charles had been on the lake about twenty minutes when he called his wife, Tina, and not so jokingly said he wanted them to move there. It is that beautiful. The best news was, we all had a great time and he felt comfortable Wanda could make her own decisions about this relationship. One in-law down, one to go.

Every three or four years, it seems, I work an event called the Florida Strawberry Festival in Plant City, Florida. It's a huge festival in that area, which includes Valdosta, Georgia, where Wanda's parents lived. I was on a collision course with the other half of Wanda's parents. I was determined to make her see how happy Wanda and I were. Her blessing would be crucial. By the time I left Florida, she would either accept me or kill me, I figured.

Having never met Clomenteen (Tina) Miller, I really had no idea which option—accept or kill—was most likely. But from our first telephone encounter, I knew Tina was a no-nonsense person. When it came to her girls, there were no exceptions—they came first. She would speak her mind freely and let you know the truth about how she felt. I must admit I liked that about her. There would be no room for misunderstanding. She and Charles were the salt of the earth. They had worked very hard to give both Tonia and Wanda a good perspective on what life was like. Now I felt like I had come in and thrown a monkey wrench into their dreams for their girls.

For forty years or so, Charles Miller had worked for the railroad as a conductor and as the main man in the caboose. His life had been, and still is to some extent, trains. This job required that he be gone from home quite a bit, but when he was in Valdosta, he forgot about the trains, and his girls were his life. Tina had a lot of time at home while the girls were in school with not a lot to do, so she had taken up cutting hair as a pastime and had become very good and very well respected in the area.

Our fateful meeting took place in Plant City, a large outdoor venue with a series of big dressing rooms. Wanda and I were set up for her to give me a haircut in one of these dressing rooms. (Wanda has cut my hair for the twenty years I've known her.) When Tina came in, I was surprised and shocked. This was not how I had hoped our first meeting would be. As I started to stand up for Wanda to introduce us, Tina politely said, "Keep your seat," and I did. As she came around behind me, I noticed she had taken the scissors from Wanda.

This would be the deciding moment, "accept or kill." Tina simply said, "May I?" Since I had never heard of anyone asking for permission to kill, I said, "Sure."

"I want you to know, I don't respect what you're doing with my daughter," she said, "but she seems happy, and that's what's important to me. I am surprised you would let me this close to your throat with these scissors, though." She smiled.

"Me too," I replied.

I had now met Tina, the other in-law, and gotten a great haircut in the process.

I left Plant City with a feeling that while we might not have had their blessings, we had her mom and dad's acceptance, and that was big for both of us.

Once we explained to her parents that we were dating and that my intentions were good, it was so much more fun to date in the open. By now the tabloids had replaced me with some other poor soul about to be fed to the masses.

All my adult life I've tended to go out for dinner every night. But things were different now. The mere thought of cooking a meal in our Las Vegas kitchen seemed oddly romantic.

Wanda and I considered ourselves the best cooks in our bunch of friends. After all, we had just been given cooking lessons from Michael, the head chef at Spago Las Vegas, and we had learned to make the best pasta marinara I've ever tasted.

Settling into our new place in Vegas, we thought it would be fun to have some of our friends over for dinner. This would not be just any dinner; this would be a party concept we had heard about that would add laughs to our evening's meal. It originally started in small towns as a way for friends to help new neighbors get the basic cooking utensils and small appliances they would need in their kitchen, and for the community to get to know them better.

The idea was for those who came to bring a gift—a mixer, an ice cream maker, a toaster, a set of bowls, and so on—for the new-comer's kitchen and leave everything at the end of the night. Knowing the game lovers in our group, we decided it would be fun to do something different; we would make it a cooking party with a twist. We all met on Friday and decided what courses we wanted the meal to consist of, then took small pieces of paper with one item written on each and put them in a bowl. Whatever you drew, you cooked. You also had to bring everything it took to make your dish, start to finish. You had to find a recipe, bring whatever pots and pans and special things you needed for your dish, and most important, be responsible for all your own ingredients. No sharing butter, milk, flour, anything. Even salt and pepper couldn't be shared.

Saturday morning, we jumped in our respective cars and went

shopping together. This group was rapidly taking on the feeling of a flash mob. We were not just a lot of people shopping; we were a lot of people shopping fast. Then everyone had to hurry back and claim their spot, their territory, in the kitchen as well as claim their times for stovetop burners, oven use, and even freezer space. Everyone had to cook in the same kitchen at the same time. What was going to make it really fun was this was a competition; we all agreed that after we finished eating, we would vote for the best dish and the worst dish of the night. The person responsible for the worst dish would have to wash everyone's dirty dishes.

The meal would be that night at seven P.M. Once we finished shopping and laid everything out, we ended up with duplicates of almost everything.

6 pounds of butter

4 pounds of flour

4 gallons of milk

3 different packages of Italian spaghetti

3 pounds of sugar

Lots of cilantro and several other bags of exotic seasonings

Here's how the drawing went:

Kenny: salad and bread

Wanda: main dish—cilantro chicken

Rob: main dish—manicotti (or "manigot" as the real Italians
     say)

Tonia: main dish—barbecue shrimp

Kelly: soup—tom kha gai coconut soup

Jill, Kelly's girlfriend: dessert—ice cream

A perfect name for this event would be: "Chaos in the kitchen."

Six people in one kitchen are both funny and frightening at the same time. People were pushing other people's food around so they could get their own dish in an oven or in the freezer or on one of the four burners on the stove. We now had flour, rice, spaghetti, and butter all over the kitchen and the kitchen floor, even out into the hall. The smell of so many different dishes cooking at the same time was in some ways actually nauseating.

Wanda's chicken would have been perfect, except it was burned. It seems she set the timer for the wrong amount of time, by about thirty minutes. She swore someone changed it for their dish after she had set it, which ruined hers. Tonia's shrimp, a recipe she had gotten from her ex-boyfriend, was exceptionally tasty and ended up winning first place as "best dish of the night." Rob, our undercover policeman, went out into the hallway to mix his priceless "manigot" so no one could steal his hundred-year-old family secret sauce, direct from Italy. I have to say his family had strange tastes. Either he didn't really know the family secret or that was their reason for keeping it a secret. He was smart to protect that personal treasure from us.

Jill, Kelly's girlfriend at the time, was making ice cream that was going to be better than Baskin-Robbins, she said. As it turned out, it ended up being a sweet soupy dish that never gelled and became ice cream. Kelly made some kind of a Thai dish no one could pronounce and no one fully appreciated. He called it "tom kha gai" soup, a form of coconut soup. Now who on earth makes coconut soup? Kelly.

Since I had been assigned to do a salad and bread, I purchased a bread mixer and put in all my ingredients. The water, the flour, the yeast, the salt. Now all I had to do was flip the switch. Then Wanda brought it to my attention that I had accidentally forgotten to put the little kneading blade in the machine. Unfortunately, the blade needed to go in first, before the dough. So this was never going to work, and there was no correcting it. This was a mess, plain and simple.

For a salad I chose to make a potato and cilantro salad. The bread had been one thing, but this was what I had drawn for the competition. I have no idea why I chose this recipe, because I don't even like cilantro in Mexican food, much less in a potato salad. Everyone agreed.

Between my bread and cilantro messes, I received five out of seven votes as the worst dish of the night, and I truly deserved them. I had tried to dress up my potato/cilantro salad with bell peppers and then even basil, but nothing I could add would salvage that disaster. It was really bad and everyone knew it. I had lost fair and square, and a deal is a deal. I would wash the dishes. Everyone's dishes, and there were a lot of them.

To add insult to injury, my son Kenny Jr. came by at the very end. After tasting everybody else's contribution, his remark stung: "Dad, I dropped everyone else's food on the ground and yours was still the worst." I got it, stated as only family can do.

Everyone offered to pitch in and help with my punishment. Everyone, that is, but Kelly. He was watching a football game and he knew the rules. The fact that he was next to last in the voting did not matter. He wasn't last.

It took me two and a half hours just to get the uneaten food in the compactor and the dishes cleaned off and ready to wash. Then at least another hour to wash all of them. No dishwashing machines were allowed, this was grunt work.

I had lost that night and had learned a very valuable lesson. Stay as far away from cilantro dishes in competition as you can and invite fewer people when playing this game. Fewer people = fewer dishes.

I continued recording music throughout this period, including what I consider one of the best albums of my career, *Timepiece,* released in 1994. It was a collection of some of the best songs of the 1930s and 1940s, standards like "I Get Along Without You Very Well," "When I Fall in Love," "My Romance," and "My Funny Valentine." I find it hard sometimes to juxtapose these songs with songs like "Just Dropped In," "Ruby, Don't Take Your Love to Town," "Lucille," and "The Gambler." How could all those songs happen in one career?

I've lived my life and made most of my career decisions based on one concept or another, so here's another one for you: "An artist in motion tends to stay in motion, while an artist at rest tends to stay at rest." I know it's not really my theory, it's Isaac Newton's, but I do believe it applies to music as well and explains how those songs I mentioned relate. Artists who stop moving forward, stop expanding their vision and setting off in new directions, become museum figures, relics of the past. Lose your momentum, lose your options.

The music of the '30s and '40s, when you analyze it, is really all insinuation and very little statement, while the songs of today are all statement and little insinuation. I think music is simply a reflection of the times we live in. During and after World War II, the music of the '30s and '40s was a form of escapism, and songwriters, composers, and singers chose romance over confrontation. In the

1960s, that all changed. As Americans realized the futility of the Vietnam War, they became angry and expressive. They protested what they didn't like and drugs became a form of escapism and the music reflected it.

So "Just Dropped In," the psychedelic song I did with the First Edition, did nothing more than show the average person how far he or she could go to avoid reality, and "Ruby, Don't Take Your Love to Town" was about the reality of war. It was another time and a socially appropriate song. You throw "The Gambler" and "Lucille" in there and you get a group of country songs with some real depth and a peek into where society and music were at the time.

I was an artist in motion. I had options.

Thanks to my friend David Foster, I was allowed to completely change course and do the *Timepiece* album of twelve standards from that earlier era. For some reason, I've always felt guilty about loving jazz. I don't know why, I just have. When I was in jazz, I felt very comfortable liking country music, but in country music, I feel this guilt about jazz. But jazz, or at least the jazz-influenced music of the '30s and '40s, is such a rich blend of melody and thought. Don't get me wrong; I actually love both forms of music, and one is not necessarily better than the other, they are just different. That is the beauty of it, and to have the opportunity to perform and record both at such a high level is a true gift.

The *Timepiece* album done and released, I can't tell you how excited I was when I was then offered a TV special to perform music from the album. No hits, just the album.

To tie my career together, we decided it would be great to reunite the Bobby Doyle Three. We had a full orchestra conducted by David Foster and Jeremy Lubbock, and the setting was the House of Blues in Los Angeles.

To get a head start and a little rehearsal in, I swung through Houston with my airplane and picked up Bobby Doyle and Don Russell. It was the first time we had seen each other, much less sung together, in twenty years. We were all genuinely excited. It would be one last big hoorah for the group—big band, big audience. Bobby suggested that we rehearse on the plane on the way. He was still the leader. We huddled together and started singing a cappella what had been our signature song, "It's a Good Day." We were halfway between Houston and Los Angeles when we realized how bad we sounded. There were no flashbacks of past brilliance, only fears of future failure.

Fortunately, the hours of practice that we had done years ago came forth when the big band started playing. We sounded great. And it's a good thing because in the audience were Dustin Hoffman, Quincy Jones, Johnny Mathis, and a host of others from the Hollywood community.

Sometimes there are unexpected benefits from things we do. It made me feel really good to share this magical moment with my old friends Bobby and Don. We had gone out with a bang.

After the show Wanda remarked she was surprised how comfortable and happy I seemed in that environment. She had only known me doing country music.

During the same period, I was doing *Gambler V* in Galveston, Texas. Once again my character, Brady Hawkes, would be placed into history with real-life characters. This time Brady's son had joined Butch Cassidy and the Sundance Kid's Hole in the Wall Gang and he had to go out and bring him back. I had promised Wanda and her sister, Tonia, that we would use them as extras in the movie. They would be dressed as saloon girls, the twin girlfriends of Butch Cassidy, and sit in Butch's lap during their scene.

Now, by definition, an extra doesn't get to speak. Once you speak in a movie, you have to join SAG (the Screen Actors Guild), and more important, the production company has to pay you.

Wanda and Tonia were told they absolutely could not speak for those reasons. So when Butch says to them, "My now, aren't you two beautiful ladies," they both answer instinctively together, "Why, thank you." There was complete silence on the set for a few minutes. The girls had no idea what they had done; they were just doing what they had been taught by their parents—always say "thank you" when you get a compliment.

Finally someone said to Kelly, who was producing, "I thought they weren't supposed to speak." Kelly replied, "If Kenny wants 'em to speak, let 'em speak. We'll just pay 'em." And so it was that Wanda and Tonia joined the Screen Actors Guild, and they still get their residual checks to this day. They also received acting credits at the end on-screen alongside future Emmy Award winner Mariska Hargitay. I guess having good southern manners does pay off after all.

Before I made my next big move, I had to write a song for Wanda:

"AS GOD IS MY WITNESS"—
A WEDDING SONG FOR WANDA

Once in a lifetime the right love comes by and with no rhyme
*   or reason, you never know why.*
You just wake up one morning . . . and nothing's the same
*   for you. The kisses taste sweeter, the touch just feels right.*
You rush through the morning to get to the night.
Then you're together, and it takes your breath away.

*So hold on with your heart, and let's think forever right from
    the start.*
But love's not forever, it's just for the rest of our lives.
You're not my first love but you'll be my last.
I give you my future. Forgive me my past.
And I know in my heart that this is what I want to do.
*If I had one life, one love, there'd be one dream, for the two of
    us.*
And as God is my witness whatever you do
Don't change a thing 'cause I love loving you.
And as God is my witness I'll give you all of my love.

I know that, as many marriages as I have been through and survived, it's hard to believe I could feel this way at this point in my life, but the words in Wanda's wedding song, "As God Is My Witness," are exactly how I felt on my wedding day. Ask anyone who knows me. Our relationship is something special.

Wanda wasn't there for the peak of my success, and in some ways that's good. At that stage of a career there is no downtime. It's just go here, go there, and try to keep up. It's great fun and very rewarding for the artist, but damaging for a relationship. I missed a lot of important moments in my son Christopher's life because of the pace I was living, and I regret that. As I said earlier in this book, there is a fine line between being driven and being selfish. I have no doubt that because success was so important to me, I crossed that line more than once.

Wanda actually came along at the best time for us. She missed the wave, but caught the crest afterward. We were still traveling in a private airplane—a 731 Jetstar—and had moved back to Beaver Dam Farms.

In 1996, I was working New Year's Eve in Las Vegas at the Aladdin Hotel and had made a momentous decision. I would ask Wanda to marry me.

So, at ten thirty that night, just before the show, in the coffee shop, with Tonia; Jim Mazza and his wife, Val; and my friend Kelly Junkermann at the table, I literally got down on one knee and asked, "Wanda Miller, will you marry me?" I think everyone at the table was dumbfounded, not so much that I had proposed, but the fact I had chosen this way to do so. It was so out of character for me to do anything like this in public. I wanted her to know she was that special to me. Wanda, obviously, said yes.

We made a decision to get married at Beaver Dam Farms on June 1, 1997, and then we would fly off to the Caribbean the next day for our honeymoon. In the course of living at BDF for many years previously, I had also been in the Arabian horse business and had built a gigantic twenty-stall, 70,000-square-foot barn with an indoor riding-training ring in the middle and a big show ring just outside with viewing stands for shows and for sales purposes. We agreed it would be a perfect spot at a great time of the year for our wedding.

As June approached, we discussed with our wedding coordinator just how to do this. We decided we would build a big white gazebo in front of the outdoor sales ring, across from the stands, with garlands of flowers wrapped around the overhead bracing and baskets of flowers all around the bottom. It would be beautiful, we all agreed. Wanda and I, her dad, the flower girls, and the rest of the wedding party would come out the side door of the indoor arena and make our entrance from there.

Now I know it's supposed to be bad luck for the groom to see the bride before the ceremony, but around two o'clock the day of the wedding, I was summoned to Wanda's area, where she and Tonia had been watching the weather report. Wanda was now convinced it was going to rain on our wedding. She asked about moving the entire event indoors. I reassured her it would not rain; there was not a cloud in the sky, and the gazebo was coming together beautifully. At three I was still confident, and she was more worried. Again I reassured her. At four, still three-plus hours before wedding time, she put her foot down as only a woman getting married can do. Her logic was, men look cute with wet hair, women don't. The wedding would be inside.

So the transition began. While Wanda's mom and sister were helping Wanda stay focused, her dad, Charles, who I swear can do anything, had recruited everyone there, staff and guests alike, to build a new gazebo, move the flowers, and polish the brass rails. Oh yeah, I forgot to mention that surrounding this indoor ring were brass rails. There must have been thirty people helping in what I honestly thought was a useless process. It was not going to rain.

Believe it or not, by six, it was done. Charles and crew had moved the wedding gazebo, baskets of beautiful flowers, and two hundred folding chairs inside. This place was ready for our wedding. Six thirty, still no sign of rain. At seven P.M. sharp, the wedding began.

Wanda was absolutely beautiful, more beautiful than ever. Tina, her mom, and Tonia, her sister, both looked breathtaking. This was one beautiful family. Even Charles in his tuxedo was a really handsome guy, a side of him you don't get to see very often. The entire wedding party looked spectacular. The barn had taken on a new look.

Outside, overhead, the tabloid helicopters were whirling around to get their shots, while outside the gates, a crowd had gathered, including some fans and, of all things, some protesters. This was at a time when I had Kenny Rogers Roasters chicken franchises all over the country. Two people in the group had dressed in chicken outfits with signs that read KENNY KILLS CHICKENS. What a sight that must have been.

Inside, things were moving pretty quickly. I had written the song "As God Is My Witness" for Wanda and had asked friends of mine, a group called the Katinas, to sing it for her. It was a special moment for Wanda, her family, and me because it said everything I felt.

So the music started and we came down the aisle with flower girls and rose petals scattered in front of us; Charles gave his little girl a squeeze and gave her hand to me. I saw Tina and Tonia in the back crying. As the minister started the ceremony, "as God is my witness," it started to downpour. Not just a little shower. It poured.

Wanda just looked at me as if to say "don't ever doubt me again." Even in the middle of the wedding, I couldn't help but visualize what the two chicken outfits out front looked like about then. What a night . . . for everyone.

My sister Barbara, her husband, Don, my sister Geraldine, my brother Billy and family, my other brothers, Randy and Roy, and my sister Sandy were all there to help us get married. My two older sons, Chris and Kenny, were there as well. I think Chris really loved Wanda right from the start. She had suggested we include him on a trip we took to Birmingham, Alabama, when Michael Jordan was playing baseball. Once he met Michael, he knew she couldn't be all bad. One of my favorite moments of that night was when Wanda, who was concerned about how my sons would react to my marrying someone so much younger, was introduced to Kenny Jr., who was two years older than her. Without even saying hello, he put his arms around her neck and said "Mom." That spoke volumes to all of us.

Here's one small example of how Wanda began to change my life, in her own words:

Kenny has always felt young at heart, but I swear sometimes I think he thinks he is indestructible. Honestly, I thought he was, too, but then again you have to remember Kenny and I weren't even married when this incident occurred. We had been dating about two years, I think, when I realized we were both wrong. At that moment, he was hurt bad, but I didn't know it and he wouldn't admit it.

Every year Kenny and the group would do a Christmas tour, with an annual show in Glens Falls, New York. There was this beautiful park in the middle of town and it was the middle of football season.

No matter who toured with Kenny at Christmas, they played touch football against each other for bragging rights. Testosterone was at an all-time high with all the guys.

Kelly would organize their traditional game every year. I got the feeling this was a big deal for everybody. I was too new to the group and really too young to say anything. I was maybe twenty-eight and most of the guys were at least forty, and though they would not admit it, they were all getting a little old for this.

This particular year, the opposition was Shelby Lynne and her group of musicians. Kenny was quarterback for his team, and as he went back to throw a pass, Shelby's three-hundred-pound trumpet player rushed in, leaped, and landed right on poor Kenny.

Kenny's shoulder went limp and made a crunch like I have never heard a shoulder crunch before. Everybody was so sure he was hurt, but with his high threshold for pain and tremendous ego, he finished the game, went on to do the show, and finish the tour. He would learn later that year that he had torn the rotator cuff in his shoulder. In January, we scheduled the surgery and we were told he would have to take a few months off while it healed.

It was early in the year, so he decided, what the heck, his other shoulder was bothering him, too, so why not get them both done. He actually had rotator cuff surgery on both shoulders at the same time. Well, rotator cuff surgery is, as I came to learn, a very painful operation and demands a good time of rehab afterward. He was all bound up and miserable.

However much he needed to lie back and recover, he immediately rushed back into action. Within a week or two after the operation, I caught him, loaded with Demerol and feeling bulletproof, out on the golf course with Rob and Kelly, attempting to hit golf balls. There was hell to pay for all of us. Ken Kragen called about then and went ballistic. He kept yelling, "Get him back in the house before he hurts himself."

I don't know what came over me but I felt I needed to say something to him since no one else would. Now, remember here I am twenty-eight years younger than him, and relatively new in his life. So what did I do?

I grounded him!

He would never admit it, but I think he was glad I made him quit.

His shoulder has never healed properly. He has never played another touch football game or loaded himself up with painkillers again but once after that. He was in so much pain he was taking enough Percocet, a painkiller, to drop a full-size horse. Since he had been grounded, the only thing he could do was watch TV. As I walked by one day, he was watching a commercial that ended with "I love alpacas." Kenny looked at me, eyes at half mast, and said, "I think I do, too." He ordered three.

CHAPTER EIGHTEEN

Comeback

Meanwhile, along with my marriage to Wanda and along with the movies and the other TV appearances that kept me in the public eye, Kelly and I were cooking up one new scheme after another.

"Success breeds confidence; confidence breeds more success."

That's the only way I can explain the stupid, unrealistic things Kelly and I have tried since I've known him. We have pulled off things that if we had ever considered failure, we would have never attempted.

It was around 1997, and I had been telling Kelly about Bryant's five-and-dime that had been such an important part of my childhood, and how Mr. Bryant had a toy soldier that had been handed down from generation to generation in his family. It had been given to him when he was a child by his father and he had placed it up on the shelf so all the kids who came in could see it, but no one could touch it.

He would tell us kids as we sat around the story of the great Civil War, the North against the South, a moment in history we could not possibly relate to except for this little toy soldier that had been in his family since 1862. It had once been his great-grandfather's. He made his story sound and feel so real, none of us could move as we listened. We were riveted every time he told it, and we couldn't hear it too many times.

At one time the toy soldier, he said, had been carrying a rifle, but when his great-grandfather went to war, he had been shot and killed by a Yankee soldier with a rifle just like that, so someone in his family had removed the rifle and thrown it away, but the soldier had been kept all these years as a way of remembering his great-grandfather's bravery. His great-grandfather had seen the need for the military at the time, but hated the killing.

The more Mr. Bryant told the story, the more real the war, the history, and the soldier became to all of us. This toy was a part of his family. Somewhere along the way, the grandkids had named the soldier "Captain William Bryant" in memory of his great-grandfather. He had been a decorated war hero in the Civil War. Mr. Bryant showed us that he was actually in the history books. You almost felt like you knew him and you were there.

Kelly loved the visual of kids sitting around a toy store being told stories about the history of old toys. He asked me what had happened to the hardware store, and I told him it had recently been forced out of business and taken over by a large chain of restaurants.

We were in about the tenth year of doing Christmas shows when Kelly and I decided to write a one-act play about the feel of Mr. Bryant's storytelling. Instead of a five-and-dime store, it would be a neighborhood toy store that was being forced out of business by a money-hungry old man, Mr. Baxter, who wanted to open a Baxter Burger store in its place. It was classic tale of good versus evil.

This toy store, we decided, would represent everything good. It had been in the neighborhood for a hundred years. In it would be large, life-sized toys that had great history and deep meaning to the affable store owner, Hank Longley, who would be played by me.

The toys would literally come to life the moment the store closed its doors. At night, while the toys were active, they would dance, sing, and discuss among themselves the problems facing the toys and Mr. Longley.

Some of the toys were old and broken but protected by Mr. Longley's theory that "Just because they weren't perfect didn't mean they didn't have value." One of Hank's most prized possessions was a carved wooden doll with only one leg. He had been named "Mr. Perfect" by the kids. On the back of Mr. Perfect was a poem that read:

ALL ARE EVEN IN THE EYES OF GOD
SOME GET BETTER STARTS.
BUT IT'S THOSE WHO HAVE THE LEAST ON EARTH,
WHO ARE CLOSEST TO HIS HEART.

Hank would tell stories to the kids about the origins and meaning of these old toys. One of them was about Hero the dog, the very first stuffed animal ever made. I loved writing both lyrics and narrative and especially loved short lines/lyrics that had heart. For the song about Hero, I wrote:

We all need heroes.
Someone to believe in.
Someone who believes in you . . .
That's why they're heroes . . .
They don't try to be heroes . . .
Just doing every day . . .
What everyday people don't do . . .

Writing all this was a daunting task since none of us had ever written anything like this before. Once we agreed on the specific toys and their backstories, we needed music. Warren Hartman and Steve Glassmeyer, both band members of mine for twenty-plus years and great songwriters, were the perfect guys to help. We each have our own strengths as songwriters.

Warren had the best sense of Broadway. He knew better than any of us how to make things flow with his unique songwriting skills and lush orchestrations. Steve had the best ability to write the fun songs the toys would sing and dance to. It was his job to make the audience laugh and smile.

I specialize in songs of the heart. It was my job to make them cry. So between laughing, crying, and Warren's music, we gave it a try. The chances against this working were astronomical. In truth, that's what made it fun for us.

So here we are, a former tennis pro, a country singer, and two musicians from the band, about to undertake the biggest gamble of our lives. More honestly, of my career. I have often said, "Kelly has had a great career by taking chances with mine." We were, I guess, too stupid to even think about what could happen if this thing didn't work, God forbid.

We had a friend, Diana Martinez, the producer of a Chicago theater group who helped us cast the toys and get the costumes made. A friend of Kelly's who had helped us on several movies, Maia Javan, designed the sets. Maia, to no one's surprise, has become one of the top Hollywood production designers.

We rehearsed and rehearsed and rehearsed. And we would write and rewrite and rewrite. At one point we needed a song where one of the children needed to learn something from Hank, and Hank needed to learn something from her. While riding my lawn mower cutting my greens at the farm, I wrote "If Only I Had Your Heart."

Help me find a way
To finish this journey we started today.
No one may know
This deed that you do.
It's simply a moment between me and you.
These are the times that set you apart
If only you have the heart.

At the time I lived in Athens, Georgia, so that would be where we performed it first. There were two halves to the show: "The Toy Shoppe" and a Christmas-hits section called "The Chosen One." We had performed "The Chosen One" and knew that it would work, so we would close with it. We would start with "The Toy Shoppe." If it didn't work, we would always have the Christmas hits to fall back on.

During "The Toy Shoppe," we were shocked to see people in the audience crying. Much to our surprise, at the end of the play, the audience gave us a standing ovation. This was a brand-new play, something they knew nothing about, yet they got it. They laughed and they cried. From that night on, we did the hits first and closed with the play.

For two years, we toured with it and honed our skills and fixed all the little things that were wrong with the show. Diana and her friends out of Chicago were a big help. This was all new to me. I had done a lot of things but never gone onstage acting with a group of kids. I was much more comfortable doing movies. You don't have the luxury of retakes in live performances. As I remember, the kids did a better job with their lines than I did.

In year three, we actually played the Pontiac Superdome at Christmas. The stage had been set up like a Broadway show, and all the action played to a "front" audience. There were more than twenty thousand people there that night. Some of them had to be seated behind the stage. That was really strange for all of us. The seats in the back got no "theater." They were treated to our set changes and all the backstage stuff you're never supposed to see. Believe it or not, they loved it.

To show you how professional we were, if you were on the tour, you were in the show. The moms of kids, including Wanda, made appearances. Doug Dean, the tennis pro who had taken Kelly's place when Kelly was on tour, had been cast as the deliveryman. He was brilliant in his delivery of the now-famous line: "Got some more toys for you, Hank." Doug was always unusually nervous. A friend of his, Robbie Halmi, a guy Doug hit tennis balls with, was the head of Hallmark Entertainment and came to see him one night. Robbie enjoyed it—so much so, he offered us six weeks at the Beacon Theatre in New York at Christmastime.

Now we had to step everything up a few notches. We needed to have Broadway quality in our little play. So we created a couple of new toys, wrote some new songs, and basically made it feel professional and more interesting for a more sophisticated New York audience.

We auditioned the best young girls in New York for the part of Katie, a little girl who, in our play, was full of magic and wonder. This role required her not just to sing, but to really sing.

We found the perfect girl for the part. She was from a little town just outside of Philadelphia. Her name was Jillian Arciero. She would be with the show for the next five years that we performed it. She was an amazing talent. As a bonus, when we went back on the road she had three sisters—Gabby, Dominique, and Olivia—who also came along to help round out the cast. We had no idea the amount of talent that the four Arciero sisters possessed. Another of our permanent cast members was Taylor Bugos, the daughter of my longtime production manager, Keith Bugos. Taylor had been doing our Christmas show since she was five years old.

As we rehearsed the new show, we realized things were totally different in New York than they had been on the road. For one thing, we would have a stationary, more permanent set. We now had a two-story set and a fireman's brass pole that I could slide down. This would get me to two fighting boys in the opening scene faster and gave me a more exciting entrance for the show. We had gone Broadway and high tech in one move. It was great.

The pole itself was pretty impressive, but the exciting part was watching me slide down every night. I found out quickly, you wrap your sleeves around the pole and slide down; if you grab the pole with your bare hands, your fingers lock on the brass and you "s-c-r-e-e-c-h" down the pole, creating blisters on every part of your hand. I did that only once. That was enough.

Of all the things I've been fortunate enough to do in my career, writing, singing, and being a part of these live acting performances may have been the most challenging and at the same time the most rewarding.

By the late 1990s, as much as I liked doing "The Toy Shoppe" and the TV movies, I needed to get back to making hit records. Jim Mazza, who originally championed me at Capitol, had become more involved in my musical career, to the point that he had found an investor and started his own record label, Magnatone Records. I recorded a couple of albums there with him. We had some success with the Christmas album *The Gift* and the Christmas special of the same name, which we shot at the famous Ryman Auditorium. *The Gift* actually became a Top 10 album and went on to be certified gold. One of the songs that we recorded was "Mary, Did You Know?" I sang it with Wynonna Judd, and it remains one of my favorite Christmas songs. Steve Glassmeyer, Warren Hartman, and I also wrote a narrative/montage that drove the album called "The Chosen One," which we went on to perform in our live Christmas show for a number of years. But it took a lot of clout to get radio airplay, and Magnatone just couldn't compete with the bigger labels.

Jim really believed that there would be more hits for me. He had another idea: Why don't we form our own company—record label, management, touring, and film and television? This time we would have a distributor who would guarantee to provide the money to promote the songs we would be cutting. Jim would head the label, Ken Kragen would head the management, Kelly would head the film and television, and a friend of Jim's, Bob Burwell, would head the touring. We would be a management team. It sounded great on paper, and we all agreed to move forward. Ken and Kelly would stay located in Los Angeles to give us a West Coast presence, and the company would be based in Nashville. We would call the company Dreamcatcher. It seemed like I had come full circle having my own label again. Many years ago, in the early 1970s, thanks to Mike Curb, it was Jolly Rogers Records.

Mike, now president of Curb Records, had put up the money for Jolly Rogers, a label that probably didn't have much of a chance as our logo was a skull and crossbones. We had a few records, none of which did well, and I felt bad for Mike. He had believed in me, and I had let him down.

Once that label closed its doors, there was a contractual payout to me for $250,000, which I split with my brother Lelan, who had been running the label. I think Lelan had had his fill of the music business and was ready to retire. He bought forty acres of land in Checotah, Oklahoma. How he picked this place to retire, I will never know. This was to be his new home. There was a cattle herd and an old farmhouse on the property. Lelan had a horse that I had given him years before named Dude. The previous owner, an older man who had live there most of his life, agreed to stay on and show him how things worked. Lelan, at about fifty years old, and this old man sat on the porch the first day just to watch the sun go down. It was what Lelan had dreamed of all his life. About three in the afternoon, Lelan noticed that his cows were gone. In a state of panic he jumped up, saddled up Dude, and took off down the road. About thirty minutes later in a cloud of dust came Lelan's cows, with Lelan herding them back into their pen. This was really Western. He unsaddled his horse, realizing he had done this all by himself and was very proud. He would survive here. At about four he glanced over his shoulder to tell the old man how happy he was to be here when he noticed his cows were gone again. As he jumped up to saddle Dude again, the old man said, "Mr. Rogers, unless you just want to play cowboy, if you just sit right there in that chair, those cows will come down that road at about five and go straight to that feeding trough. Hell, you can't run those damn cows off. They have been doing this all their life and they ain't about to change."

Back to the main story: so we now had a new company, Dreamcatcher. We were also working with Diamond Rio, Sara Evans, and Jo Dee Messina, all of whom had No. 1 albums with us. At about the same time I had come across a new Don Schlitz song, "The Greatest." Don had written "The Gambler," and as was the case with "The Gambler," other artists had been singing "The Greatest" around town, but it just didn't seem like it could be a hit. After all, it was about baseball and a little boy, not exactly what country radio was playing.

I really liked the song and was doing a radio interview in New York when they asked me if I could play something live. It seemed like a perfect opportunity to try out "The Greatest." It was just me and a guitar in a radio studio. If the song fell flat, who would care? So I said, "Well, I do have this new song that I have been playing around with. Let's try it."

Little boy, in a baseball hat,
Stands in the field, with his ball and bat,
Says "I am the greatest player of them all,"
Puts his bat on his shoulder, and tosses up his ball.
And the ball goes up, and the ball comes down,
He swings his bat all the way around,
And the world's so still you can hear the sound
As the baseball falls, to the ground.

It was a classic Don Schlitz story song. The phones at the radio station rang off the hook. Mazza gathered the "team." "We have a hit." And we hadn't even recorded it yet. So we did. It was the spring of 1999. We went to a sports supershow, and I did an interview with the legendary sports announcer Dick Schaap, who called the song the second best baseball song ever, after "Take Me Out to the Ball Game." It was there that we met with Tim Richards of Rawlings Sporting Goods. The company agreed to supply us with $10,000 worth of baseball equipment for youth baseball leagues across the country that we could use in radio promotions. To top it all off, I would travel across the country, sitting on a stool at home plate, playing my guitar and singing the song at all the major-league ball parks across the country before the game. It worked. The song, as unlikely as it was to be played on country radio, began to get airplay. Some rock stations even started playing it. I sang it live on the air for my good buddies Mark and Brian at KLOS in Los Angeles when they had me on with home run hitter Mark Mc-Gwire. I remember that interview particularly well as I gave them one of my Grammys.

There was one more piece to the puzzle. We needed a video. Kelly in Los Angeles had met a young filmmaker who was only a production assistant in the film world. Actually the only reason Kelly had met with him is that he was married to a friend who was a model I had photographed when she was just starting out years earlier in Athens. She was now Julia Roberts's stunt double. Kelly looked at this filmmaker's spec reel, and it was really well done. We didn't have a lot of money and Kelly wanted to use this new director. It was our company; we could choose whomever we wanted. We took the chance on Shaun Silva.

The simple, gritty, heartfelt video shot in black and white raced up the CMT video charts to No. 1. The song shot up the charts into the Top 20. We now had a hit song and a hit video, and we were still frantically working on having an album.

We put one together called *She Rides Wild Horses*. It included a number of standards on it, but there also was a song written by a couple of writers, Jim Funk and Erik Hickenlooper, from, of all places, Utah—probably not the hotbed of country music classics. It was called "Buy Me a Rose." It was perfect for me, as again it said what every man would like to say and what every woman would like to hear. Jim Mazza added Alison Krauss and Billy Dean to the record, and it sounded great.

Buy me a rose, call me from work.
Open a door for me, what would it hurt.

Show me you love me by the look in your eyes.
These are the little things I need the most in my life.

Again, the timing could not have been any better. The song started up the charts. This time we used another video director outside the box. My old stunt double from the *Gambler* films, Dave Cass, was now directing. Kelly had just worked with him on a film and asked if he would like to direct the video. Why not? New company, new director. We shot the video on the beach in Malibu. The video closed with Wanda and me. It seemed a perfect ending for the song. The video went to No. 1 on the video charts.

It was the spring of 2000. Our promotion staff was working with radio frantically to tie the song into Valentine's Day, again a perfect fit. But the crowning achievement was that the television show *Touched by an Angel* had written an episode based on the song and I sang the song in the show. The song went to No. 1 on the *Billboard* charts. I was now actually the oldest country artist, at sixty-one, to have a No. 1 country hit.

It was a pretty good start. We had taken my career into, really, my own hands and had come out of the gate with a Top 20 song, two No. 1 videos, and my first No. 1 single since 1987. The album had gone on to be certified platinum at that time, the first time that had been done with an independent label.

It was a bunch of firsts that could probably only be accomplished with our own company and Jim taking control of my career. We had the ability to take a chance and bring in new talent. We put together an album in an amazingly short period of time without any of the trappings of having too many decision makers. With the success of radio airplay, my touring took a jump as well. We now had some success.

All things considered, an interesting move for us was when we put together a young country "boy band," which we called Marshall Dyllon. They were young, they were fresh, they were good looking, and they sang great. Much to our surprise, the by now much respected Lou Pearlman, manager of the Backstreet Boys and 'N Sync, took an interest in them. They were that good. The rest is tabloid history. Need I say more?

You always hear about artists changing managers every day, but not me. Ken Kragen was my first manager, and we were together for thirty-three years until 2001. I felt like Ken wanted to slow down at a time when I needed to ramp up. Jim Mazza, having been president of Capitol Records, became my friend and a stabilizing force in my career, so when I decided to change managers, I went to him. For many years, he guided me and made some great decisions on my behalf. But in 2011, I needed some fresh eyes on my career, and I was running out of time. Jim and his wife, Val, have been two of our closest friends for more than twenty years, which made this separation incredibly difficult, but in my opinion, it was necessary nonetheless. Separations like this are like divorces. You can't tell what the outcome is going to be until you've made the decision. Once I decided to make the change and made it, I learned that Ken Levitan at Vector Management had expressed an interest in managing me, and that sounded really interesting. I think he has created a new interest in my music and style.

Life was good in 2004, but it was about to get even better. I was sixty-five years old, and Wanda was having twins.

TWINS!

This was such an incredible time for Wanda and me, and, for

this book, I wanted to make sure I didn't forget anything important that happened in the process, so I asked Wanda if she would
write down for me some of her memories of this special moment
in our lives.

What she wrote for me was so much more insightful, interesting, and heartfelt than anything I could have written. I thought it
would be better for you, the reader, to hear a mother's excitement—
her fears, her joys, and her thoughts—almost as she lived them,
and in her words.

Enjoy this. I did.

*Kenny and I decided early on that we didn't want to have
kids. We had an exciting life together, traveling and seeing
the world, usually on a whim. We knew that kids would
change our priorities forever.*

*Then when I turned thirty-five, BAM, it hit me. I was
worried about missing out on having children.*

*We were on a trip in China with the Mazzas, and I
called Kenny into the dressing room where I was getting
ready to have dinner. I asked him, "Should we give it a
chance to have kids, and if it doesn't work out, then let it
go?" And he graciously agreed! He said, "Yes, I would never
want to cause you to miss out on your childbearing years." So
when we returned to Atlanta, we gave it our all.*

*We came to find out that I had a low ovarian reserve,
which meant that I could not possibly do this without IVF.
We decided that we would try that. When we finally got to
the part of extracting the eggs to fertilize, the doctor was very
honest with us. "It doesn't look promising." Actually, it was
less than a 13 percent chance that the procedure would work.*

The doctor usually plans on retrieving twelve to thirteen eggs to fertilize. I produced only three. Nevertheless, we decided to carry on with our plan.

After retrieving the three eggs, they put them in a petri dish to fertilize them and hopefully turn them into embryos. What a miracle! Another problem popped up. Only one of the eggs fertilized and the doctor usually wanted at least three fertilized embryos to put back into me. We decided, even against the doctor's advice, to put the one embryo back and see what would happen.

Now, the waiting game for the pregnancy test to turn pink began.

Kenny and I heard different things from the doctor. He thought he said I would take the pregnancy test in three days. I thought he said ten days. We decided to check it in three days. It didn't change colors. Heartbroken, we called the doctor. "No," he said. "Don't test for fourteen days at least!"

We waited for maybe five more days, and I took the test again. It was only a light pink, but it was pink. I was pregnant.

It was Thanksgiving and almost time to go out on the Christmas tour. I had always been with Kenny on tour and I decided not to change that. I would find the proper doctors on the road to do these tests and we would bus from town to town, like always.

Kenny was scheduled to do a show in Billings, Montana, and there was a critical test I needed to take to make sure the baby was in the right position to develop naturally. We found a great doctor to do the ultrasound for us. We were sitting in his office and he took out a pen and notepad and started to ask us questions. This didn't sound good to me. "Tell me the truth," I said, "Is there something wrong?"

"No, my dear," he very quickly said. "The embryo has split and there are two heartbeats. You are having identical twins." Kenny thought he said "three heartbeats." All of us were overwhelmed. My twin sister, Tonia, was there with us and now doing cartwheels and cheering. We had been doubly blessed.

I could go on, detail by detail—I went into labor too early, had to have a needle in my leg for the meds to stop the contractions, got up to 197 pounds and forty-eight and a half inches around the waist—but it's enough to say despite the 13 percent chance of becoming fertilized embryos, on July 6, 2004, our boys, Justin and Jordan, were born—and life was never the same.

Both were small at birth, and Jordan had to go to the ICU to be monitored closely. I demanded at one point to go visit him. When I saw him all hooked up with wires and tubes, I fainted. I recovered to hold and cuddle him. The next visit I braced myself, and when I again saw him in the ICU, I fainted again.

Having two newborn babies is so nerve-wracking at first; then it all comes so naturally. I was so lucky to have my family. My mom stayed with us to help me with every decision. She raised twins with cloth diapers and no extra help, so she is now my hero, more than ever before.

I had a really hard time the first two to three months. I can remember going to Kenny and crying, "What have we done! I can't handle being a mom of twins!" Kenny in his

calm, patient way said, "Okay, Wanda, the babies aren't
puppies; we can't take them back. We will get through this."

My mom had been with us (off and on) for eight months,
helping me every step of the way! It was time for her to head
home and for me to take charge and handle this on my own.
I had, on several occasions, followed my mom to the back
door, crying and breaking down, letting her know that she
couldn't leave me. Kenny in his ultimate wisdom told me
that my mom was a crutch to me and I really needed to
know that I could do this. I thought to myself, He is really
gutsy saying this to me. I need my mom! When she left, I
quietly cried myself to sleep every night. Then one night I
didn't and realized I could do this. He was right. My mom
left and I had to handle everything on my on, and all of a
sudden I felt so strong and empowered. I could do this. I did
do this!

All the motherly instincts kicked in, and I just followed
my intuition. It's the best job I have ever had—the hardest
job, but still the best job!

As I watch Wanda with the boys, I can tell you this as a husband and a proud father of twins, this has truly been a wonderful
experience for both of us. I never cease to be amazed what a mom
can do when someone has confidence in them. They say that having children at my age can make you or break you. Right now I'm
leaning heavily toward break!!

CHAPTER NINETEEN

❊

Looking Back

When you break it all down, you're seventy-three years old, you've been singing songs for fifty years, and you realize that the most treasured things you have are your family, your friends, and your memories.

Fifty years! It's been fifty years of touring and I had just spent the day rehearsing and running through the songs from every decade spanning those fifty years for a television special we were taping called *Kenny Rogers: The First 50 Years*. We were rehearsing the entire show in one day, and it could be done only if I was surrounded by people I could depend on and whom I had counted on to be there for most of my career.

Every artist who travels in this business has more than one family whom he or she needs and loves. Certainly I have mine. It's really hard to believe how long I've been surrounded by this incredibly faithful group of people.

I'll describe my crew by explaining who was there that day at our taping. First (because I think he's been with me the longest) was Keith Bugos, my sound mixer for the last forty-one years. Every night when I go to work, he's there. I met Keith in 1969 at a little club in Columbus, Ohio. I had to promise his mother if she would let him go on the road with me I would personally watch over him. I'm thinking next year I'll make him responsible for himself. He's sixty now. I think I've done a pretty good job with him.

Crossing the stage as I walked off was Gene Roy, who had started out as an eighteen-year-old kid selling T-shirts at my concerts thirty-three years ago. He was now my tour manager, my photography sherpa, and the guy I turn to on a daily basis to survive. Without him I couldn't. I've watched all these guys get married and have kids. I watched Gene and his wife, Kelli, have two sons, Eron and Travis, who are now grown and young men we are all proud of.

Working with Gene was one of my favorite employees, Debbie Cross. She was with me for ten years, then jumped ship and went with Alan Jackson. It didn't take her long to realize that she really missed me, and we gladly accepted her back. Together Gene and Debbie don't miss a thing. I promise you this, if she leaves me again, I'm not taking her back.

My band was there for me, flawlessly running through the songs for each artist. Steve Glassmeyer, one of my three keyboard players, who at one time played with Phil Harris, has been with me the longest of any of my band members—thirty-six years. He was a part of the first band I put together immediately after the First Edition broke up. He was also a part of the now-infamous Saudi Arabia tour we did for Aramco Oil in 1977. That was one of the most fascinating tours I have ever been a part of. I'm so glad he's still around to keep the story straight. I have a feeling I might have blown things completely out of proportion without him.

Randy Dorman is an incredible jazz guitar player who has been with me for thirty-five years. But jazz is kind of an elitist music and not the most commercial. We all love it and everyone in the band plays it for the fun of it. He has also become quite a photographer on the tour, having shot one of my latest album covers. I wonder sometimes how people go from jazz to country; then I remember, they are no different than anybody else—they have to eat.

I remember something Bobby Doyle told me about playing bass in his group. He said, "Look around, every band has a bass player." But when I got my first band in Nashville you can imagine how shocked I was that there was no bass player. So when my keyboard bass player left, I got one. Chuck Jacobs is a bass player's bass player. He's been with me thirty-three years and never missed a show. He played a lot around New York and played with Wayne Cochran, so he has had a lot of musical influences. He knows how to play each genre, and he lets each retain its integrity.

I actually met my keyboard player/arranger, Warren Hartman, in a little club in St. Louis called Mother's. He was playing with a group called Stanley Steamer. If my memory is correct, I think I produced an album for them. If I didn't, I should have. Warren has been here twenty-two years, and his use of electronic strings and his orchestral arrangements add such a thickness to my songs, particularly the ballads. Warren has now branched out as a producer, coproducing my *The Love of God* album. What a different sound we would have without him.

Lynn Hammann has been with me for twenty-three years, and before that he played with Frankie Valli. He's an amazingly understated but highly effective drummer. Sadly, he has just given me notice that because of physical constraints, he will no longer be able to play on the road. I will miss him because he is head and shoulders the most sane guy in our band.

Gene Sisk played with Eddie Rabbitt and now he's been with me sixteen years. He has the greatest recall for songs of anyone

I have ever met. If I ever do a covers album, he's my guy. One of his greatest attributes is that he can sing high and hard and enjoys performing every night, or at least he appears to enjoy it. He's the only person in the whole band, including me, who warms up his vocals before each show.

Brian Franklin's dad, Paul Sr., is a famous steel guitar maker, and Brian's brother, Paul, is one of the best-known steel guitar players in the world. Brian's wife, Rosie, sings at the Grand Ole Opry with The Whites. As you can see, Brian is surrounded by the royalty of country music, and it shows. He's a great guitar player who's been with me eleven years, and I think he is the only band member who cares about how his hair looks.

Ten years ago I decided to add a fiddle player to the band so that I would sound more country. I always let the band hire new members, because they have to travel with them and be around them dealing with their personalities. When they brought me Amber Randall, she was beautiful and she played great, but not just great—she took second place in a national fiddle contest. She has been such an amazing addition and, boy, has she cleaned up the language on the band bus. She has since married one of our tech guys in the crew, Aaron Corr, who has been here just a little longer than she has. Aaron and Amber have recently welcomed their first son, Owen, into the world. They are a great couple, and I am thrilled and lucky to have them both.

Rounding out my crew are some very unique guys. Technical director Frank Farrell has been with me for seventeen years, having worked with the Who, Paul McCartney, and Steve Miller. He is a techie's techie. He not only can mix monitors to my very deliberate liking, he also has kept our show ahead of the curve in these fast-paced technological times. If that's not enough, when our drummer Lynn went down with an injury on our Christmas tour, Frank amazingly stepped in the next night and played drums for the rest of the tour.

Years ago I wanted to expand the look in my lighting department. What better way to expand than to take a lighting director from the Grateful Dead. Jeff Metter has been with me for sixteen years. He may have made the biggest transition of all my guys, coming from the Dead tour to mine. I can honestly say we approached our lighting scheme from a whole different place.

Our newest crew member came fresh out of music school. He was determined to learn the music business as I had, by jumping right in and actually doing it. Brian Parkos has been with me for six years now. He is also an accomplished percussionist. If we lose another drummer and Frank goes down, Brian can step in to take over. We are covered as far as drummers go!

During the taping of the special, I thought about how these guys were my extended family and had been there with me through all my ups and downs, and what a ride it has been . . . for all of us.

It was the night of the show, and it was beginning to feel like "This Is Your Life, Kenneth Ray Rogers," and it felt good. My mom and dad would have been proud of me.

I was onstage singing and looked out at the people in the audience. I swear it was as if my entire life flashed before me. These were all my friends, and they were performing the songs I had recorded over the last fifty years. It didn't take long to realize that the first fifty years had been great, but the second would be a bitch!

I saw my older sons, Chris and Kenny, in the audience. They had my younger sons, Justin and Jordan, sitting on their knees. And there was my wife, Wanda, as beautiful as ever, sitting next to them. That was my family. I could honestly say through them, "I have accomplished something," and this was no small thing.

I noticed the theater was filled with all three of the important things—family, friends, and memories. It was so great to see my manager and one of my best friends for the last twenty-five years, Jim Mazza. Who would have believed the day we met in his office at Capitol Records that he and his wife, Val, would play such a pivotal role in my life and my career? They are such a part of so many special memories and events, and I love how closely entwined our lives have become.

I had to smile when I looked out and saw my good friend Kelly Junkermann. I've always loved the idea of giving someone a chance and an opportunity to grow. I realized Kelly was the producer of the very TV show we were now doing. I was very proud of him and flattered to have been a part of his amazing growth.

Speaking of old friends, there, in front of me, sat all the members of the First Edition. They represent such an important and fun part of my life . . . what memories there were: Terry Williams, Thelma Camacho, Mike Settle, and me convincing Terry's mom, Bonnie, to talk to Jimmy Bowen about getting a record deal on a major label, and we got it; Mary Arnold taking over for Thelma when she left on one day's notice and doing a great job; Mickey Jones strapping that big Dual Showman amplifier on top of the station wagon and it blowing off as we drove down the highway; the group opening the show for, and getting to spend time with, Richard Pryor.

This wasn't just my personal life but my professional life as well. Dolly Parton, who had probably single-handedly added ten years to my success with "Islands in the Stream," was there, cutting up as usual. One of the highlights of the night for me was to hear Alison Krauss and Dolly sing the song I had written, "Sweet Music Man." It's a song that is very personal to me, and to hear those two voices together was really quite amazing.

As Lionel Richie took the stage, I remembered how much fun we had had on my boat in the Bahamas and what a milestone in my career it had become when he wrote the song "Lady." Lionel happens to be the most unique songwriter I've ever encountered. He writes the most beautiful melodies, and his lyrics are like musical conversations. Not many people can do that. I've asked him time and time again for another song, but now that he is so successful I think he feels that if they are good enough for me, they are good enough for him.

They just kept coming: there was Smokey Robinson, Wynonna Judd, Billy Dean, Linda Davis, Chris Isaak, Sheena Easton, all there onstage. Tim McGraw, Billy Currington, and Darius Rucker couldn't make it live, but they had taken the time out of their busy schedules to film songs and congratulations for me. Believe me, I know how hard it is to interrupt your schedule for something like this, and it did not go unappreciated.

The Oak Ridge Boys were there sitting in the front row. These guys had been my friends both musically and personally since this whole thing started. In 1981, they helped me headline the tour with Dottie West when Jerry Seinfeld had missed his opening.

What a night and what a way to remember my life and my career. The one thing I am certain of is that you can never underestimate the value of true fans. There are two women who have been to 1,078 of my concerts, Susan Bradley and Sharman Pirkle. They've even dragged James, Sharman's husband, to the majority of the concerts. There they were sitting out in the audience. They have never expected special treatment, so we try to give it to them.

At one point we were doing a show and the opening comedian noticed the girls in the front row with the roses that they traditionally give to me. Attached to the roses was a card with the number of the shows they had attended. Having no idea what the number represented, he asked, "What are the flowers for, girls?" They replied, "They are for Kenny. We are big fans," at which time he focused on the number on the attached card. He immediately replied, "You girls are no longer fans. You are stalkers!" They were both shocked and delighted. If that's true, I wish there were more stalkers like them.

As the lights went out, the music stopped, and all my friends went home, my thoughts went from what I *had* done to what I *will* do.

Professionally I have started a new album for Warner Bros. Records, produced by Dann Huff, who produced my favorite of my albums, *Water and Bridges*. I am convinced that my musical career will take care of itself, one way or the other, but my personal life has always seemed a little more daunting.

Wanda and I just celebrated our fifteenth wedding anniversary. We've been together for twenty years now, and I know a lot of people who would have lost a lot of money on that bet.

This has been by far the most compatible relationship I have ever been in. I don't know why, but from day one, with all its age complications, it has simply . . . felt right.

Wanda is a rare, unique woman, who I think understands me better than anyone else and accepts me with all my quirks and silly needs. I am honestly so blessed to have a wife that provides me with such a secure-feeling future. I love her more than she knows.

Now Justin and Jordan present a whole different set of problems, all good, just different. You have to remember I wasn't around for the terrible teens with my first two boys, Kenny and Chris, so I really have no idea what to expect. I do know this: I want to be there this time with Justin and Jordan and help shape their lives and their thought processes as they get older.

Interestingly, I have no idea what their interests will be, just as my mom and dad could have never been prepared for my choices. But I think if we instill good values in them, let them know they are loved, help them with the difficult choices but let them make their own when they can . . . they will survive. I am so proud of the men Chris and Kenny have become; I can only hope Justin and Jordan turn out as well.

And with a little luck or something like it, they will.

ACKNOWLEDGMENTS

Alvin Toffler once wrote a book called *Future Shock,* in which he laid out a theory that in every life there are what he called crisis moments. These are moments that happen to everyone, after which your life can never be the same.

Since this book was written more anecdotally than sequentially, I am sure there are people I have failed to mention who have certainly been important in the shaping of my life and career. No matter how well intentioned I am, or how hard I've tried, I am sure I have forgotten someone, and for that I am deeply apologetic.

Let me at least take a moment to mention some people who were there at career-turning points for me.

My mom and dad, who made me the person I am today. I will be forever grateful for the foundation you laid for me.

My brother Lelan, who always believed I had talent and helped me find my first outlet.

Jimmy Duncan and Larry Kane, who changed my name and recorded my first record, "For You Alone."

Bobby Doyle, for giving me a great musical foundation and a belief that I could make a living in music.

Kirby Stone, who mentored me through the confusing times and taught me the business of music. I have to wonder, without him, where I might be today.

Terry Williams, Mike Settle, and Thelma Camacho, who allowed me to be a part of something really special—the First Edition—and get my first taste of success.

Jimmy Bowen, for giving me both the courage and the opportunity to record and produce music at a very high level.

Mike Post, for producing "Just Dropped In," a truly career-changing piece of music.

Ken Kragen, who as my manager for thirty-three years took me to career heights I didn't really deserve, none of which would have happened without his knowledge, caring, and guidance.

Larry Butler, who produced most of the biggest hits I have had in my career and did it in a six-year period. What a ride that was. I will be forever indebted to him.

Kelly Junkermann, for teaching me tennis and probably adding years to my life by making me exercise. I have always jokingly said that he was never afraid to gamble with my career, but he helped me transition from music to acting. Along with Ken Kragen, he has produced almost every piece of film I've been a part of.

Jim Mazza, who stepped into my life first as a friend and then as a manager for a total of some twenty years. Jim kept the boat afloat and encouraged country music to accept me. He represents so much in my life. I can never repay him for that and wouldn't even know where to start.

Dick Lowry, who through five *Gambler* movies took this country boy and made him a cowboy. He actually made me feel like Brady Hawkes. I love the character, and I love how Dick made me look. I hope someday I can be more like Brady. Who wouldn't want to be a cowboy?

Barry Gibb, for having the foresight and the brilliance not only to write "Islands in the Stream" but to suggest we bring in

Dolly Parton to save us. This was definitely a crisis moment in my life.

Dolly Parton, for infusing me and my career with an energy I didn't know I had, and teaching me how much fun friendship and music can be. Every note in every performance was a joy.

Lionel Richie, who with one song—"Lady"—gave me a connection with every woman in the world. He was, and still is, in every sense of the word, my soul brother.

Ken Levitan, for bringing new thought and new respect to an otherwise stagnant point in my life. I am more impressed with him every day.

PERMISSIONS

———————————— ✦ ————————————